SHELTON STATE COMMUNIT
COLLEGE
JUNIOR COLLEGE DIVISION
LIBRARY

DISCARDED

D0968589

LC
3075
.S26
L68
1982

Low, Victor.

The unimpressible
race

DATE DUE

| | | | |
|---|---|---|---|
| | | | |
| | | | |
| | | | |
| | | | |
| | | | |
| | | | |
| | | | |
| | | | |
| | | | |
| | | | |
| | | | |

# The Unimpressible Race

# THE
# *UNIMPRESSIBLE*
# RACE

## A Century of Educational Struggle
## by the Chinese in San Francisco

## Victor Low

DISCARDED

**East/West Publishing Company, Inc.**
San Francisco

Cover design and figures by Sherman Fong

Copyright © 1982 by Victor Low
All rights reserved
Printed in the United States of America

First printing 1982

Library of Congress Catalogue Card Number: 82-71121

ISBN: 0-934788-03-0 hardcover
      0-934788-04-9 paperback

Published by East/West Publishing Company, Inc.
838 Grant Avenue
San Francisco, California 94108

To all educators who are committed to cultural pluralism

# Contents

# Foreword

THE CHINESE AMERICANS have the longest history of any Asian group in this country, with the first pioneers setting foot on American soil just a few years after the Declaration of Independence. However, the Chinese population in the United States remained sparse until the 1850s when the California gold rush opened the door for development of the Western frontier and immigration took a quantum jump.

These Chinese immigrants found themselves in a milieu where a young, aggressive Republic of the United States of America had proclaimed her manifest destiny to assert sovereignty over a vast territory stretching from the Atlantic to the Pacific. Native Americans, Mexicans, and others who interfered with this grand design were brushed aside or eliminated summarily. As a companion piece to this process, the notion of the superiority of white America was fostered to provide ideological justification. By mid-century such racist ideas had permeated practically all levels of American society, with the principal victims being the non-white groups in this country.

From the beginning, American society regarded the Chinese as inferior and unassimilable into its own social order. The Chinese were tolerated as long as their labor was useful in mining, railroad construction, reclamation, agriculture, light industries and other endeavors, especially in the rapidly developing economy of labor-short California. Their continued immigration during this period in the state's development increased the number of Chinese to about a tenth of the California population. The use of Chinese labor became common throughout the West.

The completion of the first transcontinental railroad facilitated immigration from east of the Mississippi to California, and thus speeded the settlement of the Golden State. However, the railroad did not bring with it the expected prosperity. With the advent of hard times in the 1870s, jobs became increasingly difficult to find. The unemployed and malcontents, egged on by demagogues, searched eagerly for scapegoats.

Concurrently, a fierce struggle was being waged by a coalition of labor unions, small proprietors and small farmers against the railroad, large corporations and large landowners who together were dominating California's economy and politics. Chinese labor was dragged in as part of this struggle by being identified as the tool of these monopolies. The Chinese were accused of taking jobs away from white workers. They were blamed as the cause of various economic and social problems. An anti-Chinese movement developed, fueled by prevailing racist sentiments and capitalized upon by opportunistic labor leaders and politicians. Harassment of the Chinese became a common occurrence. Violence and riots increased in intensity and frequency. Eventually, events led to Congressional enactment of the 1882 Chinese Exclusion Act, the first immigration law in this country to bar the entry of members of a specific ethnic group.

For the next sixty-one years, until the law was repealed in 1943 during World War II as a concession to wartime needs to counteract Axis propaganda, Chinese Americans suffered the ignominy of belonging to an unwanted minority in this, their native or adopted land. It was under this shadow that they developed a Chinese American society. From the beginning they had to struggle to have America even recognize their basic rights as Americans, and it was only after continuous efforts over many decades that their status in this country gradually improved. This, then, is the background which is necessary to understand the significance of the developments described in *The Unimpressible Race.*

During the nineteenth century, stimulated probably by the fact that San Francisco had the largest concentration of Chinese in the country, this city was also the center of the anti-Chinese movement. Thus it was natural that Chinese Americans in San Francisco would be motivated to play a leading role in the efforts of all Chinese Americans to attain equal status in American society. The story of the struggle of Chinese American parents against bureaucrats and politicians of the city's educational establishment was an example of the obstacles they had to overcome.

From the early years of San Francisco's Chinese American community, the Chinese as taxpayers had continually asked the city to allocate to their community a fair share of funds for public education. But it was only after persistent efforts that the Chinese were able to induce city officials to take heed of their needs and make halfhearted moves to establish classes; however, at that time, the impact was limited due to the small number of Chinese American children.

Education of the Chinese in the public school system expanded just when Chinese fortunes in this country were near their nadir during the exclusion era. During this period the number of Chinese children had increased to such an extent that the San Francisco Board of Education no longer could afford to ignore the situation and had to admit them under segregated conditions into the public school system.

The public school experience had deep and far-reaching effects, beyond that which anyone could have foreseen at the time, upon the young Chinese American students. It became a powerful tool for Americanization and disproved the racists' pet assumption that the Chinese were unassimilable into American society. Second generation Chinese Americans rapidly adopted American customs and behavior and abandoned many of their parents' traditional ways, often leading to generational conflicts within their families. This acculturation was also taking place under an atmosphere of racial discrimination which no doubt affected Chinese American psyches. Certainly many students must have smiled cynically within themselves as they listened to teachers extolling the blessings of American democracy in the classrooms. But the status of Chinese Americans slowly improved, due to the unceasing efforts by Chinese Americans as well as changes in attitudes in American society, especially in the decades after World War II.

Equal opportunities for all ethnic groups is now an accepted doctrine in this country, even though at times its observance still seems to be more lip service than true dedication to principle. The uphill battle waged by the Chinese for equal rights in education as described in this book is one facet of the total struggle to gain these objectives. But not all battles have been won, nor have all obstacles been removed. The road ahead is still beset with numerous roadblocks. Therein lies one of the main reasons for this publication: to enable us to learn lessons from the past, so that we can better manage the present and hopefully help posterity steer a better course in the future.

H. M. LAI
*Past President Chinese Historical Society of America*
*July 7, 1981*

# Introduction

*" ...If missionaries after a life-long devotion to the spiritual regeneration of this unprogressive and unimpressible race, show but little fruit of their exhaustive labor, surely no sudden or extensive progress of American ideas can distinguish the only Chinese public school-house outside of the Celestial Kingdom...."*
— *San Francisco School Superintendent George Tait, 1864.*[1]

ONE HUNDRED AND TEN YEARS after School Superintendent George Tait in his annual report expressed his negative views of the Chinese, the United States Supreme Court declared, on January 21, 1974, in *Lau v. Nichols* that the San Francisco Unified School District had violated Title VI of the 1964 Civil Rights Act.[2] The *Lau* lawsuit, initiated in 1970 against the president of the school board, Alan Nichols, and the school district, was the culmination of the increased social activism in San Francisco Chinatown during the 1960s. Lau was one of approximately 1,800 Chinese students in San Francisco who did not speak English. The federal decision meant that English could no longer be the sole language of instruction in the public schools of America.[3]

The 1960s saw the abolition of the national origins quota system which had up until that time mandated an annual entry quota of 105 Chinese immigrants to the United States. The influx of newcomers exacerbated problems in education, health care, housing, employment, recreation, delinquency and poverty in the Chinese American community.

Service associations sprang up in Chinatown to answer these social needs. The we-take-care-of-our-own image of the Chinese community was shattered as Chinese American professionals and civil rights activists challenged the traditional leadership in Chinatown.

The rapid increase of Chinese-speaking students in the public schools in and around Chinatown resulted in a change in instructional policies. In 1966, the school district in San Francisco established an Office of Bilingual Education and Chinese American teachers in schools outside Chinatown were recruited to return to the community.

At colleges and universities, Chinese and other minority Americans, spurred on by the civil rights movement, established ethnic studies departments which probed their heritages and became involved in their communities.

In Chinatown, many social service agencies formed a new organization called the Chinatown/North Beach District Council. Subcommittees were formed in the areas of youth, housing, recreation, immigration, and education. Under the direction of project coordinator Alessandro Baccari, the subcommittees, in conjunction with Chinatown citizens, updated Chinatown's problems in the *San Francisco Chinese Community Citizens' Survey and Fact Finding Committee Report.*

In 1968, the National Teachers Corps Program was started in San Francisco to explore new alternatives in teaching minority children. This joint endeavor of San Francisco State University, the San Francisco Unified School District, and the United States Office of Education had as its underlying assumption that minority children have low educational attainments and/or low self-esteem because of their dissimilar school experiences and cultural backgrounds. To remedy this problem, interns were trained in Chinatown to raise the Chinese children's academic achievement and self-image. The first training program there took place at Jean Parker School.

On February 26, 1969, in an educational forum held in Chinatown at the Commodore Stockton School auditorium by Superintendent Robert Jenkins, the image of the obedient Chinese student was shattered. Youths, frustrated by empty promises by the district to provide more Chinese American teachers, counselors, classrooms and curriculum materials, ended the meeting by throwing firecrackers at the school staff. Many Chinese American teachers employed by the school district were in the audience and the incident led to the formation of TACT—The Association of Chinese Teachers.

By the late 1960s there was a national concern that non-English-speaking students needed more than English as a Second Language (ESL) classes in their educational program. The Bilingual Education Act, passed by Congress in 1967 and signed into

law in 1968, was incorporated into the Elementary Secondary
Education Act as Title VII. It provided federal funds for school
districts to set up bilingual/bicultural demonstration projects.
San Francisco's proposal to the federal government's Office of
Education was funded in 1969. Housed at Commodore Stockton
School, the program used the children's language as the basis for
education while introducing them to the language and culture of
their new environment.

The latter part of the 1960s also saw the long-overdue publishing of books on the Chinese experience in America. With *Mountain of Gold* by Betty L. Sung and *A History of the Chinese in
California*, edited by Thomas W. Chinn and published by the
Chinese Historical Society of America, there was finally in print
a more balanced picture of the Chinese in America.

While the turbulent events of the 1960s made it seem to the
media outside Chinatown that the Chinese were finally gaining
their voice, in fact they had been exercising their right to protest
against educational discrimination for over a century. But their
voice had not been heard outside the confines of Chinatown, nor
was this information systematically passed on to the young.

The *Lau* decision pinpointed a problem for the linguistically
different students which had needed to be addressed since the
beginning of public schooling in the United States. This very
need has generated this study of the Chinese in San Francisco,
long the urban center for the Chinese in America.[4]

In the early days of San Francisco, the Chinese needed to maintain their cultural and social traditions in their new environment. Residential and social restrictions were a harsh fact of life
for them, and these two realities limited the public schooling
of the Chinese to Chinatown for nearly a century. This book is
an edited version of a dissertation, "The Chinese in the San
Francisco Public School System: An Historical Study of One Minority Group's Response to Educational Discrimination, 1859–
1959," submitted in 1981 to the University of San Francisco
School of Education's Multicultural Program. It traces the education of Chinese children in the San Francisco school system
during a hundred-year period by centering upon the systematic
actions of San Francisco school boards and the corresponding responses from individuals and groups in the Chinese community.

This study substantiates Charles Wollenberg's assertion that
minorities were not passive victims of discrimination, but active
participants in a social process.[5] The Chinese involvement with
the educational hierarchy in the city and the state has been a

steady struggle since the middle of the nineteenth century. The *Lau* decision was therefore not an isolated judgment, but an overdue confirmation of the justness of a continuing protest.

Contemporary studies of the Chinese in the San Francisco school system by Dolson,[6] Fernandes,[7] Hendricks,[8] Wollenberg[9] and Lum[10] deal primarily with one aspect of school discrimination—the segregation of the Chinese from the public schools of San Francisco. This study goes further by pointing out in addition other forms of discrimination in education.

Lum's study documented the Chinese community's response to educational prejudice by examining the issue of school desegregation from the late 1960s through the early 1970s. Traced here is a continuum of response since the beginning of public education of Chinese in San Francisco.

The first half of this study illustrates the pattern of city and state school officials withholding school privileges from the Chinese. Schooling for Chinese was not a right, but depended upon the favor of school authorities.

The second half of the book concerns the accomplishments of the Chinese and their gradual entry into the school system as educators. These achievements occurred in the midst of lingering racial, cultural and linguistic discrimination by school officials and by society in general.

The search for documentation followed the techniques of historical research of Borg and Gall.[11] As a starting point, the writer posed a number of questions concerning the development of schooling for Chinese pupils in San Francisco. How did the educational authorities view the presence of Chinese pupils and teachers? How were Chinese treated? What was school like? How did the Chinese respond to their education?

Major attention was given to primary source materials in both English and Chinese. The materials in English included the California State Statutes, legal cases, state and local school superintendents' reports, school board minutes, circulars, memorabilia, enrollment reports and certificated payroll records. Newspapers, books, journals and pamphlets in each time period were researched. Chinese materials included the Chinese press, minutes of the Chinese-American Citizens Alliance, and interviews with Chinese American educators who were employed in the San Francisco Unified School District before 1960.[12] Grammatical mistakes in the primary source material have not been corrected, in order to maintain the flavor of the period.

The interest to do this study grew out of a personal and professional need. Born and raised in San Francisco Chinatown, I grew up in a tightly knit family and was immersed in the customs and practices transplanted from the villages of China. It was before the socially activist period of the 1960s and it just didn't occur to us during our adolescent years that there were social problems.

The world of my childhood was the YMCA, the church, Cameron House,[13] the playground and the Chinese Recreation Center—all within walking distance of where I lived. It was a predictable world where everyone knew everyone else on a first-name basis.

The public schools I attended in San Francisco were Commodore Stockton, Francisco Junior High and George Washington High School. Commodore was practically an all-Chinese school with virtually an all-white staff. At Francisco, there were two main ethnic groups, the Italians and the Chinese, with the Chinese in the majority. In high school at George Washington I first experienced the feeling of being different, of being part of a minority a little apart from mainstream high school activities.

All during this period there was a separation of the American-born Chinese from the immigrant Chinese. They spoke better Chinese and were more oriented to the values and customs of China. We spoke better English and were more "Americanized." At Commodore, a small number of immigrant students were in special classes. There were immigrant students at Francisco, but the only time they mixed with the American-born was at lunch or during physical education classes. Otherwise the immigrant Chinese were in Americanization classes. They continued on to Galileo High, while the American-born went to George Washington and other high schools in the city.

When I attended San Francisco State College and declared education as my major, I was told by a department screening officer that I had to take a speech course to correct my English. At the time I considered it part of my career preparation. After repeating the course three times, I realized that the majority of those taking the course had speech impediments rather than a different linguistic orientation, and that during my developmental years, too much time was given in public school to paper and pencil activities, while oral language development was ignored.

After I graduated from San Francisco State College in 1960, I taught in the San Francisco school system for seven years at Marshall School Annex to predominantly Spanish-speaking students. By 1967, the heavy influx of overseas Chinese students to the Chinatown schools required bilingual teachers like myself to be recruited. Since I had never taught Chinese-speaking students before, I felt somewhat unprepared, a feeling that never left me though I later became a team leader of the National Teachers Corps Program in 1968, project manager of the Chinese Bilingual Pilot Project in 1971, and project head of the state bilingual program since 1975. I never felt myself to be the "bilingual expert" that the assignments required, because neither my public school experiences nor my teacher preparation period accounted for the needs of the linguistically and culturally different students.

These experiences have shaped my desire to systematically document how educational discrimination impacted upon one ethno-linguistic community. Hopefully this study will shed some light upon, and facilitate an understanding of, the current thrust for bilingual education shared by many minorities across this nation. While political pressure sometimes has to be utilized to achieve bilingual education, the motivating factor behind that drive should always be an education for one's children that is worthwhile.

The author would like to thank the members of his dissertation committee: professors John Tsu, Francis Hsu, Uldis Kruze and Reverend James Chuck. A special note of thanks to Professor Tsu and Reverend Chuck for support beyond the immediate approval of the dissertation itself. The author is indebted to Helen Jacobsen, the school district's librarian, for invaluable assistance in providing school district documents, and to the various departments of the San Francisco school district, particularly to Julia Schneider, the school board secretary, who made available the school board minutes.

The chief archivist of the San Francisco History Room in the San Francisco Main Library, Gladys Hansen, provided helpful tips, and information from her book, *The Chinese in California: A Brief Bibliographic History*, has been included in the narrative.

A giant among Chinese American researchers, Him Mark Lai, has been helpful and gracious in sharing his collection of information on this topic from Chinese and English sources. Information gleaned from his preliminary research necessitated that this study be conducted in both languages.

Leonard Louie, president of the Chinese-American Citizens Alliance, and Reverend T. T. Taam, an officer of the Chinese Six Companies, assisted in gaining approval to review documentation from those two organizations. Robert Sung, curriculum writer in the San Francisco school district's Chinese Bilingual Pilot Program, was the author's Chinese language mentor and helped in the understanding of materials written in Chinese, particularly those written in Classical Chinese.

Special mention has to be accorded Dr. Jose Llanes, under whose leadership the multicultural program was established at the University of San Francisco. Another deserving individual is Gordon Lew, editor and publisher of *East/West Journal*, department chairman of Chinese studies at City College of San Francisco, and consultant to the Chinese Bilingual Pilot Project at Commodore Stockton. He gave assistance at various stages of this project.

Thanks also to Richard Springer, who prepared the manuscript for publication, and to Rachel Hum, Edna Gee, Carrie Won, Estela Estrada, Teresita Galura, Linda Wong and John Chiang for technical assistance. A heartfelt thanks to my wife, Melanie, and my mother-in-law, Madeline Wong Findlay.

Finally, I must express my grateful appreciation for the willingness of the Chinese American teachers and parents who so graciously shared their time and their unforgettable experiences about their struggles with the school system.

—V.L.

# Chapter 1

# The Early Years
# 1850–1858

## The Chinese Response to
## Racial Prejudice

EARLY CALIFORNIANS welcomed the arrival of peasants and merchants from Guangdong (廣東), a province situated in southeastern China.[1] Needing the Chinese population to develop the rich resources of the state, Governor Bigler said on January 7, 1852:

It would probably be for the interest of the State to adopt, in regard to the lands designated as Tule, a system of grants to individuals, on the condition that the lands so granted shall be drained by them within a given time. By this course a large portion of the State now lying in a useless condition, would be made productive, contribute largely to the State Treasury, and to induce a further immigration and settlement of the Chinese—one of the most worthy classes of our newly adopted citizens—to whom the climate, and the character of these lands, are peculiarly suited.[2]

The large numbers of Chinese arriving in California didn't alarm the most influential newspaper in the state at that time, the *San Francisco Daily Alta California*:

Scarcely a ship arrives here that does not bring an increase to this worthy integer of our population.... They are amongst the most industrious, quiet, patient people among us.... They seem to live under our laws as if born and bred under them, and already have commenced an expression of their preference by applying for citizenship, by filing their intentions in our courts.... Hats and other American garments succeed and soon the chief distinction consists in the copper color, the narrow angular eyes, the peculiar gibberish and beardless faces. When these national costumes shall have passed away, national prejudices, whether of politics, morals or religion are pretty certainly on their road to amalgamation. The China Boys will yet vote at the same polls, study at the same schools and bow at the same Altar as our own countrymen.[3]

Nearly four months later, on April 23, 1852, Bigler changed his mind. Seeking re-election in 1852, he stigmatized the Chinese as "coolies"[4] and seized upon the question of Chinese immigration to attempt to capture votes.[5] He proposed that the state use its taxing power to check the indiscriminate Asiatic immigration and demanded that the United States pass an act to prohibit "coolies" shipped to California under contracts from laboring in the mines of the state.[6]

The terms of Bigler's message were considered offensive by many intelligent and liberal-minded Americans.[7] However disturbing to some the presence of the Chinese might be, there were those who felt it was not the place of the governor of the state to encourage the outrages that were being committed against them.[8] He articulated many of the anti-Chinese slogans used for over half a century in California and set a vicious example for labor and political leaders who wanted to increase their popularity in California.[9]

On April 29, 1852, the Chinese in San Francisco published a long letter in response to Governor Bigler's message.[10] One paragraph in this ably written document reads:

If the privileges of your laws are open to us, some of us will doubtless acquire your language, your ideas, your feelings, your morals, your forms and become citizens of your country. Many have already adopted your religion as their own, and will be good citizens. There are very good Chinamen now in the country; and a better class will, if allowed, come hereafter—men of learning and of wealth, bringing their families with them.[11]

The *San Francisco Daily Alta California*, which had been warmly pro-Chinese, had a change of editors at this time and went over to the Bigler party.[12] In an article entitled "Chinese Citizenship," the editor stated that treaties with China did not obligate the United States to confer citizenship on the Chinese, and that the only important question was the desirability of large numbers of Chinese. The article concluded with the following:

They [the Chinese] are morally a far worse class to have among us than the negro. They are idolatrous in their religion—in their disposition cunning and deceited, and in their habits libidinous and offensive. They have certain redeeming features of craft, industry, and economy, and like other men in the fallen estate, "they have wrought out many inventions." But they are not of that kind that Americans can ever associate or sympathize with. They are not of our people and never will be, though they remain here forever.... They do not mix with our people, and it is undesirable that they should, for nothing but degradation can result to us from the contact.... It is of no advantage to us to have them here. They can never become like us and they are not of that race or native character which will ever elevate the social condition of California. If great numbers of them should continue to be imported, the manner of treatment to be observed towards them is destined to be an important question in our State politics.... Will they amalgamate with Americans? The last hypothesis is too disgusting to entertain.... It is therefore unwise to encourage them in coming hither. They cannot or ought not to become citizens, and the whole advantage in having them here at all may be summed up in these words—it benefits American commerce at the expense of American civilization.[13]

The above was but one of a series of anti-Chinese editorials published in the spring of 1853. To show that the *Alta* was willing to present an opposing view, the editor printed a letter from Lo Chum-Qui that he felt displayed "originality, ingenuity, and 'chopstick' logic." Lo, whose letter provided a glimpse of the way Chinese were treated in California, castigated the newspapers for "delighting to stigmatise my poor countrymen as a set of 'nasty furriners' who are sunk so low in the depth of degradation that extrication is impossible."[14]

He probed the editor:

Why do you wish to create a feeling of prejudice against my countrymen through the columns of your paper? Are we not already sufficiently ill-treated by those that profess to know better—so much so that we cannot pass along the streets without being subject to insult many times of the vilest kind.... Translate a portion of your laws into our language, and you will no longer complain of our ignorance. We do not pretend to be initiated in all the wisdom of the Fan qui.[15]

He concluded with:

We wish to be friends to those that will use us well. My countrymen are very apt to remember what they see. They have always regarded the American as their best friend. Do you wish them to cultivate those feelings, use them at least as human beings. The most that are in California, at home were poor men; but what they tell about the American will be duly remembered by those that have been fortunate enough not to come to California.[16]

By 1852, San Francisco's Chinese population numbered from three to four thousand. Though they resided and carried on business in every quarter of the city, the chief district was the Chinese quarter or "Little China,"[17] an area that forms the inner core of present-day San Francisco Chinatown. This concentration provided a visible target to those in sympathy with Governor Bigler.

Toward the end of 1853, in the process of reviling the Chinese in San Francisco, the *Alta* provided a description of the boundaries of early Chinatown (to see how the boundaries of Chinatown have expanded in the past hundred years, see Figure 6, page 155):

The Chinese Quarter, which occupies Sacramento Street, between Kearny and Dupont Street [Grant Avenue], Jackson from Kearny to Stockton, and Dupont Street between Sacramento and Jackson is now occupied almost entirely by Chinese. They seem to have driven out everything and everybody else, and to have monopolized this portion of the city. Sacramento Street is devoted by them to trade, while the other streets mentioned are filled with low establishments of the vilest description...disgusting to look at...excessive filth...houses are mere shells and tinder boxes, which could be fired almost by a single spark....If we are to have a Chinese community amongst us, and we see no prospect that we shall not always have, they ought to inhabit a portion of the city by themselves, and that ought to be farther removed from the heart of the city.[18]

The *Golden Hill News*, published in 1854 and considered the first Chinese newspaper in the United States,[19] argued its cause:

The Chinese is said to be unfitted for Caucasian civilization. Give them a fair trial before condemnation.[20]

On another occasion the paper commented:

The outrages upon these unfortunates is on record in the public Annals. The press almost unanimously have spoken against them with contempt and has excited an aggressive prejudice against them in the public mind....Everybody in this country has been reluctantly forced to confess that the Chinese are industrious (when we allow them), peaceable and are no burden to our taxation. They neither crowd our almshouses, hospitals nor prisons.[21]

The argument in defense of the Chinese was ignored. In 1854, the Supreme Court of California held that "Chinese and all other people not white are included in the prohibition from being witnesses against whites."[22] Since the Chinese could not testify, they were mortally afraid of the American courts.[23] For many years the Chinese would have no legal protection against insults, robberies, murder and lynchings by hoodlums.

In a January 30, 1855, reply to Governor Bigler's favoring a policy of excluding Asiatics,[24] the Chinese merchants of San Francisco responded:

It is said that "henceforth you would prevent the emigration of people of the Flowery land" [China]. Hitherto our people have been imbued with your sacred doctrines; we have tried to exercise modesty and reason. If we can henceforth be treated with mutual courtesy, then we shall be glad to dwell within your honorable boundaries. But if the rabble are to harass us, we wish to return to our former homes. We will speedily send and arrest the embarkation of any that have not yet come, And now we, who are here, do earnestly request that a definite time may be fixed, by which we may be governed, within which we can return our merchandize, and make any necessary arrangements. We trust that in that case the friendly intercourse of previous days will not be interrupted; and that your honorable nation may maintain its principles in tenderly cherishing the strangers from afar. If there be no definite regulation upon this subject, but only these incessant rumors about forbidding the Chinese emigration, we fear the result will be that the class who know nothing, of every nation, will be ever seeking occasions to make trouble; that our Chinese people in the mines will be subjected to much concealed violence, to robbery of their property, and quarrels about their claims. Thus there will be unlimited trouble; and where will be the end of it? Further, if there be no definite date and regular method fixed for our return to Canton, where can we make preparations in San Francisco for the accommodation of several tens of thousands of the Chinese? We most earnestly request the officers of the government early to issue a definite enactment. Such a course will be the best for the interests of our nation. It will be the best for the Chinese here.[25]

This wish to return to their former homes was disregarded. Governor Bigler needed Chinese laborers to plow the soil, sow crops, and build dikes and irrigation systems to ease California's transition from a frontier society to an agricultural settlement.[26] It was a double injustice. First, taxes were unfairly imposed on the Chinese to secure revenue for the support of the government. At the same time, legislation was passed to force the Chinese to withdraw from profitable industries or entirely from the state.[27] Given the climate that produced these miseries and the loss of legal protection, it is not hard to follow the progression that led to the Chinese and other non-white children being denied the right to public education.

## State Superintendent Moulder and School Segregation

RACE WAS NOT MENTIONED in the early school laws of California. The laws of 1851 and 1853 only provided for the distribution of state educational funds in proportion to the number of school-age children in a particular community. In 1855, the year after school authorities in San Francisco established a separate "colored school" for black children,[28] race was mentioned. Section 18 of the 1855 school law stated:

The Marshals selected and designated by the Trustees under the provisions of this Act, shall, in the month of October, annually, take a specific census of all the white children within their respective precincts, between the ages of 4 and 18 years, specifying the names of the children, of the parents or guardians of such children, and the town, city and school district within which they reside, and make full report thereof, in writing, under oath, to the County Superintendent of Common Schools, and deliver a true copy thereof to the Trustees in their respective school districts by the 10th day of November next, thereafter.[29]

This "white children" clause codified the denying of public-school attendance to all non-white children.

The act of 1856 reinforced the 1855 school law by stating how an additional school or schools could be provided in the state:

Sec. 34. Upon the petition of fifty heads of white families, resident citizens in any district, the Board of Education may, in their discretion, establish a common school or additional common schools therein, subject in all respects to the laws and regulations governing the other common schools, awarding to such school or schools its proportionate share of school fund.[30]

This law placed the establishment and organization of public schools entirely in the control of the white population, while the state refused to recognize the need of non-white families for public education. The stage was set for the Chinese and other non-whites to struggle via the courts to obtain their rights in the public schools of California.[31]

After the establishment of a separate school for black children in San Francisco in 1854, it was only a matter of time before the San Francisco Board of Education discussed the question of educating the Chinese in the English language. When the subject was brought up on January 13, 1857, the board was unanimous in its opinion that it was very desirable that the "Asiatics, and particularly the Chinese youths, should have every opportunity to acquire a knowledge of the English language." However, the board decided not to admit Chinese into the evening school because "they were liable to insult by rude boys before and after school hours."[32]

The board debate is instructive as to the thinking of the time. Board member Mitchell on the one hand made a motion to admit Chinese to the evening school, but he also said that if "Chinamen" were admitted, it would drive many other students away.[33] Board member Blake doubted the power of the board to exclude Chinese under 18 years of age, but President Sherman was of the opinion that the board had that power.

A Mr. Goddard supported the motion and said it should be the main object of everyone to "Americanize the Chinamen," since they paid heavier taxes and behaved themselves better than what he called the low class of American citizens. Goddard thought that if the board could not provide for them in this school, it should make some other arrangement. Further, he said that "Negroes and Chinamen" were different sorts of people, and that he did not see any reason to exclude Chinese because their skin was a little darker. The motion to admit Chinese into the school lost by a vote of seven to two.

The editor of the *Evening Bulletin*, while acknowledging that the Chinese were eager to be instructed and could pay for their tuition, referred the problem to the missionary schools. His argument was that the church should instill the Christian religion into the minds of the Chinese, and that the best way was through the teaching of English. He referred the matter to Reverend William Speer of the Presbyterian Board of Missions.[34]

Reverend Speer's reply to the newspaper communicated the idea that the Chinese were determined to improve the quality of their education. His reply said in part: "Their pride rebels against being taught children's knowledge out of children's books which are unfortunately the only ones we have adopted to the end in view."[35]

Speer regretted the board's decision and was convinced the public schools should educate the Chinese. He believed the Chinese would endure any inconvenience and rudeness for the sake of educational advantages. He argued:

I would urge that the Board of Education ought to take some steps towards the intellectual improvement of this large and important class. As taxpayers they have a civil right to school privileges. No portion of a miscellaneous population can without detriment to the general peace and welfare, without injustice to them and indeed to all others, and without ultimate great pecuniary disadvantage, be left unenlightened.... I will lend my efforts and acquaintance with the Chinese people towards the formation of a separate school and will advocate it through the Chinese columns of the Oriental newspaper.[36]

Since the board would not set up a separate evening school, Speer proposed a separate school, free of charge, for the Chinese in his church building, but under the auspices of the board of education. The board didn't seriously consider Speer's offer until the matter of a day school for the Chinese was brought up two years later.

By the late 1850s, allowing blacks into the city's high schools had become a problem in San Francisco. The issue before the board was "the degree of whiteness." A black child named Lester entered the city's high school in 1858. Other girls "as white as Lester" had previously applied for admission, but the superintendent, Henry B. Janes, delayed their admission pending a board ruling, since he was denied power until such action.

The board meeting over the question of colored children in public schools produced a lengthy debate, but the subject was indefinitely postponed. The various resolutions proposed by the board are listed below because they had far-reaching implications for the non-white students of the time.

Resolved, that no "colored children" be admitted into any Public School except the school established for colored children, and that the Committee on Classification be directed to remove to said school any "colored children" who may be in attendance in other Public Schools.

The above resolution clearly made a separation between the rights of white students and the rights of colored students.

Whereas, the Board of Education has provided a school for the education of the children of the African race by themselves — and whereas this Board do not deem it expedient that the white and colored children should be brought together in the same school — therefore Resolved, that no applicant shall be admitted into or be allowed to attend the schools designated for white children unless removed from the African race at least to the eighth degree. And it shall be the duty of the Director of each District to visit and examine the school or schools in his district for the purpose of ascertaining whether there are any scholars that should be excluded therefrom, and report the same to the Board.

This second resolution dealt with the "degree of whiteness" and was offered by Goddard.

Resolved, that white children who desire to attend the public schools of this city shall be required to attend the schools assigned to white children and children who are manifestly of African descent shall be required to attend the schools which now are, or may hereafter be assigned to colored children.

The third resolution was more emphatic than the first in suggesting a total separation. White families would be prohibited from allowing their children to attend school with black children.

Resolved, that no colored children be admitted to any public school, except the school established for colored children: provided, this resolution shall not exclude any children now in the public schools.[37]

The fourth resolution dealt with the question of exceptions to the regulations. The board wanted the policy to exclude colored children, but didn't want Lester removed, since she was already admitted into the high school by the board's own examining committee. Sending Lester back to the Colored School would have called into question the competence of the examiners. The board was particularly opposed to the fourth resolution, because, by allowing exceptions, it went against the prevailing notion that blacks were inferior to whites.

The matter was resolved a week later, when a resolution was passed that "no colored children be admitted to any Public School except to such as are provided for colored children."[38] After this ruling, Lester had to leave the city's high school and attend the Colored School. This local decision for separate schooling for whites and blacks antedated by two years the segregated school laws of California.

Echoing the prejudice that existed in San Francisco and every other American community, the *Evening Bulletin* lauded the school board's decision and advocated separate schooling also for Chinese:

Then let us keep our public schools free from the intrusion of the inferior races. If we are compelled to have Negroes and Chinamen among us, it is better, of course, that they should be educated. But teach them separately from our own children. Let us preserve our Caucasian blood pure. We want no mongrel race of moral and mental hybrids to people the mountains and valleys of California.[39]

Separate schooling for whites and non-whites was officially sealed in California when Andrew Jackson Moulder, California's third school superintendent and a Southern Democrat, brought his long-cultivated prejudice against the black slaves of the South to the state.[40] He was influential in the development of public education in California from 1850 to 1895.

Moulder's report to the state legislature marked him as the first California school superintendent to prevent non-white children, in general, and Chinese children, in particular, from attending public schools with white children. His 1858 report,[41] the first official document from the state school authority concerning the public education of Chinese children in California, predated even the full-scale anti-Chinese outcry from the California labor movement.[42] Moulder's actions played a major role in obstructing Chinese children from going to schools with white children in San Francisco in the mid-1880s.

The opening and closing sentences in Moulder's report revealed his belief in racial and class superiority. Criticizing the "mock philanthropists for forcing Africans, Chinese and Diggers into our white schools," he insisted that this persistence would result in the ruin of public education. Moulder mentioned his power "to resist, to defeat and to prohibit their admission into the white schools." He regretted he couldn't do more under existing law and recommended he be given the power to withhold public funds from any district that admitted the children of "inferior races" into the common schools.

Moulder maintained that non-whites should not be brought up in "ignorance and heathenism" and he allowed school districts to establish separate schools for "inferior races," with some public funds for their support, provided citizens did not object.

During Moulder's second term of office, two of his recommendations—that school districts which mixed the schooling of whites and non-whites be punished and that separate schools be established—became law. His direct involvement in the education of Chinese children in San Francisco will be discussed in Chapter 4 of this book.

In early 1858, San Francisco School Superintendent Henry B. Janes appeared before the school board to recommend that a rule be passed "confining children of African and Negro descent to schools established for colored children."[43]

Though Janes was a product of his time, he had some reservations regarding separate schooling for non-white children. This can be seen in his 1858 *Annual Report*. (Except for the word "now," the italics, for emphasis, are mine):

There is, also, "power consistent with a free government" which I hope soon to see exerted—that is, the power of the State to protect against corruption and internal foes, by requiring that *every child* shall receive, sometime during its minority a common English education, *leaving the choice of schools entirely free.* "The intelligence and virtue of the people are safeguards of the Republic," is a saying as common as it is true. If true in theory—and we have as a people the right to guard our free institutions from any and every kind of foe—why not *now* act upon it? Negatively, this power is already recognized: we exclude Chinese and Negroes from the ballot box and witness stand, because of their real or assumed ignorance and liability to corruption. *Why not, then, by positive enactment, prevent the same evil tendencies in those who by birthright or adoption may demand the exercise of those rights for themselves and their children.*[44]

The advocacy of a free education for every child was a minority viewpoint. Janes's position was put to the test four years later when John Swett ran for the position of State Superintendent of Public Instruction. Swett was accused by his opponents of being an "abolitionist with amalgamating proclivities," because he had allowed black and white children to attend the same school while he was a principal in San Francisco. Janes was the superintendent at the time, and he was officially directed by the board to visit the schools and carry out their order to confine "colored children" to the Colored School. Swett's accusers asked Janes for a response, since board minutes did not document Swett's "amalgamating" activities.[45] Janes made his survey and replied that he found Negroes classed with white children in three schools and that the Rincon School of John Swett was one of them. Steps were immediately taken for the removal of black children to the Colored School.[46]

Sacrificing principle in the face of political pressure, Janes didn't maintain his egalitarian stance for long. The combined power of the San Francisco School Board, State School Superintendent Moulder, the press, public opinion, and Swett's accusers was too overpowering. Janes gave the following reply to Swett's opponents: "The effect of these facts [black and white children in the same school] upon the charge to which you refer [attack on John Swett], I leave to your own opinion."[47] Separate schooling for non-white students in San Francisco was a soundly established fact when the Chinese began their petitioning for public schooling.

# Chapter 2

# The Struggling Years
# 1859–1871

## The Initiative for a Chinese School

WHEN THE SUBJECT of educating the Chinese was brought up again in 1859, the San Francisco Board of Education showed a more conciliatory attitude. At a meeting held on January 18, board member Stoddard moved that the Chinese be admitted to the foreign class at the evening school, and the motion prevailed.[1] This move enabled the men and the older boys to have an education. However, the problem of "rude boys" and the inconvenience of attending the evening school outside of the Chinese quarter caused Chinatown's leaders to petition the board for a school for the Chinese.

The board discussed the request for a separate evening school and informed the Chinese applicants that there was insufficient money to authorize the opening of a school during the fiscal year, but consideration would be given to their plea.[2]

With day schooling still not provided for the Chinese children, thirty Chinese parents petitioned the board on August 23, 1859, to establish a primary school for their children. This subject was referred to the committee on textbooks.[3]

Previously, on August 13, Mr. Knowles, a board member, had stated that when he had visited the school for Chinese children organized by the Presbyterian Board of Missions, there were 17 children present. He said he was told there would soon be about 25 boys and 10 girls. The subject of board involvement in educating Chinese during the day was still pending before the board by the end of the month.[4]

September 12, 1859, was the official date Chinese children were allowed to attend public school in San Francisco. The school established for them was simply called the Chinese

School. The incentive for the board to start the school was Reverend Speer's offer of a large room in his church. Thus, the Chinese School began, free of charge, on the corner of Sacramento and Stockton streets. The only cost to the board was to pay Mr. Lanctot, the teacher, the amount of $75 per month.[5] Thirty-two students were enrolled at the school and an average daily attendance of twenty-one pupils was soon established.[6]

Commenting on converting the church school to a public school, School Superintendent James Denman said:

I believe this to be the only school in the Union that provides a school exclusively for the Chinese learning our language; and there is none other, having in its midst a heathen temple, established and used for the worship of idols, whose worshippers may also enjoy the blessings of the free Common Schools.[7]

Adults and older children also attended the Chinese School and no longer had to attend the evening school outside of Chinatown.

But four months after its official opening, the board discontinued the school due to lack of funds.[8] This reason did not satisfy the *Evening Bulletin*. Its editor chided the school board:

The only excuse we hear for this, is lack of funds. But we are convinced that it is a mistaken policy—a piece of two penny economy. It seems a great pity that an experiment, commenced with so many difficulties, and which was proving so eminently successful, should be abandoned at the very outset. Chinamen are required to pay school taxes. It is but decent that they should have some remuneration for their taxes. Certainly it is not to our credit that heathen, for whom we afford no educational advantages, should help to school our children. The glory of the Free School System is that it extends its privileges to all, white or black, outside barbarians or the tailed Celestials—to any who have, by the most charitable construction, a soul or an intellect that ranks above instinct.[9]

A day later the *Alta* printed a letter from a person named "J" who claimed that a large proportion of the people of San Francisco wanted the Chinese School to continue:

Surely our worthy Board of Education can find some other means of compromising to the extent of $75 per month, and thus continue this laudable work of educating the Chinese children; for it is only by doing so that we can prevent their becoming the degraded and pernicious pests of society.

So long as we continue to permit, and indeed invite the Chinese to immigrate hither, and require them to pay taxes, it is our business duty to furnish them with the means of acquiring a knowledge of our institutions.[10]

The press made an impact on the board, for the subject of reopening the school was discussed at the next meeting. Janes said he would not vote for rescinding the resolution if the Chinese had access to any other schools, but as they had not, he thought it best to continue the school. Brewer was originally opposed to continuing the school because of the board's lack of funds, but when he heard his fellow board members classifying Chinese with baboons and monkeys, he felt he could not side with his associates.[11] A motion by Eldridge to rescind the resolution to abolish the Chinese School carried, and Superintendent Denman was directed to reopen the Chinese School on Monday, January 9.[12]

On April 17, 1860, Superintendent James Denman presented a report to the board on his visit to the school:

I have visited the Chinese School during the week, and found the few pupils in attendance anxious to learn the rudiments of our language. I was surprised to find so few present, there being only three children and seven adults in attendance. I was informed by the teacher that the usual average was but little greater than this number. I very much question the justice and propriety of expending the public funds to sustain this school, when those for whom it was established manifest so little interest in availing themselves of its advantages.[13]

Denman's comments were devastating to the school and it was scheduled to be closed again. The school operated until the end of the school year only because board member Eldridge wanted to give the school time to build up its enrollment. He proposed that, if after a certain period the number of scholars was still insufficient, the school be discontinued. This recommendation was adopted by the board.[14] Superintendent James Denman's remarks on the small number of pupils and the lack of interest on the part of the Chinese would be echoed again and again over the next twenty years by school superintendents in San Francisco in their *Annual Reports.*

The school struggled on until the end of the term. When Superintendent Denman reported on July 24 that the average attendance was ten scholars, the board passed a resolution requiring that "the Chinese School be suspended after the 31st of July for want of sufficient members to continue the school."[15] The reason for the low attendance at the school was found in the *Evening Bulletin* rather than in the board minutes:

It appeared during the discussion which this provoked, that the Chinese School started on the 12th of September with 15 scholars, and that during the last week its average attendance was 21 and a half. Mr. Brewer urged forcibly the arguments for sustaining the school. Mr. Eldridge wanted it understood that if the school was reopened, it should be upon precisely the basis that the other schools are on. He believed that the school had been injured before by the religious teaching that had been introduced — by long prayers, and reading the Bible. The school professed to be established for the purpose of teaching the Chinese our language. It unnecessarily offended the intelligent scholars, and taught them nothing, to give it so decided a religious cast. So long as the school was supported by the public moneys, it was wrong to allow it to be construed into a religious school; if the religious community could support a religious school for the Chinese, let them do it — but better teach them the alphabet, which the scholars are anxious to learn, before trying to force the gospel on them.[16]

The board suspended the daytime operation of the school for three months, but pressure from the Chinese community and its advocates led to its reopening. On October 25, the board considered a resolution that the school "be reopened forthwith, and that Mr. B. Lanctot be employed as the teacher thereof at a salary of $75 per month."[17] However, the resolution was passed with the understanding that the school would resume operation only in the evenings,[18] so Chinese children were still denied a proper public education in San Francisco.

The closings of the Chinese School in December 1859 and July 1860 occurred during Denman's administration. While the records didn't show that he was solely responsible for the closings, remarks by him in the press and particularly in city school reports revealed his prejudicial attitude toward the school.[19] He promulgated the opinion that the Chinese lacked scholars and an interest in education. He stated this opinion twice in the *Annual Report* and in his April 17 presentation to the board. Denman felt the Chinese people's "caste and religious idolatry" precluded their education in America. However, he acknowledged the inequality of the law as one possible reason the Chinese showed little interest in education. As superintendent he could have used his influence to keep the Chinese School in operation. Instead, Denman labeled the school a "doubtful experiment" and cautioned the board to give careful consideration before appropriating public funds for its support.

State Superintendent Moulder's recommendation that his office be given the power to withhold public funds from any district that admitted non-whites into public schools became law during his second term. The California School Law of 1860 reflected Moulder's 1858 report and showed his racist influence:

Negroes, Mongolians and Indians shall not be admitted into the public schools; and whenever satisfactory evidence is furnished to the Superintendent of Public Instruction to show that said prohibited parties are attending such schools, he may withhold from the district in which such schools are situated, all share of the State School Funds; and the Superintendent of Common Schools for the county in which such district is situated, shall not draw his warrant in favor of such district for any expenses incurred while the prohibited parties aforesaid were attending the public schools therein; provided that the trustees of any district may establish a separate school for the education of Negroes, Mongolians and Indians, and use the public school funds for the support of the same.[20]

To be sure district superintendents understood the intent of the law, Moulder remarked:

This salutary regulation will be rigidly enforced. Whenever satisfactory evidence of its violation is furnished to the State Superintendent, he will take prompt action.[21]

This was the first school law in California that expressly discriminated against the children of black, Chinese, and Indian parentage. While earlier laws emphasized schooling for white children, no penalties were exacted from school districts that permitted the enrollment of non-white students. Moulder's law became a prototype for later state laws and city ordinances to prevent non-white children in general, and Chinese children in particular, from attending the public schools of California.

The Chinese evening school resumed operation from November 1860 to May 1861. Fearing that the evening school would suffer a fate similar to that of the day school, the *Alta* on May 23, 1861, appealed to the city school authorities to keep the school open through the summer months.[22]

The appeal by the *Alta* had no impact on the board. Two days later, a committee on the evening school reported it was inexpedient to keep the Chinese School open for the present, a position adopted by the board.[23] On September 3, 1861, the board was asked again to reopen the Chinese School,[24] but this appeal had very little effect, and from May until September 1861, public education was not available to the Chinese in San Francisco. It was true, however, that, in an apparent economy move, all evening schools in San Francisco were closed down in the summer of 1861.

On September 23, 1861, the board ordered all evening schools reopened. However, the salary of Lanctot was reduced from $75 to $50 per month. Lamenting this cut in salary, the *Evening Bulletin* said:

We are sorry...for it was little enough before for a duty that very few can perform, and which must be performed by somebody, if as citizens and Christians, we are true to our own interests.[25]

Two months later, Lanctot's salary was restored to $75. The reason given was the increase of Chinese students—Lanctot was teaching at the Chinese School during the day and in the evening.[26]

## State Superintendent John Swett Bucks Anti-Chinese Trends

THE STRUGGLE FOR PUBLIC SCHOOLING took place within the larger social context of race prejudice against the Chinese. In Governor-elect Leland Stanford's January 10, 1862, inaugural address, he reiterated his predecessor's anti-Chinese policy:

There can be no doubt that the presence of numbers among us of a degraded and distinct people must exercise a deleterious influence upon the superior race, and, to a certain extent, repel desirable immigration. It will afford me great pleasure to concur with the Legislature in any constitutional action, having for its object the repression of the immigration of the Asiatic races.[27]

This message from the highest officer of the state gave official sanction to white workingmen to organize anti-Chinese societies. Anti-coolie clubs were formed as early as 1862 in San Francisco.[28]

The increased conspicuousness of Chinese in San Francisco after the mining period made them victims of violent pranks by rowdy toughs. Sporadic incidents of brutality against Chinese by bands of hoodlums were the subject of frequent news reports in the 1860s.[29]

In an *Evening Bulletin* article, "Cowardly Business for American Boys," the editor wrote:

Can't something be done to stop the boys from insulting and abusing Chinamen? They are a cowardly set, those boys that throw stones at those inoffensive people, and shamefully ill-mannered. And I must tell you, confidentially, (for I am ashamed to have it known out of the family) that many of the city schoolboys do these things. I saw a little squad at it yesterday, right by a church, where we were praying for pardon for our National sins! Won't you speak to the parents of our boys, or their school masters, or Sunday School teachers, and drop a word in Chief Burke's ear, for him to pass to his officers about the city?[30]

The sporadic insults and abuses toward the Chinese would become systematic and violent in the 1870s.

Just when city school authorities were taking a harder line in denying school privileges to the Chinese, the state began to recognize their right to an education. This came about when John Swett replaced Moulder as the state's fourth school superintendent. This Yankee schoolmaster's most important period of service to California began on January 1, 1863, the day President Lincoln's Emancipation Proclamation became effective, and extended until 1867.[31] As superintendent during the Civil War period, Swett fought against the prejudices of his time to make schools an instrument of democracy.[32] He attempted to reach an accommodation between the contradictory American commitments to equality of opportunity and racial segregation.[33] Swett, determined to achieve the goal of free education for all, said in his report:

If all classes pay taxes on their property for the support of the schools, there is no reason why the children of all classes, whether white, black, tawney, or copper-colored, should not be educated.[34]

While in office, he gradually removed racial demarcation in his first, second, and third revisions of the state school law. He "recognized separate schools merely as a minimum right of the children of Chinese, Indian and Negro parentage; not as a maximum limit of their educational opportunity."[35] A simple reading of these school laws might give the impression that Swett was a segregationist, but his efforts improved the status of non-white

students in California. School law revisions under his administration reflected his change of policy. The School Law of 1863
mandated that non-whites be included in the school census:

It shall be the duty of such School Census Marshal to take ... a special census of all the white children in his district between the ages
of four and eighteen years ... ; to include all children who may be attending private institutions of learning ... ; to report the number not
attending school, the number between the ages of eighteen and
twenty-one years, the number under four years of age, the number
born in California, the number of Indian, Mongolian, and Negro
children, respectively.[36]

Swett, a pragmatist, preferred not to argue his case until he had
substantial data. By this first revision, the census marshals were
able for the first time to describe the educational situation of the
Chinese in California:

The number of Mongolian or Chinese children returned by the
School Census is four hundred and fifty-five; none of whom attend
school. There is a School for Chinese in San Francisco, but it is de-
signed principally for adults.[37]

This was the earliest official report of the number of Chinese
and other non-white children in California and established their
need for public schooling.

In 1864, the second revision of the state school law took a de-
finitive step forward in establishing separate schools for non-
whites:

Negroes, Mongolians, and Indians shall not be admitted into the
public schools; provided, that upon the application of the parents or
guardians of ten or more such colored children, made in writing to
the Trustees of any district, said Trustees shall establish a separate
school for the education of Negroes, Mongolians, and Indians, and
use the public school funds for the support of the same;- and provided, further, that the Trustees of any school district may establish
a separate school, or provide for the education of any less number of
Negroes, Mongolians, and Indians, and use the public school funds
for the support of the same, whenever in their judgment, it may be
necessary for said public schools.[38]

This revision advanced the status of non-white students in
three ways. First, the punishment of withholding school funds
for admitting children of the "inferior races" into the public
schools was deleted. Second, while the School Law of 1860 permitted trustees to establish separate schools for non-whites, this

law made it an obligation in certain circumstances. Third, fewer than ten non-white children could be considered for public schooling by trustees.

Swett's third and final revision of the state school law took place in 1866. That same year saw the civil rights bill passed by the United States Congress which granted citizenship to all emancipated persons and the passage of the Fourteenth Amendment to the Constitution, which provided that no state could deprive any citizen of equal protection by the laws. These two federal enactments aided Swett's cause of improving the educational status of non-white children in California., The salient sections of the third revision are enumerated below:

Sec. 43....It shall be the duty of the School Census Marshal to take...an exact census of all children under fifteen years of age. He shall take specifically and separately a census of all white children, Negro children, and Indian children who live under the guardianship of white persons, between five and fifteen years of age.... The Census Marshal shall further report, separately, the number of white, Negro, and Indian children under five years of age, and the whole number of Mongolian children under fifteen years of age.

Sec. 56.... Any Board of Trustees or Board of Education, by a majority vote, may admit into any public school half-breed Indian children and Indian children who live in white families or under guardianship of white persons.

Sec. 57.... Children of African or Mongolian descent, and Indian children not living under the care of white persons, shall not be admitted into public schools, except as provided in this Act; provided, that upon the written application of the parents or guardians of at least ten such children to any Board of Trustees or Board of Education, a separate school shall be established for the education of such children; and the education of a less number may be provided for by the Trustees in any other manner.

Sec. 58.... When there shall be in any district any number of children, other than white children, whose education can be provided for in no other way, the trustees, by a majority vote, may permit such children to attend school for white children; provided, that a majority of the parents of the children attending such school make no objection, in writing, to be filed with the Board of Trustees.[39]

This third revision was the most liberal in dealing with the education of non-white children. Note the phrasing in Section 43 where "Mongolian children under fifteen years of age" is inserted clumsily at the end of the sentence. "All children" should naturally include the Chinese, but it was not *natural* to provide schooling for Chinese children in Swett's time. Chinese children in 1866 were totally excluded from the public schools of California, according to the *Second Biennial Report:*

No schools for Mongolian children are reported. The Chinese in San Francisco are entitled to a separate school under Section 58, but during the past year it has not been maintained.[40]

This passage showed school administrators that a segment of the population was being ignored, and the census data in that same report indicated the scope of the problem. It showed that 218 Mongolian children were attending private schools, with 179 in San Francisco, 20 in Sacramento, and 8 in Alameda.[41]

Section 56 of the School Law of 1866 advanced the educational status of those who had the "privilege" of living with white families. Such was the case of some Indian children in California.

The section of the School Law of 1864 regarding the education of fewer than ten African, Mongolian, and Indian children was changed in Section 57 of the School Law of 1866, so that school boards could use means at their disposal outside school funds to finance this education.

Section 58 provided that non-white children could attend the same schools as whites through a majority vote of the trustees, provided a majority of the parents of the children attending the school made no written objection to the board of trustees.

Under the leadership of State Superintendent John Swett, the status of non-white children was raised from non-recognition to one theoretically equal to that enjoyed by whites. Swett followed the policies of Andrew Moulder by prohibiting non-whites from entering California's public schools, but he also lessened the racial prejudice in school legislation. These revisions document the wisdom and tactics of a great educational administrator who aided the socially oppressed.

# City Superintendent Denman and the Demise of the Chinese School

CHANGES IN THE STATE LAW provided the incentive needed for the Chinese in San Francisco to continue the struggle for public education. The on-again, off-again Chinese School operated from 1861 to 1866, with morning and evening sessions. This plan accommodated the larger number of students who had to work during the day. The city school report of 1864 showed an average daily attendance of 30 pupils—a high mark during those shaky years.[42]

Though the school was successful, the new superintendent, George Tait, denigrated the idea of educating Chinese in his annual report:

This School, although small, deserves notice, if not for the good results manifested, at least to express our admiration of the philanthropy which suggested its organization.

If missionaries after a life-long devotion to the spiritual regeneration of this unprogressive and unimpressible race, show but little fruit of their exhaustive labor, surely no sudden or extensive progress of American ideas can distinguish the only Chinese public school-house outside of the Celestial Kingdom. Regarded from this stand point, this school should be famous, even though its habitat is only a gloomy basement of the Chinese Chapel, whose obscure walls, are nevertheless not repugnant to Mongolian tastes and habits.

For one not acquainted with the Chinese language, or population, it is difficult to note the progress made from year to year, by the school, and hence, we can only infer from the increasing attendance that advantages of the school are becoming better known and appreciated by the Chinese, and that therefore the school is doing its peculiar work not ineffectually.[43]

Neither did the Chinese School's success please the editor of the *Daily Morning Call*. In an editorial entitled "Mongoliana," he concluded with the following:

No person can show in what respect this expenditure is ever to benefit the American name or fame, its interests, its civilization, its society. It is simply a gratuity thrown at the expense of our own pockets, and to the detriment and injury of our own children. When the city shall have provided Schools and Teachers for all our children, will be time enough to throw away its extra funds upon people who cannot and never desire to become citizens, and not till then.[44]

Despite these unfavorable attitudes, peak support for the Chinese School occurred during this period. The board allowed the teacher and his students to take their vacation during Chinese New Year instead of the regular vacation period[45] and granted the teacher's request to have the day session at the Chinese School changed from morning to afternoon in order to accommodate a larger number of working students.[46] Evidently holding morning sessions was inconvenient to those students who had to work at night. The board also acted on a recommendation from 14 Chinese merchants[47] to replace Lanctot with William Dye, a teacher of a Chinese private school.[48]

Removing Lanctot turned out unfavorably for the Chinese. As soon as Dye started teaching, Lanctot asked that his removal be referred to a committee for investigation. The board honored his request and referred the subject to its judiciary committee.[49] Apparently this meant closing the school until the Lanctot/Dye controversy was resolved.

Complicating the issue was a third applicant for the teaching position, James T. Doylan, who had taught in China.[50] With three men contending for the job, the subject of re-establishing the school was under board consideration from March 1867 to the end of the year. During this interval, the school reverted back to its former status as a private enterprise. Dye taught in the school until the issue was resolved.

The *Alta* had this to say of Dye:

He has devoted himself to the work without compensation of any kind, hoping that the city will at an early day take the matter in hand and extend to the Mongolian population, who contribute fully their share of taxes, the same privileges enjoyed by other classes. . . . Being interested in the people, knowing them well, and having the confidence of their leading men, Mr. Dye undertook charge of the school. . . . [51]

As to Lanctot's removal, the records did not indicate why the Chinese merchants wanted to get rid of him. In the formative years of the Chinese School, he seemed to have the respect of the Chinese pupils. They gave him a Christmas gift every year and, the Christmas prior to his termination, he received $117 from them. A bilingual dictionary written by him may have been the first of its kind.[52]

The only clue to Lanctot's unpopularity was his overzealousness in religious teaching.[53] Apparently the fact that the Chinese did not learn enough English to cope in an English-speaking environment led the Chinese merchants to petition for a reorganization of the Chinese School.[54]

Of all the San Francisco school superintendents during these struggling years, John Pelton was the most progressive in wanting to extend the benefits of public education to the Chinese. He reminded the board of the difficulties the Chinese School had encountered and said the school needed a teacher who could speak both languages or two teachers — one American and one Chinese. He recommended that the subject be referred to a committee. He felt the Chinese had rights to school funds, rights that they could enforce through the courts.[55] Pelton's recommendation for a teacher who could speak both languages preceded bilingual education in the United States by a hundred years. Pelton's far-sightedness was exemplified in his *Annual Report* to the board:

From the census returns we find that there are 179 Chinese children in this city, under fifteen years of age. Of these only thirty-seven are attending school. None are in public schools, such being excluded from all except the Colored School, which they will not attend. They are provided with no school for their special accommodation. Here we have a striking instance of taxation without representation; a principle and practice which we are accustomed to condemn as wrong. The Chinese, it is estimated, pay about one twentieth of our total taxation, this year amounting to about $120,000, and of this amount $14,000 goes to make up our school fund. Should not at least the very small portion of this sum necessary for that purpose, be devoted to the support of a school especially for the Chinese children now seen in groups upon many of our streets? Would not police and moral considerations, as well as those of justice, urge this same measure? There are many of our citizens, too, who, in view of our probable future relations with the East, desire and intend to give their sons a knowledge of the Chinese language. A department of the proposed school might, if properly organized under the instruction of teachers familiar with the English and Chinese languages, supply this opportunity to such as desire it, at no increased expense to the Department.[56]

This school report marked Pelton as an educator of vision. Though his recommendation for a special school didn't come to pass, it is interesting to note his additional suggestion for a centrally located building for the school at the corner of Sacramento and Powell streets.[57] This would have moved the site from the chapel and provided initial contact between the Chinese residents and their white neighbors near the western border of Chinatown. Moreover, it would have made schooling accessible to those who feared venturing from the Chinese quarter.

Second, so concerned was Pelton to overcome the impediments to the Chinese School that a Mr. Choy Cum Chew[58] was elected as teacher in 1867, even though the school was still suspended because of the Lanctot-Dye controversy. Though Choy Cum Chew was never hired, the fact that his election was recorded in the *Annual Report* showed that Pelton considered the Chinese School seriously. Had he continued as San Francisco school superintendent, the re-established school (which opened again as an evening school in February, 1868, with Dye as the teacher) would have been on a firmer foundation. Unfortunately, the office went back to James Denman, who had closed the Chinese School ten years before.[59]

Events did not go well for the school. First, Dye asked that his salary be not less than $80 per month,[60] but the board fixed it at $75 per month[61] and denied him a salary increase the following year.[62] Dye was most unhappy over this and tendered his resignation.

The Chinese School facility, located for ten years in a gloomy basement at Sacramento and Stockton streets, was moved to the north side of Powell Street, between Jackson and Washington streets.[63] It was not reported why the school was moved or whether the new facility was more suitable to the Chinese students. However, the recognized western limit of Chinatown was Stockton Street,[64] and the new location fell in Caucasian territory. The common practice of insulting, abusing, and throwing stones at Chinese caused a decline in attendance at the Chinese School. The rehiring of Lanctot in 1870 probably angered the Chinese merchants who wanted him removed back in 1866. Lanctot's term didn't last long. He submitted his resignation on February 14, 1871.[65]

These events contributed to the declining attendance at the Chinese School from 1868 to 1870. All Denman needed was legal sanction to terminate the school. He found it in the School Law of 1870, which was sparked by an upsurge of racism against the increasing number of Chinese in California.[66] A key section read:

Sec. 56. The education of children of African descent and Indian children shall be provided for in separate schools. Upon the written application of the parents or guardians of at least ten such children to any Board of Trustees or Board of Education, a separate school shall be established for the education of such children, and the education of a less number may be provided for by the Trustees, in separate schools, in any other manner.[67]

The principal change was the omission of Mongolian (Chinese) children from the provisions of the law. It should be noted that the education of African and Indian children was provided for in separate schools. The bitter hatred toward the Chinese in many quarters was the real racial problem confronting early California.[68]

The School Law of 1870 gave Denman the legal right to close the Chinese School permanently. In 1870 Denman wrote in his report:

The whole number of pupils attending the Chinese School was 202, with an average daily attendance of only 20. This irregular attendance is mainly owing to the fact that the pupils are young men who only attend school long enough to acquire sufficient knowledge of our language to enable them to transact business with us, when they leave school to act as clerks and interpreters for their countrymen.

Since the last Legislature repealed the law authorizing the establishment of Chinese Schools, I question the legality and propriety of expending the public funds to educate these young men, while we have not the means to furnish suitable accommodations for the large number of our own children constantly applying for admission.[69]

The Chinese School was terminated on March 1, 1871, the same day other evening schools in the city stopped operating. Savings to the district in closing the Chinese School amounted to $75 per month.[70] This time the school stayed closed.

## Popular Support for Anti-Chinese Forces

ANTI-CHINESE FEELING INCREASED. In a period of labor shortages, agents, sent to China to lure Chinese to America, gave false promises of a return trip home. Since the agents were paid $4 for every Chinese brought over, they told fabulous tales of opportunities in the newly discovered "Gum Shan," or "Land of the Golden Mountains."[71]

The arrival of the immigrants from China provided leisure time for other Californians, since Chinese were performing the less desirable work. But as road construction was completed, Chinese laborers were dumped in San Francisco in spite of promises to send them home to China. They were not unemployed for long, because there was a market for their services in newly created industries in San Francisco.[72]

At this time there was an increase of white foreign-born and the Chinese found themselves at the mercy of politicians and workingmen.[73] Propagating the coolie image begun by Bigler and reiterated by Stanford, workingmen by 1866–1867 formed anti-coolie clubs in the wards of San Francisco to stop the influx of these competitors.[74]

Violence occurred in San Francisco on February 12, 1867, when a mob drove Chinese laborers who were excavating a lot at Second and Townsend streets from their work and burned their shacks. The mob then proceeded to the Potrero district and drove off the Chinese employed on the rope walk of Tubbs and Company and set fire to their cabins.[75]

Violence toward the Chinese then broadened to a state issue. So strong was the feeling against Chinese that, during the election of 1867 and in subsequent campaigns, political parties seized upon the issue to win the support of the people, particularly workingmen. Both the Democratic and Republican parties included anti-Chinese planks in their platforms.[76]

The Democrats passed an anti-Chinese resolution in 1867:

That the power to regulate foreign immigration being vested in Congress, it is the duty of that body to protect the Pacific states and territories from an undue influx of Chinese and Mongolians, and it is the duty of the legislature of this state to petition Congress to endeavor to obtain the adoption of such regulations as shall accomplish this object, and the legislature should use all its power to prevent the introduction of Mongolian laborers.[77]

The new governor of California, Henry Haight, urged on December 5, 1867, that the influx of Chinese be discouraged by all lawful means. He warned that the people of Europe and of the Eastern states woud not migrate to California upon the completion of the Pacific railroad if the labor market was filled by Chinese. The governor concluded his prejudicial inaugural address: "We ought not to desire an effete population of Asiatics for a free State like ours."[78]

With the completion of the Central Pacific Railroad in 1869 came a decided turn in public sentiment against the Chinese. The Western labor market was filled with men discharged by the railroad, while immigration from the Eastern states was increasing. California markets were opened to Eastern competition, which further reduced profits from local commodities. The increase in Chinese immigration created more labor competition, and made inevitable a readjustment of occupations and wages.[79]

The concentrated visibility of Chinese laborers aroused the antagonism of the unemployed. The 1869 Republican Convention took the following stand:

We are opposed to Chinese suffrage in any form and to any change in the naturalization laws of the United States.[80]

The struggle by the Chinese to gain access to public schools took place during the Civil War period. Reconstructing the nation had taken the tension off of local affairs, but ratification of the Burlingame Treaty of 1868 between the United States and China aroused anti-Chinese feeling more violently than ever before.[81]

Anson Burlingame was the American diplomat dispatched to the Imperial Court in 1860. During the six years of his mission in China, he became a trusted advisor to the Chinese government. When he was about to resign in 1866, the Chinese government, in an unusual move, asked him to represent China as their envoy to the United States and the principal European nations. He helped negotiate the Burlingame Treaty, which opened trade and commerce between China and the United States.

In the opinion of labor, the treaty increased Chinese immigration by encouraging the use of Chinese labor by men like Charles Crocker, a California industrialist.[82] Article 7 of the treaty provided that "citizens of the United States shall enjoy all the privileges of the public educational institutions under the control of the government of China; and reciprocally, Chinese shall enjoy the same privileges in the United States which are enjoyed in the respective countries by the citizens or subjects of the most favored nation."[83] The closing of the Chinese School in San Francisco was in violation of that treaty. Chinese children should have been allowed to attend school under conditions similar to those for children of "most favored nations."

The year 1870 is most often identified by historians as the time when anti-Chinese forces in California and the United States first achieved a high degree of popular support.[84] By the winter of 1870–1871 there were three men—two white and one yellow—for every job in San Francisco.[85] The restless unemployed joined the city's hoodlums in the persecution of Chinese, who were in turn being used by the city's industrialists to break the back of nascent attempts to organize for higher wages and better working conditions.[86]

In San Francisco, two large meetings were held in 1870 to oppose Chinese labor. An anti-coolie mass meeting was held at

Platt's Hall on July 9 and the "Anti-Chinese Convention of the State of California" was held at the Mechanics' Pavilion on July 15.[87] The object of these meetings was to stop Chinese immigration and to cultivate public opinion for the abrogation of the treaty with China.[88]

The delegates to the state meeting were from organized labor and trade associations. They requested that the Chinese Six Companies inform the Emperor of China that it was unsafe for any more Chinese to come to the United States.[89]

State and local governments continued to pass anti-Chinese laws[90] in spite of the fact that Congress on May 31, 1870, restricted states from enacting legislation directed at special groups.[91] By 1871, the physical attacks against Chinese became grave enough to be mentioned by Governor Booth in his inaugural speech.[92]

One Chinese letter-writer to a magazine responded eloquently to these events:

We ask nothing but that you treat us justly. We are willing to pay taxes cheerfully when taxed equally with others. We think the tax of five dollars collected from each Chinamen coming into this State is not right if this is a free country. We also think the special tax of four dollars per month collected only from Chinese miners is not according to your treaty with our government. Most of all we want protection to our lives and property. Your courts of justice refuse our testimony, and thus leave us defenseless. Our country can furnish yours with good, faithful, industrious men, if you wish to employ them, and will enact laws to make them feel safe, and insure them equal justice with people of other nations, according to the terms of their treaty with your government. We live here many years in quiet; all we ask for is right and justice.[93]

## Denman's Reasons for Closing School Do Not Hold Up

IT MUST NOT BE FORGOTTEN that Denman had terminated the Chinese School even before there was strong popular support from anti-Chinese forces. His pattern of public statements shows that he would have closed the Chinese School in 1871 even without that support or the new school law.

Denman cited the reasons for his closing of the Chinese School, but the data do not substantiate them:

**Insufficient Number of Pupils.**[94] During its first year of operation, the Chinese School showed an average daily attendance of 21 pupils.[95] According to press reports, there were more than 40 students before and after the Christmas vacation.[95] The reason for the high number of students was that, in both cases, school was in session during the day for adults and children. Even under George Tait, who viewed the Chinese as an "unprogressive and unimpressible race," the school was well attended in morning and evening sessions. Forty pupils were reported at the missionary evening school when the Chinese School was closed in 1866 and 1867.[97]

This contradicts Denman's "want of scholars" theme. The lowest attendance at the Chinese School—in 1860 under Denman's administration—was an average daily attendance of just twelve pupils. Moreover, a significant number of Chinese pupils enrolled from 1868 to 1870. The average daily attendance at the Chinese School dwindled to less than ten percent of the total enrollment, because Denman limited the operation of the school to the evening. Table 1 supports the view that Denman misrepresented the numbers of Chinese scholars.

**Young Men as Students.** Denman's subtheme was the preponderance of adult male students,[98] who, when they learned to speak and write a little English, left the school to become clerks and interpreters.[99] Only one article could be found to substantiate this theme. The writer of the article shared Denman's view of serving white children before wasting funds on Chinese who didn't want to become citizens.[100]

Historical information doesn't support Denman's position. When the Chinese School opened as a day school, the *Evening Bulletin* reported only seven pupils out of a class of 41 students who were over 18 years of age.[101] Prior to the opening of the Chinese School, 17 children were reported to be attending the school when it was a private enterprise.[102]

When the Chinese School operated morning and evening sessions, the *Alta* reported that the school had many young boys, a number of young men, and several middle-aged men.[103] The *Evening Bulletin* also reported that the male pupils were both children and adults, generally the latter and mainly from the mercantile class.[104] It commented on the working male students:

As soon as they learn to read and write many of them leave the school for the Chinese counting room. This takes about two years. There are some however, who have been in the school three years and still attend.[105]

It is not clear from the article whether it was the children or the adults who stayed in school three years or more. It is also not clear whether those who stayed this long attended the morning or evening session or both. Some adult students may have taken longer to learn English, or younger male students, not of working age, may have been attending day sessions.

One more piece of evidence to dispute Denman's claim came at the time the Chinese School reverted back to a private enterprise during the Lanctot-Dye controversy. The *Alta* reported that one-half of the boys who attended the school in the evening were "sons of merchants; the other half work in families."[106]

The meager accommodation of having the Chinese School reopen only in the evenings meant Chinese children could not

## TABLE 1
### Chinese School Attendance Data, 1859–1871

| Year | Enrollment | Average Daily Attendance | Page Located in Superintendent's Annual Report |
|------|-----------|-----------|-----------|
| 1859* | 32 | 21 | 64 |
| 1860 | 69 boys<br>8 girls | 12 | 30–31 |
| 1861 | 60 boys | 21 | 18 |
| 1862* | 33† | ... | 227 |
| 1863* | ... | 26 | 227–228 |
| 1864 | 119 | 30 | 45 |
| 1865* | 40<br>8 boys | 29.8 | 312 |
| 1866 | ... | ... | ... |
| 1867 | ... | ... | ... |
| 1868 | 179 | 38.8% | 90 |
| 1869* | 277 | 29.5 | 301 |
| 1870 | 202 | 20 | 53 |
| 1871 | ... | ... | ... |

* School Superintendent *Annual Reports* located in San Francisco *Municipal Reports* for the respective years.

† This figure is the average number of pupils enrolled—not the total number of pupils enrolled for the year.

attend school, but the *Annual Reports* (see Table 2) showed significant numbers of Chinese children in San Francisco.

A cursory reading of Denman's 1869 and 1870 annual reports could lead to the mistaken conclusion that there were no Chinese children to be taught and therefore it was a waste of public funds to educate Chinese adults. This, in fact, was not the case.

To a limited extent Chinese girls attended the Chinese School when it operated during the day. Board member Knowles had anticipated that ten Chinese girls would enroll in the first Chinese public school,[107] but only eight girls registered, according to the 1860 *Annual Report*.[108] Another report to the board showed there were five girls in the Chinese School in 1861.[109] When the Chinese School opened day and evening sessions, one or two girls attended, according to the *Evening Bulletin*.[110] During the final years of the Chinese School when it was opened only in the evening, no mention of female students was made. When the school closed in 1871, 166 Chinese girls under fifteen years of age were recorded in the superintendent's *Annual Report*.[111]

The crucial point to be made here is that Chinese boys and, to a limited degree, Chinese girls would have attended the Chinese School in San Francisco if it had been open during the day. The

### TABLE 2
### Chinese Children in San Francisco, 1868–1871

| Year | Between 5 & 15 Years of Age | Under 15 Years of Age | Between 6 & 15 Years of Age Attending School | Page Located in Superintendent's *Annual Report* |
|---|---|---|---|---|
| 1868 | ... | 233 | 9 | 19, 68 |
| 1869* | ... | 48 | ... | 282 |
| 1870 | 139† attending school | 298 | ... | 39 |
| 1871 | 9† attending school | 311 boys 166 girls | ... | Found in back of report— pagination not cited. |

* School Superintendent *Annual Report* located in San Francisco *Municipal Reports*.
† Since the Chinese School was opened during these years for adults, these figures represented children who were attending mission or private schools. The fact that there were nine children attending the reopened Chinese School in 1868 indicated some anticipation by the Chinese community that daytime operation would eventually be restored for their children.

failure of the day school was caused not by the "want of scholars" but by Denman's prejudicial attitude as chief school administrator. By closing the day school during his first term (1859–1860) and having only night school during his second term (1868–1870), Chinese children in San Francisco were denied the benefits of public education.

**Lack of Interest.** Denman's most insistent reason for closing the Chinese School was "the lack of interest among the Chinese to appreciate the benefits of free school instruction." Subsequent school superintendents repeated his remarks in their reports to the board whenever the Chinese School was mentioned.

Surprisingly, Denman was one of the few superintendents to say anything positive about the strong interest of Chinese for public schooling. When the Chinese School was a day school, he found the few pupils in attendance "anxious to learn our language."[112] When the school operated in the evening, he remarked that "greater interest has been manifested by a few of the more intelligent Chinamen to sustain the school."[113]

There was an increase in attendance for both children and adults as a result of day and evening sessions during Tait's term of office. The press indicated that some of the students even attended both sessions.[114] Superintendent Tait remarked that "considerable interest is said to be manifested by the most respectable portion of the Chinese."[115]

The most dramatic evidence for the continual interest in public schooling shown by the Chinese occurred on February 12, 1867. It was dramatic because that was the day of anti-Chinese violence in San Francisco. The leading Chinese merchants petitioned the board that same evening for a reorganization of the Chinese School.[116] Dr. Ayer, one of the members of the board, remarked that the Chinese strongly desired to have the school reestablished.[117] The petition vividly portrayed the interest of the Chinese in public schooling, and the violence in San Francisco did not diminish this concern.

A less dramatic but nonetheless important indication of strong interest occurred when the Chinese School reopened in 1868 as an evening school. As Table 1 shows, the school recorded the highest average daily attendance and the highest enrollment in the midst of growing anti-Chinese sentiment.

The Chinese "lack of interest" in education was manipulated

by Denman's lack of support and the momentum of the anti-Chinese movement. Despite these twin obstacles, the records show that the Chinese attended school anyway. The young men who continued to go to the Chinese School exhibited bravery and the determination to secure an education.

The fact that the Chinese School had to struggle for its existence during this turbulent period (1868–1871) was due in no small measure to the chief school administrator. When Denman returned for yet a third term (1874–1876), the school was nonexistent. By this time, the anti-Chinese movement was no longer confined to the laboring class but had spread to the general populace. The national concern with restricting Chinese immigration overshadowed the local problem of public schooling.

•

BEFORE CLOSING THIS CHAPTER, it is helpful to mention the four areas noted by those who had visited the Chinese School: the students' aptitude, the curriculum, their learning habits, and their social attitudes. The first three are well documented by press accounts and are a further rebuttal to Denman.

**Aptitude.** Superintendent George Tait, when visiting the Chinese School, was "attracted by the stillness prevailing in the classroom, each scholar being seemingly absorbed in studying his book, which is usually Sargent's Primer."[118] After a brief English lesson with them, Tait "became conscious of the patience and aptness with which the Chinaman acquires knowledge."[119]

Lanctot reported that "his congregation of little Celestials were very apt at learning. The younger ones knew nothing whatever of the English language on entering, but they picked it up with marvellous facility. Writing they learned with even greater ease than Yankees."[120]

Lanctot also told Superintendent Tait of an example of their zeal for knowledge. Eleven of his pupils copied an English and Chinese dictionary that he prepared himself—a task requiring ten hours of daily labor for three months for its completion.[121] While teaching at the Chinese School, he found only one scholar who couldn't read and write in his own language. That was a little boy whose parents died while he was very young and who was brought to this country at that time.[122]

The *Alta* reported on the Chinese pupils' aptitude when the

Chinese School operated in the evening, when it held double sessions (morning and evening), and when it was a private enterprise. The following statements are quoted in that order:

We are reliably informed that the children learn with great facility and give promise of reasonable improvement if properly encouraged.[123]

Many of the pupils...make surprising progress in the branches taught, considering the dissimilarity in our language and that of their native land.... A more studious class of pupils we have never seen anywhere and for good order and general decorum, the school is a model.[124]

They are attentive to their studies, orderly in their deportment and it is stated, advance rapidly in acquiring a knowledge of the English language.[125]

The last quote was an attempt by the *Alta* to secure public aid for the mission-sponsored school, because the Chinese School was closed during 1866 and 1867.

Just before the Lanctot-Dye controversy, the *Evening Bulletin* made this comment on the Chinese pupils:

They are very orderly in their behavior and do not give their teachers much trouble.[126]

**Curriculum.** The initial thrust of "Christianizing the heathens" was replaced by teaching the rudiments of the English language. When Superintendent Tait visited the school he remarked that they were "experts in figures and other scientific lore. However 'John' fails to appreciate the value of any other English studies than those of spelling and reading."[127]

The *Alta* reported that "the branches taught are reading, writing and spelling only, but maps have recently been furnished to the school, and geography will be added to the list of studies at the next term."[128]

The most detailed report on curriculum appeared in the *Evening Bulletin*:

The pupils commence with Sargent's Primer. In two days they will acquire the English alphabet. After mastering this primer, they take up Town's First, Second and Third Readers. In connection with reading and spelling, they also learn to write. Beyond reading and writing English, they care but little about other studies. Once a week outline maps are studied. At first they could not be induced to pay any attention to these maps. "We believe the earth is level," said they, "but suppose it is wrong, what difference will it make to us? We won't make any more money whether it is round or square." Now, however, they are beginning to take more interest in geography since the teacher has pointed out to them on the map the places from which they originally came. In addition to the maps, there are charts hung up about the room from which they are taught the pronunciation of letters and words. This was very difficult for them at first, and they could not see the use of it. But now they are beginning to appreciate it and comprehend its importance. They care nothing for arithmetic. They have a system of their own for computing by means of a board, which they think goes ahead of any Yankee multiplication table ever invented; and it is truly a valuable thing and very accurate. But in the absence of the board, figures are a maze to them.[129]

**Learning Habits.** The pupils' study habits in China were carried over to America. As noticed in the *Alta:*

All the pupils learn to form their letters with great precision, and with so much mechanical accuracy, that a distinctive individual handwriting, as with us, is hardly to be recognized.[130]

As observed by the *Evening Bulletin:*

They all study aloud in the school, which is the custom in their native land. They say that they can learn quicker and better in this way, getting the exact pronunciation of the word by hearing the sound of their own voices.[131]

All the above comments generally portrayed the Chinese students in a positive light; unfortunately they swayed neither Denman's nor his successors' anti-Chinese attitudes. For the next fourteen years, 1871–1885, public schooling was not offered to the Chinese in San Francisco.

# Chapter 3

# The Exclusion Years
# 1871–1884

## Chinese Respond to
## Anti-Chinese Momentum

IN THE EIGHTEEN-SEVENTIES, white sentiment toward Chinese became more virulent. The Eastern panic of 1873 precipitated a large influx of white immigrants to California, helped by the ease of transportation and encouraged by rumors of prosperity in the West. As many white immigrants came to the state in the three years before 1874 as came from 1857 to 1867.[1] In San Francisco they were confronted with severe competition from Chinese laborers. They also found themselves unable to buy land for small farms in California because it was held in huge parcels by men who were developing it with teams of Chinese workers. Politicians, sensing a volatile situation that they could turn to their advantage, came to rely on stirring up popular feeling against the Chinese.[2]

Both the 1872[3] and the 1874[4] sessions of the state legislature passed resolutions calling upon California lawmakers in Congress to secure treaty amendments to discourage Chinese immigration. Potential officeholders knew they had to adopt the anti-Chinese cause.[5]

This "zeal" extended even to the Catholic Church, one of the few supporters of the Chinese. On February 25, 1873, Father Bouchard delivered a lecture at the St. Francis Church in San Francisco entitled "Chinaman or White Man—Which?" Lamenting the inability to convert the Chinese and repeating the coolie fiction espoused twenty years earlier by Governor Bigler and the *Alta*, Bouchard wanted the "white man to perpetuate our glorious institutions, to maintain our self-respect at home and our influence abroad, and to make this American Republic eternal."[6] His racist views were used later by Governor Irwin in his speech at a huge anti-Chinese mass meeting at Union Hall in San Francisco on April 5, 1876. Senator Sargent also used Bouchard's notes in his report to a Congressional commission on the Chinese question.[7]

Father Bouchard's lecture was refuted by Reverend Otis Gibson, a Methodist missionary, in a speech delivered at Platt's Hall in San Francisco on March 14, 1873.[8] Three days after delivering his lecture, Rev. Gibson received the following communication:

The leading Chinese gentlemen of this city have just learned of your able defense of the treaty rights of the Chinese in this country. They wish me to assure you of their high appreciation of your services, and to convey to you their grateful thanks for what you, unsolicited by them, have done for our people. The "Six Chinese Companies" also ask the privilege of paying the expense of publishing an edition of your "Reply to Father Bouchard." With sentiments of profound respect. In behalf of the Chinese in America, Yours very truly, A. Yup, Hop Kee and Co.[9]

As the white workingmen's outcry against the Chinese became incessant, the Chinese Six Companies telegraphed Hong Kong on May 28, 1873, to urge an end to emigration to San Francisco.[10] The Chinese Consolidated Benevolent Association, commonly known as Chinese Six Companies, is made up of the titular heads of Chinese who originally came from the six districts of Guangdong. This organization acted as an intermediary between the Chinese quarter and white society in San Francisco, arbitrated disputes between the various factions in Chinatown, and provided vital social services to the new arrivals.[11]

The next day, at Dashaway Hall, a large anti-Chinese meeting was held.[12] In June, the San Francisco Common Council (board of supervisors) passed a number of ordinances which, if enforced, would have stopped immigration, if not driven the Chinese population from the state. Mayor Alvord's subsequent vetoes of the proposed queue and laundry ordinances were endorsed by the Eastern press, because the legislation was a breach of treaty obligations. The Eastern writers ridiculed California in general and San Francisco in particular for "trying to make it appear that Mongolian labor is gradually undermining Caucasian industry and will eventually wreck them upon the shoals of skill and cheapness."[13] Said the *St. Louis Republican:*

In their efforts to prove this point they put the Chinese in the position of the superior race and their own [white] population inferior in enterprise, skill and capacity to labor and endure.[14]

So from a national perspective the Chinese problem was viewed by the press as a local and state phenomenon—a peculiarity of a frontier western state.

In 1874 and 1875, a temporary prosperity absorbed the surplus immigrant labor and diverted the discontented classes, but the political and social upheaval which found its outlet in Kearneyism and the Workingmen's Party, was now inevitable.[15]

In 1876 the bottom fell out of the financial markets. A severe drought in the winter, the death of thousands of cattle, and the decline by one-third in the output of the mines, now added unemployed farmhands and bankrupt miners to the mass of drifting workers in the city.[16]

In the winter of 1876 there were estimated to be ten thousand unemployed men who congregated in San Francisco.[17] Two labor societies were established that same year which were avowedly anti-Chinese—the United Brothers of California and the Anti-Chinese Union of San Francisco.[18] Before these white laborers organized sufficiently to form an appreciable voting bloc, the attacks on Chinese laborers were occasional and sporadic, though at times severe. From 1876 onward they became increasingly systematic and irrational.[19]

Without a strong Chinese government to protest effectively on their behalf, the Chinese were helpless before an epidemic of mob violence. The Chinese Six Companies held a meeting on April 1, 1876, to take action on three items. The first was to petition its government across the sea to appoint a consul who could take up residence in San Francisco. His main tasks would be to protect the Chinese in emergencies and allay the ill-feeling against them. The second action was to send another telegram to China for the purpose of preventing further emigration to this country. After deliberating, they made the third decision and sent the following communication to Chief of Police H. H. Ellis with copies to Governor Irwin and Mayor A. J. Bryant:

Sir: We wish to call your attention to the fact that at the present time, frequent and unprovoked assaults are made upon our Chinese people while walking peacefully the streets of this city. The assaulting party is seldom arrested by your officers, but if a Chinaman resists the assault he is frequently arrested and punished by fine or by imprisonment. Inflammatory and incendiary addresses against the

Chinese, delivered on the public streets, to the idle and irresponsible element of this great city, have already produced unprovoked and unpunished assaults upon some of our people, and we fear that if such things are permitted to go on unchecked a bloody riot against the Chinese may be the result. Regretting that the Chinese are so obnoxious to the citizens of this country, and quite willing to aid in seeking a repeal or modification of the existing treaty between China and the United States, yet being here under sacred treaty stipulations, we simply ask to be protected in our treaty rights.

> Respectfully submitted,
> Yeong Wo Co.,
> Ning Young Co.,
> Kong Chow Co.,
> Hop Wo Co.,
> Yin Wo Co.,
> Sam Yap Co.[20]

From the days of Governor Bigler, the Democratic Party in California had been anti-black, anti-Chinese, anti-corporation and pro-workingman. Their return to power in the overwhelming state election victories of 1875, combined with a large Irish immigration and an impending United States presidential contest in 1876, brought the Chinese question again to the forefront as a campaign issue.[21]

As the tide of discontent swelled, the Democratic Party, anxious for re-election, sought to capitalize on the antagonism toward Chinese. In April 1876, it announced the formation of a committee of the California Senate to investigate the problem of Chinese immigration. The "evidence" gathered by this committee, stressing sensational claims of vice and immorality among Chinese, was distributed freely in pamphlets all over the city.[22]

When the national campaign opened in March 1876, the Republican State Committee published a mild resolution in favor of a modification of the Burlingame Treaty. The Democrats, on the other hand, organized a gigantic mass meeting on April 5 to petition Congress to stop Chinese immigration.[23] Fortunately the meeting concluded without a riot, although extra police and the militia had been prepared for difficulties.[24] A committee of twelve was appointed at this meeting by the mayor of San Francisco to spearhead a concerted movement against Chinese throughout the state.[25]

Alarmed, the Chinese Six Companies again telegraphed China to stop emigration and called on the San Francisco authorities for protection. Many Chinese, fearing an attack, purchased pistols and other arms to use in case of assault. The day before the mass meeting, the Chinese sent the following communication to Mayor Bryant:

Sir: We the undersigned Presidents of the Chinese Six Companies of this city, desire most respectfully to call your attention to the fact (which may not have escaped your notice) that widespread rumors are abroad all over the city, to the effect that a riotous attack upon the Chinese is about to take place. It is widely reported that tonight, while the more respectable class of citizens are peacefully devising means to prohibit further Chinese emigration, another class, mostly of foreign birth, will commence riotous proceedings against the Chinese who are already here. We notice that anti-Chinese societies are being formed in every ward of the city and in many towns of the State. Denunciatory and incendiary addresses against the Chinese, publicly made upon the streets of the city to large crowds of idle and excitable people, have already produced acts of violence and unprovoked, and we are sorry to say it, unpunished assaults upon our countrymen. We have noticed that for two or three weeks past the city papers have failed to observe the violent assaults made upon the Chinamen; or, if they have observed them, they have neglected to notice them in their columns. We have also noticed that the daily press of the city is constantly warning the people to abstain from riotous proceedings against the Chinese, which we think would hardly be done without some cause existed to fear that such proceedings are intended. All these things are causing the Chinese people great anxiety. And in the immediate dangers which seem to threaten us, as well as to threaten the peace and good name of this city, we appeal to your Honor the Mayor and chief Magistrate of this municipality to protect us to the full extent of your power in all our peaceful treaty rights against all unlawful violence and all riotous proceedings now threatening us. We would deprecate the results of mob violence, for we not only value our property and cherish our lives, which now seem to be in jeopardy but we should also regret to have the good name of this great and honorable country tarnished by the riotous proceedings of her own citizens. Our countrymen are better acquainted with peaceful vocations than with scenes of strife, yet many of them have lived long enough in this country to learn that self-defense is the common right of all men: and should a riotous attack be made upon the Chinese quarters, we have no power, even if we had the disposition, to restrain our countrymen from defending themselves to the last extremity and selling their lives as dearly as possible. But we trust and believe that it is in your Honor's power and in accordance with your high sense of justice to prevent these threatened evils. That we may do all in our power, as good citizens, to preserve the peace and avert a riot, we most respectfully submit these statements and make this earnest appeal to your Honor,

Respectfully submitted,
Lee Ming How, Sam Yup Co.,
Saw Yun Chong, Kong Chow Co.,
Chan Lung Kok, Ning Yung Co.,
Lee Cheong Chip, Hop Wo Co.,
Lee Chu Kwan, Young Wo Co.,
Chan Kong Chew, Yan Wo Co.[26]

By May 1876, the agitation against the Chinese lowered their attendance at Sunday schools. As explained in the *Evening Bulletin,* "The [Chinese] scholars are shrewd enough to think that the religion of a land which advocates open violence against an inoffensive people is not just the faith which it is desirable to embrace."[27]

By the summer of 1876, the level of panic and agitation in San Francisco became high enough that even the pro-Chinese business class and Governor Irwin began to consider exclusion as the only way of regaining domestic order.[28]

After nearly all the legislation by the coast states against the Chinese was declared unconstitutional or a violation of treaty, it was evident that effective measures could only be obtained by a new treaty and federal legislation. An organized effort was begun by the Pacific Coast congressmen to obtain the federal restriction of Chinese immigration. But they were met with indifference, if not active opposition, and the sole result of six years of effort on their part was the appointment of a joint special committee of Congress in 1876 to investigate Chinese immigration.[29] These hearings were held in San Francisco and Sacramento, and the testimony in support of Chinese immigration came from international diplomats, clergymen who had lived in China or worked with Chinese, and from California capitalists. The latter paid a moving tribute to the tremendous Chinese contribution to the economic development of California, but their support for Chinese immigration revealed a mixture of economic self-interest and racial chauvinism strikingly similar to that of their opponents.[30]

In January 1877, a drastic drop in the output of the Comstock Lode mining region sent stock values in San Francisco plummeting. Merchants and clerks saw their life savings disappear. The unemployed, transient population of the city grew to even greater proportions, with one-half of it consisting of foreign-born immigrants.[31] That spring, boycotts, fires, and intimidation were directed at businessmen who hired Chinese. Governor Irwin said that so long as the working class had grievances, they were justified in agitation until the situation was remedied.[32] His speech certainly did not check the rising spirit of mob rule. Persecution of the Chinese, which had been sporadic throughout the state, became general. Law-abiding members of society disapproved, but no politician dared protest, and many businessmen stopped employing Chinese.[33]

Frustrated by the lack of protection, the Chinese strongly appealed to the mayor and chief of police:

We have already called Mayor Bryant and Chief of Police Ellis' attention to the hoodlum gang which infests the neighborhood of Sixteenth Street between Mission and Folsom, and commits daily outrages on Chinese pedestrians, but without effect. Now we wish to inform these worthy authorities that if they fail in their duty to protect the Chinamen from hoodlum outrages, the Chinamen will protect themselves as they have a right to do, and they will be responsible for the consequences. Moreover we will see that this lack of protection refused to Chinamen by our civil authorities is well noted by the State and Federal Government as well as by the people and press, and when Mayor Bryant and Chief of Police Ellis will ask the votes of the people for re-election, we will cordially help them to step down and out.[34]

For three days in July 1877, the rioters sacked and burned buildings occupied by the Chinese and raged almost unchecked.[35] Many Chinese escaped destruction by taking down their signs, putting out lights and transforming the appearance of the shops to escape discovery.[36] The San Francisco police weren't able to handle the situation, and, under the presidency of Wiliam T. Coleman, the Committee of Public Safety was formed to repel the outbreaks.[37]

Workingmen gathered in vacant lots, and delivered violent harangues against their twin enemies—the huge California corporations and the Chinese they employed.[38]

It was in these turbulent times that Dennis Kearney, an Irish drayman who had earlier been repudiated by his associates in socialist circles, formed the Workingmen's Party in 1877 and capitalized on the popular feeling against the Chinese. Organized labor had stirred the feelings against the Chinese in the state before Kearney's arrival, and all that was necessary was a demagogue to crystallize public sentiment into action.[39]

In September, the Workingmen's Party was formally organized.[40] The goals were to unite laboring men against the encroachment of capital and to get rid of Chinese employed in the state. While the party didn't encourage rioting, it didn't strain itself suppressing the activities of rash individuals.[41] The party's slogan was, "The Chinese Must Go!"[42]

The party addressed Mayor Bryant on the large numbers of unemployed in the city. The mayor submitted their message to the board of supervisors and requested that "a resolution might be passed setting forth the necessities and distress of workingmen and women and asking the residents of the city, as far as possible, to furnish employment to the deserving poor, discharging the Chinese and putting in their places men and women of our own race who are literally starving for want of bread."[43]

In the rallies that followed, Kearney inveighed against millionaires and scoundrel officials, threatened to lynch railway magnates, burn the Pacific Mail docks, and drop balloons filled with dynamite into Chinatown.[44] His wrath was directed against both the Chinese and the land and rail monopolies; but the latter were powerful, impregnable, organized, while the Chinese were eager to avoid conflict and ineffectual in court.[45]

Sensing more mob violence in the Chinese quarter, the Chinese Six Companies on November 3 appealed once more to the mayor for municipal protection:

Sir: We the undersigned Presidents of the Chinese Six Companies of this city and state desire to call your immediate attention to a state of things which seems to us to threaten the lives and property of the Chinese residents, as well as the peace and good name of this municipality.

In the multitude of responsibilities which tax your time and strength, it may possibly have escaped your notice that large gatherings of the idle and irresponsible element of the population are nightly addressed in the open streets by speakers who use the most violent, inflammatory and incendiary language, threatening in plainest terms to burn and pillage the Chinese quarter and kill our people, unless, at their bidding, we leave this "Free Republic." The continuance of these things for many days, with increasing fury, without any check or hindrance by the authorities, is causing the Chinese people great anxiety, and in the immediate danger which seems again to threaten us as well as to threaten the peace and good name of your city, we (as on a former occasion) appeal to you, the Mayor and Chief Magistrate of this municipality, to protect us to the full extent of your power, in all our peaceful, Constitutional and Treaty rights against all unlawful violence, and all riotous proceedings now threatening us. We would deprecate the results of mob violence, for we not only value our property and cherish our lives, which now seem in jeopardy, but we should also regret to have the good name of this Christian civilization tarnished by riotous proceedings of its own citizens against the "Chinese heathen." As a rule, our countrymen are better acquainted with peaceful vocations than with scenes of strife, yet we are not ignorant that self-defense is the common right of all men; and should a riotous attack be made upon the Chinese quarter, we should have neither the power nor disposition to restrain our countrymen from defending themselves to the last extremity and selling their lives as dearly as possible. But we trust and believe that it is entirely within the scope of your Honor's power, and in accordance with your high sense of justice, to prevent these threatened evils. That we may do all in our power, as good citizens, to preserve the peace and avert a riot, we most respectfully appeal to your honor.

> Respectfully submitted,
> Lin Check Fung, President Sam Yup Co.,
> Lo Ming Ho, President Kong Chow Co.,
> Lan Kong Chai, President Ning Yung Co.,
> Chan Fung Chin, President Yen Wo Co.,
> Lee Cheong Tip, President Hop Wo Co.,
> Lee Jee Yuen, President Yeong Wo Co.[46]

In 1878, pressure was put on the board of supervisors to remove the Chinese quarter to another section of the city. The board made an inspection and found "ample cause for removal," but justified inaction on the grounds of lack of authority.[47]

The apex of their strength was reached when Workingmen's delegates helped rewrite California's Constitution.[48] With the help of farm delegates, anti-Chinese regulations were inserted into the new document. These forbade the employment of Chinese by corporations, penalized corporations who were found importing "coolie labor," and endowed the state legislature with power to protect itself from certain aliens.[49]

The California Senate Address and Memorial, as well as a congressional committee report, later helped influence Congress to pass the Exclusion Act of 1882. The California document was constantly referred to by Pacific Coast congressmen as representing the opinion of the majority in the Far West.

The Chinese Six Companies sent a challenge to Congress regarding the truth and conclusions of the joint committee's report.[50] They, along with their supporters—the missionaries, humanitarians, and scholars—formed a group called the Pro-Chinese Minority. They held that among their constitutional rights was the right to hold opposite views on the question of

Chinese immigration, to protest against all incendiary appeals and threats against life and property, and to require each side to acquiesce fully to the decision of the National Congress as required by the Constitution.[51]

In the test vote in September 1879, only 224 of the 41,258 voters of San Francisco voted in favor of the continued admission of the Chinese.[52] Furthermore, disregarding the provisions of the Burlingame Treaty, Congresss passed an exclusion bill in 1879 prohibiting further immigration of Chinese laborers. Since this bill was in contravention of the treaty, President Hayes was forced to veto it.[53]

Success finally came to the Chinese exclusionists when the Burlingame Treaty was modified in 1880. China conceded permission to the United States to regulate, limit, or suspend immigration, but not absolutely prohibit it. The limitation or suspension was to be in good faith, and applicable only to the laboring classes. Those who were already in the country were entitled to stay or come and go of their own free will. The new treaty reaffirmed the responsibility of the United States to protect all Chinese subjects from abuse and mistreatment.[54]

Just prior to the enactment of the national exclusion legislation, Governor Perkins became an active leader in the Chinese question. Since the immigration bill pending before Congress was so important to Californians, Perkins issued a proclamation declaring that March 4, 1882, was to be a legal holiday in order that Californians might demonstrate their sentiments to Congress. He called for a demonstration against immigration. Perkins wrote his regrets to Mayor Maurice C. Blake of San Francisco that he (Perkins) could not be present to join in the anti-Chinese meeting. Perkins said that he thought it "the duty of Congress to immediately restrict Chinese immigration to our country, that free American labor may not be overwhelmed and degraded by contract-slavery and coolie competition!"[55]

Those who favored permanent exclusion did not achieve a total victory, because the Exclusion Act of 1882 only suspended Chinese immigration for ten years.[56] This legislation was accomplished through the efforts of the representatives from California. In fact, the bill had the unanimous support of the block of congressmen from the Far West and was passed over the opposition of a small minority of New England Republicans and signed into law by President Arthur.[57] This exclusion law was the first of many similar enactments, each one more restrictive than its predecessor.

Violence against the Chinese, which had begun in the late 1870s, intensified after the exclusion law was passed. There were more mass meetings and burnings.[58] The only difference was that the violence was national in scope rather than limited to the Far Western states.

One tactic of the anti-Chinese movement in the next decade was a boycott of goods manufactured by Chinese in the United States. The cigar makers and shoe and boot manufacturers faced direct competition from Chinese labor and the union label was employed to distinguish their products from goods made by Chinese. The Trades Assembly of San Francisco called a state convention of labor and anti-Chinese organizations in 1882 and formed the League of Deliverance to direct the boycott. The Knights of Labor held an anti-Chinese convention in San Francisco in 1885, and delegates came from Los Angeles, Sacramento, Stockton, and Vallejo.[59]

By the mid-1880s, Chinese workers in the once thriving white-owned cigar industry had virtually disappeared. Employment of Chinese by shoe and boot factories ceased. Competition from Eastern mills and the pressure to fire Chinese workers eventually led to the end of the woolen industry in San Francisco.[60]

# Omission of Chinese Children from School Codes of California

PROVISIONS FOR THE SCHOOLING of Chinese were omitted again in the School Law of 1872. This revised code reiterated that public schools were for white children:

Section 1662. Every school, unless otherwise provided by special statute, must be opened for the admission of all white children between five and twenty-one years of age residing in the district, and the Board of Trustees or Board of Education have power to admit adults and children not residing in the district, whenever good reasons exist therefor.[61]

Other non-white children were designated for separate schools:

Section 1669. The education of children of African descent and Indian children must be provided for in separate schools.[62]

Section 1670. Upon the written application of the parents or guardians of such children to any Board of Trustees or Board of Education, a separate school must be established for the education of such children.[63]

However, the word "shall" in the clauses "shall be provided for in separate schools" and "shall be established for the education" in the 1870 law was replaced by the word "must" in 1872. This forced blacks and Indians to be educated in separate schools only. Dismal as this may seem, at least they were acknowledged.

Pressure from the black community in San Francisco to gain entry into the public schools forced a revision of the state school law. In 1874, in *Ward v. Flood*, the California Supreme Court declared that citizens of California had the right to attend public schools and that no child who was a citizen of California could be excluded by reason of color or race. The decision in part said:

The exclusion of colored children from schools where white children attend as pupils cannot be supported, except where separate schools affording the same facilities for education are actually maintained for the education of colored children....

Unless such separate schools be maintained, all children of the school district, whether white or colored, have an equal right to become pupils at any common schools organized under the laws of the state.[64]

Thus the legislature rewrote the 1874 School Law to conform to the new court decision:

Section 1669. The education of children of African descent, and Indian children, must be provided for in separate schools, provided, that if the Directors or Trustees fail to provide, such children must be admitted into the schools for white children.[65]

Blacks and Indian children, even without written application, could now attend the public schools of California unless separate and equal facilities were otherwise provided. This separate school policy remained as law in California until 1947.

Chinese children born in California, however, were not recognized by state school authorities. According to the 1874 state school census there were 2,131 Mongolian (Chinese) children under seventeen years of age.[66] The only way to secure their right to public education was to fight out the issue as did the black community. It was a right that would be secured eleven years later.

As early as 1872, attempts were made to eliminate the words "white" and "colored" from the state school law.[67] Although arguments against the wording were unsuccessful in the 1874 legislative session, mention of race was finally removed from the school law in 1880 after the *Ward v. Flood* decision. Legislators realized their white-only designation was in conflict with this court decision and the word "white" was removed from Section 166a. Admission into the schools was made general.[68] The new law read:

Section 1662. Every school, unless otherwise provided by law, must be open for the admission of all children between six and twenty-one years of age residing in the district, and the Board of Trustees, or City Board of Education, have power to admit adults and children not residing in the district, whenever good reasons exist therefor. Trustees shall have power to exclude children of filthy or vicious habits, or children suffering from contagious or infectious diseases.[69]

The Chinese should have been admitted into the public schools under this law, but school trustees continued to bar them. From 1871 to 1884, Chinese children in San Francisco were excluded from public education, at first by being omitted from school codes, and later through the tactics that they were considered "children of filthy or vicious habits, or children suffering from contagious or infectious diseases."

## The Anti-Chinese Movement's Effect on Education

RACE HATRED TOWARD THE CHINESE was so deep that it was inevitable that the school community would reflect the anti-Chinese movement. San Francisco's school children did not escape the anti-Chinese hysteria of their elders. First- and second-graders wrote sentences during their trial examinations which caught the attention of Superintendent Widber. To him, their compositions were either examples of literary gems or specimens of bad English. Widber inserted these writings into his 1873 *Annual Report*. They were used as part of the final exam for San Francisco students, who were directed to punctuate and "put

[them] into good English." Many of these compositions dealt with anti-Chinese themes. An example of a "literary gem":

Chinese are of no importance to San Francisco, they take away a great deal of labor from our people, because they work cheaper and not so good. You may see in going around to all these large manufactories, there are a great many chinese compared with white men and also on all these great railroad's and steamer's. Chinese are employed all together, there were many working during the building of these great railroad's, in the mountain's and during the snow blockade's. There are a great many coming and going from here on the Chinese steamer's, and when they get here that is the time for the Express men for cheating them and making them pay double the price for riding. These Chinese can be seen daily over the hill's carrying there basket's loaded with vegetables and fruit to sell to people where these Italian's do not go with there wagons because it is to steep for the horse's to pull up. there is a great quantity exported from China. In the shape of tea's.[70]

Below are examples of "bad English" included in the 1873 *Annual Report*:

Many people have acussed him [Chinese] with cowardice (Second Grade)

In San Francisco, there is about nine thousand Chinamen who only pay about one-half as much taxes on property; as one man in this city. I think it shall ruin United States. (Second Grade)[71]

The *San Francisco China News* reported on April 2, 1875, that students from Hayes Valley School, while on a field trip, mocked, insulted, and scolded a group of Chinese they encountered. The "braver" ones threw rocks. The police arrested four youngsters and put them into jail for a day. One child was fined $20 and the other three were fined $10 each. The writer hoped the white children were taught a lesson and that they would be more respectful of Chinese in the future.[72]

James Denman, serving yet a third term as school superintendent, noted in his 1874 *Annual Report* the lack of attendance of Chinese children in San Francisco public schools.[73] This report was the only documentary evidence to show the absence of schooling for Chinese children during this tumultuous period. The other annual reports from 1875 to 1884 only provided the census data required by law.

The word "Chinese" was used in a disparaging sense in the 1875 *Annual Report*. The superintendent did not like the existing practice of hiring only women educated in the California public school system. He claimed that experienced teachers from other sections of the country were denied teaching positions in San Francisco:

This Chinese policy of exclusiveness which shuts us out from the march of progress of the older institutions of other countries, is dwarfing our system of instruction and rendering us provincial and unprogressive. It is filling our schools with young and inexperienced teachers.[74]

The 1878 *Annual Report* also made the association of being Chinese with exclusiveness. In advancing an alternative to the compartmentalizing of students by assigning them to grades by age, the superintendent commented:

In reality, a mixed school is a school organized, so to speak, on nature's plan; while the system that prevails in this city, of assorting our pupils and arranging them in eight different grades, which are separated from each other by a Chinese Wall of exclusiveness, is purely artificial and in some respects positively detrimental.[75]

One passage from the 1875 report shows that Denman's earlier appraisals were repeated almost verbatim in the later reports:

The Chinese School was first organized in September, 1859, under the instruction of Mr. B. Lanctot, in the basement of the Chinese Chapel, corner of Stockton and Sacramento streets. For want of pupils, and a lack of interest among the Chinese to appreciate the benefits of free school instruction, it was suspended in June 1860, as a school until February, 1871, when it was discontinued.[76]

The "want of pupils and a lack of interest among the Chinese to appreciate the benefits of free school instruction" first appeared in Denman's 1860 report,[77] was condensed in his 1870 report,[78] was slightly revised in his 1875 report, and was simply inserted into the *Annual Reports* of 1879, 1880, and 1882.[79] Moreover, Denman's 1869 report[80] was copied word for word in the 1878 report![81] Denman was the author of half of these *Annual Reports* (1860, 1869, 1870, and 1875), and the other reports (1878, 1879, 1880, and 1882) merely copied his conclusions.

The subject of continued Chinese immigration was hotly debated during this period and became a test item for teacher applicants in California. One candidate responded as follows in answer to a question on immigration:

There can be no doubt that it [Chinese immigration] is a great disadvantage to all classes of people.

First by rendering physical labor so cheap, it deprives many of our own poor, of the employment by which, alone, they subsist; making them, either work at such prices that they have to starve both body and mind, or quit work and live by some dishonest means; thus, filling the country with a bad class of people, instead of having our poor respectable and honest.

By putting it within the power of the higher classes, to avoid manual labor entirely, they are made effeminate and weakly, both in body and mind. For, the body is made strong only in proportion as it is exercised, and the improvement of the mind depends on the body; if the body be strong and active so also will the mind be; or, if the body is weak the mind will correspond.

Thirdly, if we as a nation have any hope of ever converting the Chinese to Christianity, it will be far better to send missionaries to them, than to allow them to come here; for when they do, they see persons that profess to believe in the Christian religion, acting so different to their professions, that they become skeptics, and worse than ever they were before hearing of God.

Shall then a few speculators, for their own selfish purposes, fill the country with this class of people?[82]

# The Persistent Drive for Public Schooling

As WAS STATED PREVIOUSLY, the Chinese Evening School was closed along with other evening schools in San Francisco in February of 1871. As can be seen in Table 3, alternative schooling was available through missionary and private efforts during this period.

According to the table, the average number of Chinese children in San Francisco under seventeen years of age was 1,725 during this period. The average number of Chinese children attending non-public schools was 305. There isn't information available on the number of pre-schoolers, but even granting the fact that some of the total of 1,725 were not of school age, only 20 percent of the Chinese children in San Francisco were receiving any formal education.

Chinese attendance at non-public schools can also be seen by the following statement:

While the legislators of California seem to have exhausted their wisdom in divings [sic] from time to time all the contrivances to tax and fine these people which could be brought to bear on them, their real friends were opening schools and meetings, and showing them wherein the true glory of this land consisted.[84]

However, the low percentage of students attending private schools plus the unfairness of taxation without representation resulted in the relentless drive by the Chinese community and their supporters to secure the right of public-school attendance.

On October 22, 1872, when it appeared that the Chinese School would not be reopened, the Chinese petitioned the board for a Chinese night school:

From Chy Lung & Co., Lun Wo & Co., Quoy Ling Kee, Tai Kee and others, parents of children entitled to school privileges, asking the Board to establish an evening school for Chinese boys who are prevented from attending day schools. Referred to the Committee on evening schools.[85]

On November 8, 1876, Reverend Otis Gibson, one of the few supporters of the Chinese, testified before a joint congressional committee that while the Chinese paid for the support of the public schools, their children weren't allowed to attend. He had made an application to the school district on behalf of a Chinese pupil, but permission had been refused. Gibson said it was a wonder that the Chinese knew so much of our language instead of so

**TABLE 3**

**Chinese Children Attending Non-Public Schools, 1874–1884**

| Year | Under 17 Years of Age* | Between 5 & 17 Years of Age Attending School | Page Located in Superintendent's Annual Report |
|------|------|------|------|
| 1874 | 1,286 | 308 | 25 |
| 1875 | 855 | 61 | 18 |
| 1876 | 1,115 | 36 | 47 |
| 1877 | 2,082 | 109 | 12 |
| 1878 | 1,505 | 161 | 14 |
| 1879 | 2,221 | 622 | 17 |
| 1880 | 1,779 | 475 | 301 |
| 1881 | 1,728 | 585 | 17 |
| 1882 | 2,616 | 186 | 47 |
| 1883 | 2,537 | 513 | 73 |
| 1884 | 1,252 | . . . | 65 |

*This column represents the totals from the annual census of Chinese children taken under oath by San Francisco census marshals.[83]

little. Gibson's testimony appeared in the committee's 1877 report to Congress:[86]

It is objected to the Chinese population that they do not learn our language, do not attend our schools. The fact is they are taxed to support our schools but are peremptorily refused admission to their privileges. I, myself, applied to the school department of this city in behalf of an intelligent Chinaman who wished to be admitted, but the application was refused on account of race prejudice. There are many young children in Chinatown, but neither the State nor the city is providing any schools for their education.[87]

Reverend Gibson was questioned by the committee as follows:

Q. You said something about the schools. Do I understand you to say that Chinese children are not admitted into the public schools here?

A. I make that statement. I had a Chinaman come to my school who had been to some other schools and could read very well; had studied geography, arithmetic, history, etc., and he took a notion that he wanted to go to the public schools. I told him I did not think it would be pleasant to admit him; that he had better not try; that there was prejudice against the Chinese; but he insisted. I wrote a letter to the school board, stating that this man wanted to go to school, that he was cleanly in his person, well behaved, and had such and such scholarship. They said personally they would not object, but they did not think the public sentiment would allow it, and they did not dare admit him.

Q. Are they excluded on account of their color or race?

A. It was race prejudice in this case.

Q. Is there any law by which they can exclude a Chinese child from school?

A. I think not; I think the Chinese child has a right to go to the schools.[88]

For siding with the Chinese, Gibson's reward was to be hanged in effigy twice; once by the Ninth Ward Club and again by the Tailors' Protective Union.[89] During the anti-Chinese labor riot on July 23, 1877, a mob went to Rev. Gibson's Chinese Mission at 916 Washington Street and broke the windows of his residence.[90]

When the Workingmen's Party was gathering momentum in 1876 and 1877, a few supporters of the Chinese reiterated their right to public schooling.

...it is neither to burn, nor in any way to damage the buildings in which their schools are taught, as in some instances has been the case, for that is a blind and reckless lawlessness which every respectable citizen must condemn.[91]

Every youth has a right to the benefits of our free schools. The Chinese have this right in common with all others; and they pay into the School Fund of this State, in this city alone, over $42,000 per annum, and a large sum in other parts of the State, while all Chinese youth are excluded from the public schools. We ask, will you unite in securing to them this right, and protecting them in the enjoyment of it?[92]

In 1877, the Chinese Six Companies addressed Congress to challenge the joint congressional committee's report, part of which stated that the Chinese have never adapted themselves to the American educational system. The Six Companies' response:

The injustice of this extract becomes apparent when it is undeniable that State laws have been passed, and are now in force, denying us the privilege of your educational institutions.[93]

The *Chinese Record*, a bilingual newspaper, published two articles on education. The first one, printed in Chinese on February 5, 1877, concerned the denial of school privileges for the Chinese. Since Chinese bore a large proportion of the school taxes, the article said, this justified their securing educational rights through the judicial system.[94]

An article written in English on May 21 lamented the fact that free education wasn't extended to the Chinese:

The next and most important question is: Have we free education in this city and State? We wish we could answer it in the affirmative; but when we consider that it is but yesterday since the public schools were indiscriminately opened to white and colored children and that as yet the education granted to the latter is only elementary; when we discover that the Chinese population are denied entirely the benefit of education on account of antipathy of race, notwithstanding they are entitled to it by reason of the pro-rata of the school tax which they pay in common with other people, we must with mortification confess that contrary to the spirit of the age and the national boast of the American Nation, we have not FREE EDUCATION in our city and State.[95]

Less than a month after an anti-Chinese labor riot, thirty-nine of the most prominent Chinese businesses[96] requested that schools be opened by the city to educate the Chinese and that a building be furnished for that purpose:[97]

Your Honorable State levies poll and other taxes for the support of education, and makes no difference between natives and foreigners. If from the first, Chinese and Americans had been placed on the same footing in the schools, it would have been in accordance with right and justice, and there would have been subsequently no distinction, but our Honorable State has established schools of all grades, and has not admitted Chinese, which is contrary to the original intention [that they should be open to all].

We therefore respectfully and earnestly beg that you will open schools for the benefit of the Chinese, and that you will appoint Mr. Kerr, who is familiar with our language, to have charge. Thus the original excellent design will be realized, and the learning of your honorable country will be disseminated.[98]

Getting no response from the San Francisco Board of Education, the Chinese merchants petitioned the committee on evening schools for a class to accommodate their children. This committee, feeling it was a question of law, recommended that the matter be referred to their judiciary committee.[99]

Thoroughly dissatisfied with the board's reply to their petitions, the Chinese took the issue to the state legislature in 1878. On March 6, 1300 Chinese, including the principal Chinese merchants of San Francisco, Sacramento, and the interior California cities, petitioned the state for school privileges. They argued that three thousand Chinese children in the state were denied the privilege of attending public schools, and that the Chinese pay in taxes "a sum exceeding $42,000, which money has been used in part for the education of the children of colored and white people, many of the latter being foreigners from European countries, while our youth, (the Chinese) have been excluded from participation in the benefits."[100] This action by the Chinese dramatically demonstrated their continual interest in public education even in the midst of a hostile environment.

The *Daily Morning Call* was quick to respond to this petition for public schooling by asking its readers to ponder the consequences of continued Chinese immigration:

The petition gives a new and more serious aspect to the Chinese question. The race is striving to take root in the soil. They desire or profess to desire, to mingle their youth with ours, with a view, doubtless, to more thorough assimilation in the body politic. They prefer separate schools for a time, but seem determined to insist upon what they call their rights. This new phase of the question should awaken the people to the consequence of Chinese immigration, if it is permitted to continue.[101]

Another request to admit Chinese youths to the public schools in San Francisco came on July 7, 1882. The communication came from the Ministerial Union, composed of clergymen of all denominations. They argued that there was no law to exclude the Chinese from the public schools, and that the school codes required that all children be admitted.[102] When their resolution was presented to President Stubbs of the Board of Education, he said he was unable to understand why the communication should have been presented. He knew of no case of a refusal to admit a Chinese child into the schools![103]

This request from the city's clergymen demontrated their awareness of the provisions of the 1880 School Law. That the board did not provide educational services prior to 1880 could have been rationalized by the reasoning that Chinese children weren't mentioned in previous state school laws. But the School Law of 1880 was explicit on the point that all children had a legal right to attend public schools. Like all previous petitions, the clergymen's request went no further than the school board's classification committee.[104] The educational issue had to be fought out in the courts during the height of the anti-Chinese movement.

# Chapter 4

# The Chinese Primary School
# （華人皇家書館）
# and Legalized Segregation
# 1885-1905

## Tape v. Hurley;
## Moulder Reappears

THE ANTI-CHINESE ATTITUDE of the school board was shared by other governmental bodies in the city such as the board of supervisors. The supervisors were adamant about keeping Chinese children out of the public schools, as indicated in this passage from one of their reports:

Meanwhile, guard well the doors of our public schools, that they do not enter. For however hard and stern such a doctrine may sound, it is but the enforcement of the law of self-preservation, the inculcation of the doctrine of true humanity, and an integral part of the enforcement of the iron rule of right by which we hope presently to prove that we can justly and practically defend ourselves from this invasion of Mongolian barbarism.[1]

To the Chinese, this educational inequity couldn't go on any longer. Fourteen years of persistent appeals to the school board hadn't yielded results. The turning point came when the Chinese initiated legal action, a change in tactics that came about because of two events.

First, the Exclusion Act of 1882 caused the Chinese in the United States to shift their attention to the question of the rights of American-born Chinese. Prior to the legislation, the Chinese concentrated upon their treaty rights to trade and reside in this country.[2]

The second factor was an 1884 decision of the United States Circuit Court for the Ninth Judicial District to allow Look Tin Sing, a Chinese boy born in Mendocino County, California, to disembark in the United States after a five-year visit to China. At the time of his arrival at the port of San Francisco, immigration officials refused him entry on the grounds that permitting an alien Chinese to enter would be a violation of the Exclusion Act. The court ruled against the officials and said that "birth within the dominions of the United States of itself creates citizenship and that every person born within those dominions, whatever the status of his parents, is a natural-born citizen."[3] The court further ruled that "no citizen can be banished from his country except in punishment for crime. Banishment for any other cause is unknown to our laws and beyond the power of Congress. The petitioner must be allowed to land, and it is so ordered."[4]

These two events revitalized the Chinese community's effort to seek public education for their children. On October 4, 1884, less than a week after Look Tin Sing's victory, F. A. Bee, the consul of the Imperial Chinese Consulate, complained to San Francisco School Superintendent Moulder that an application by Joseph Tape, a native of China, to admit his eight-year-old daughter to the public schools of the city had been denied, even though Tape had lived in San Francisco for fifteen years. The Chinese consul-general protested this treatment:

The reasons given by you, if correctly reported through the press, are so inconsistent with the treaties, Constitution and laws of the United States, especially so in this case as the child is native-born, that I consider it my duty to renew the request to admit the child, and all other Chinese children resident here who desire, to enter the public schools under your charge. An early consideration of this request will greatly oblige.[5]

Moulder immediately wrote to State Superintendent Welcker regarding the recent court decision and asked for instructions in reference to the admission of Chinese children to the public schools.[6] In his reply to Moulder, Welcker stated:

Finally, it is a question, as yet, in my mind, whether a Federal Court has the power to condemn the State of California to undergo the expense of educating the children of Chinese, when the presence of such foreigners is declared by the Constitution to be "dangerous to the well-being of the State."[7]

This was good enough for Moulder. A few days later, he replied to Consul Bee:

In conformity with the instructions contained in the State Superintendent's letter, I must decline to admit Chinese children, resident here, into our public schools.[8]

Moulder conveyed the above exchange to the board of education at their October 21, 1884, meeting. Board member Platt moved that the action of Moulder be approved and ratified. Another member of the board, Isidor Danielwitz, said he expected that this was only the beginning of the subject. He said a court order might be served upon the members of the board at any time. Danielwitz said he would rather go to jail than allow a Chinese child to be admitted to the schools. A stiffer resolution was offered as a substitute for Platt's motion:

Whereas, the admission of Mongolian [Chinese] children into the public schools of this city and county is about to be made an issue with the department, and whereas, such issue should be promptly and resolutely met, therefore be it

Resolved, That each and every principal of each and every public school throughout this city and county, under the instruction of this Board, be, and he or she is, hereby absolutely prohibited from admitting any Mongolian child of schoolable age, or otherwise, either male or female, into such school or class;

Resolved, That a violation of the foregoing resolution will subject such principal or teacher to immediate dismissal from the department;

Resolved, That the Superintendent of Schools be directed to have immediately transmitted a copy of the above resolutions to all principals in the Department for their guidance and for that of their assistant teachers.[9]

Not all members of the board were sympathetic to the motion. Board member Cleveland considered it wrong in principle and maintained that it was the objective of our government to educate those who may exercise the right of franchise. If Chinese may sometimes be allowed to vote, they certainly ought to be educated, Cleveland said.[10]

The resolution was adopted by a vote of eight to three. After the vote, a Mr. Brand disclosed the fact that he had been contacted by W. F. Gibson, an attorney who had threatened to make a test case if the petition of the Chinese consul was denied. The board's judiciary committee, which had the power to hire an attorney,[11] was authorized to look after the matter should it be taken into the courts.[12] The next day, Superintendent Moulder issued Circular No. 52 to all the principals in the San Francisco public schools to enforce the above resolution.

At the November 12 board meeting, it was announced that the members of the board had been summoned to appear before Judge Maguire on Friday, November 14, to show cause why the daughter of Joseph Tape, an "Americanized Chinaman," should not be allowed to enter the public schools. The matter was referred to the judiciary committee.

The main defendant was the principal of the Spring Valley School, Miss Jennie Hurley, who refused to receive Mamie Tape as a pupil. Joining her as defendants were Superintendent Moulder and the San Francisco Board of Education.

On January 9, 1885, Superior Court Judge Maguire decided the case in favor of the plaintiff. According to the report of the *Evening Bulletin*, the defendants had raised a number of interesting points, which Judge Maguire discussed at length. The judge eloquently penetrated to the essence of the question:

The Fourteenth Amendment to the Federal Constitution secures equal protection, rights and privileges of every nature to all persons born within the United States and subject to their jurisdiction. Our Legislature has enacted that all children within the State shall have equal facilities for education, so far as regards the right to attend the public schools. To deny a child, born of Chinese parents in this State, entrance to the public schools would be a violation of the law of the State and the Constitution of the United States. It would, moreover, be unjust to levy a forced tax upon Chinese residents to help maintain our schools, and yet prohibit their children born here from education in those schools. Ignorance is a prolific source of crime and the interest of the State demands that school facilities should be open and free to all. A decision to this effect would not open our public schools to the slums of the Chinese quarter. The Board of Education have ample power to keep out all children who are blighted by filth, infection or contagion, or who are daily brought in contact with population of any kind. But any such objection should be personal to each particular child so barred out, without regard to its race or color. In the case at bar, it is admitted that child is healthy and of cleanly habits, and of healthy and cleanly surroundings, and her application for admission as a pupil in the Spring Valley School is proper and lawful and must be granted.[13]

When the reading of the opinion was concluded, Danielwitz, who had earlier said that he would rather go to jail than allow a

Chinese child to be admitted to the schools, stood and told the judge that, while he had been a member of the board when the case was instituted, he was a member no longer. After announcing his resignation to the court, Danielwitz said that board policy made it mandatory that Hurley be fired if she admitted the Chinese girl to the school. Judge Maguire responded to this challenge by threatening to punish the board members with contempt citations in that eventuality.[14]

Following the decision, Tape's attorney said he would not press matters to force a confrontation. He said there would be an opportunity for carrying the question to the Supreme Court or giving the board of education time to amend its regulations, before presenting the Chinese girl again to Miss Hurley.[15]

On January 14, 1885, the Tape petition was formally presented to the board. As recorded in the *Evening Bulletin:*

Joseph Tape, through his attorney, W. F. Gibson, submitted a petition setting forth that he is the father of the girl Mamie Tape, who is between the age of eight and nine years. That he is the husband of Mary McGladery Tape, having been married to her on November 16, 1875, in the First Presbyterian Church by Rev. A. W. Loomis, assisted by Rev. J. M. Condit. That Mamie Tape was born August 28, 1876, at their house, corner of Gough and Vallejo Streets. Since her birth, the family moved to the house 1769 Green Street, Chinatown. That the petitioner and his wife have resided in this city for over 15 years, the petitioner being an expressman and drayman. That more than 15 years ago, petitioner discarded his queue and has never since worn one. That both petitioner, his wife, and Mamie, their child, now dress in American costume. That petitioner and his wife have established a Christian home, in which the habits and customs peculiar to Americans have been adopted and the English language spoken by the family. Mamie is much more proficient in English than she is in Chinese. It is asserted that she is not a child of vicious habits or suffering from any contagious disease. That her playmates attend the Spring Valley School; that she applied for admission, was refused but subsequently appealing to the courts was granted the right. Wherefore your petitioner pray your Honorable Board: "First—That it may repeal and rescind the said resolution adopted by the Board of Education on the 21st day of October, 1884. Second—That Miss J. M. A. Hurley, the Principal of the Spring Valley Primary School, be directed to admit said Mamie Tape forthwith and your petitioner will ever pray," etc.[16]

It was moved to refer the matter to the rules committee, but the motion was amended and the matter referred to the judiciary committee.[17]

Moulder viewed the Tape petition and the court's ruling direct-
ing Hurley to allow Tape to enter Spring Valley School as alarm-
ing. He asserted that the legal decision met with the disapproval
of nearly every citizen and predicted it would be reversed by a
higher court. He again brought up the defamatory accusations
against the Chinese—that they were a "nation of liars" and that
they were "filthy and impure." [18]

Moulder then read the board a long letter from State Superintendent Welcker stating the latter's surprise at the judge's decision. Welcker thought a recent decision in an Eastern court had
established that the Fourteenth Amendment to the Constitution
didn't apply to the Mongolian race. Judge Maguire's decision, according to Welcker, was bad law. The letter continued:

If this ruling should prevail, I would not be surprised to see gray-
haired Chinamen applying for admission to our public schools, and
with plenty of witnesses to swear that they had been born in California and less than 17 years ago. The fact is, a terrible disaster is
threatening our institutions, and it is this consideration which will
not allow me to keep silent at this time, although I cannot but believe that the wisdom and public spirit of your Board has caused you
already to appeal against this decision. As to the assertion that separate schools might be provided, it was suggested that thousands of
children are now unable to gain admittance to the schools. Shall we
abandon the education of our own children to provide for that of the
Chinese, who are thrusting themselves upon us in spite of treaties,
Federal Restriction laws, and Custom House officials? Can anyone
believe such to be the true intent of the law? [19]

The board meeting closed with H. E. Platt, special counsel to
the board in the Tape case, asking whether the board wanted to
appeal to the Supreme Court. On Superintendent Moulder's motion, an appeal was decided upon by a unanimous vote.[20]

On March 3, 1885, the California Supreme Court confirmed
the Superior Court's decision. Judge Sharpstein quoted from the
appropriate legal codes and gave the following written interpretation of his ruling to the San Francisco school authorities:

"Every school, unless otherwise provided by law, must be open for
the admission of all children between six and twenty-one years of
age residing in the district.... Trustees shall have the power to exclude children of filthy or vicious habits, or children suffering from
contagious or infectious diseases."—(Political Code, Sec. 1662).

That is the latest legislative expression on the subject, and was
passed as late as 1880. Prior to that time the first clause of the section read, "Every school, unless otherwise provided by special stat-

ute, must be open for the admission of all white children between five and twenty-one years of age, residing in the district."

As amended the clause is broad enough to include all children who are not precluded from entering a public school by some provision of law. And we are not aware of any law which forbids the entrance of children of any race or nationality. The Legislature not only declares who shall be admitted, but also who may be excluded, and it does not authorize the exclusion of any one on the ground upon which alone the exclusion of the respondent here is sought to be justified. The vicious, the filthy, and those having contagious or infectious diseases, may be excluded, without regard to their race, color or nationality.

This law must be construed as any other would be construed. "Where a law is plain and unambiguous, whether it be expressed in general or limited terms, the legislature should be intended to mean what they have plainly expressed, and consequently no room is left for construction." (*Fisher v. Blight*, 2 Cranch 358, 399). "Where the law is clear and explicit, and its provisions are susceptible of but one interpretation, its consequences, if evil, can only be avoided by a change of the law itself, to be effected by legislature and not judicial action." (*Bosley v. Mattingly*, 14 B. Mon. 73). This rule is never controverted or doubted, although perhaps sometimes lost sight of. In this case, if effect be given to the intention of the legislature, as indicated by the clear and unambiguous language used by them, respondent here has the same right to enter a public school that any other child has.[21]

While the state court dismissed the San Francisco school superintendent and the board of education as defendants in the case and made the writ solely against Hurley, in other respects the decision of Judge Maguire was affirmed.[22]

Moulder anticipated that the decision would be in favor of the respondent. During the Supreme Court's deliberation, Moulder proposed a separate educational facility for the Chinese. Had he waited for the Supreme Court's decision, he would have lost valuable time in setting into motion a change of legislation. But in fact it was the Superior Court judge himself who had spelled out a way for Moulder to extricate the school district from the situation: "If evil results followed this decision, it was not the fault of the judiciary. The Legislature possessed the power to provide separate schools for distinct races."[23]

Moulder realized that the doctrine of "separate but equal" hadn't been challenged by the courts. The legislature could provide segregated all-Chinese institutions.[24] Moulder was faced with a legal dilemma. Admitting the Chinese girl to Spring

Valley School was too much against traditional practice, yet maintaining the rigid policy against the Chinese meant contempt of court. The *Evening Bulletin* reported that Moulder on May 4, 1885, sent the following telegram to W. S. May, a San Francisco delegate to the California Assembly:

I fear the decision of the Supreme Court admitting Chinese will demoralize our schools. But the one remedy is for the Legislature to declare urgent the passage of the bill already introduced by you to establish separate Chinese classes.

Without such action I have every reason to believe that some of our classes will be inundated by Mongolians. Trouble will follow. Please answer.[25]

At Moulder's urging, Assembly Bill 268 was introduced by Assemblyman May on January 23, 1885, just two weeks after Judge Maguire's decision.[26] According to the *Evening Bulletin*, Moulder wanted the legislature to repeal the law that excluded the Chinese from the school count, since school funds were apportioned on the basis of the number of children in each county between five and seventeen years old.

It was Mr. Moulder's desire to have this law repealed, in as much as the Court declares that Mongolians may be educated. He holds that the duty to educate implies the duty to enumerate. It is also the desire of the San Francisco School Department that the Legislature pass a law authorizing the establishment of Chinese classes separate from the schools attended by Caucasians. An Act of this kind would remove the irritating influences of race feeling. There is a strong and well-founded conviction that the association of Chinese and white children would be very demoralizing mentally and morally to the latter, and should the Chinese be admitted to the classes as now organized, trouble and turmoil would ensue. It is hoped by the School Directors, Superintendent and teachers that prompt action will be taken by the law-making body to amend the statutes at this session of the Legislature. The additional amount which San Francisco would receive from the State school fund by the enumeration of Mongolian children in the census for apportionment of money would enable the Board of Education to establish sufficient day and evening schools for all applicants coming under the recent decision of the Court. The Superintendent believes that the Chinese care mainly for instruction in the English language, and therefore evening schools in Chinatown would be well attended.[27]

The bill was passed by the California Assembly under an "urgency provision" and sent to the State Senate.[28] Moulder then asked San Francisco's Senator Lynch to use his influence for quick Senate passage.[29] Two days later, with Superintendent Moulder and Board of Education President Ira G. Hoit in attendance in Sacramento to lend support, Senator Lynch brought the legislation to the Senate floor by declaring a state of urgency.[30] The bill moved quickly through both houses under a suspension of rules with almost unanimous approval.[31]

Before amended, Section 1662 of the Political Code of 1880 read as follows:

Every school, unless otherwise provided by law, must be open for the admission of all children between six and twenty-one years of age residing in the district, and the Board of Trustees, or City Board of Education, have power to admit adults and children not residing in the district, whenever good reasons exist therefor. Trustees shall have power to exclude children of filthy or vicious habits, or children suffering from contagious or infectious diseases.

The new bill amended this section by putting a comma after the word "diseases" and then adding the following passage:

and also to establish separate schools for children of Mongolian or Chinese descent. When such separate schools are established Chinese or Mongolian children must not be admitted into any other schools.[32]

The 1885 amendment was "promoted by the same able educational leader who advocated the theory of segregation as early as 1858 and who put his theory of segregation into practice as early as 1860. With ability, prestige, and persuasive appeals to racial antipathy, he secured cooperation from all San Francisco delegates and obtained a speedy passage of the bill. The exclusion of Chinese children from public schooling was neither for gaining political favor among the massive laboring classes, nor for any other social or economic advantages for the school authorities, nor for any known or written protest from white parents of the city. It was chiefly because the Superintendent and some other School Directors believed that the association of Chinese and white children would be very demoralizing mentally and morally to the latter."[33]

The establishment of a separate school wasn't required by law but was an option open to school districts. San Francisco elected to have a separate facility. The segregation of Chinese students in San Francisco had always been by right of law (*de jure* segregation), and not due to residential patterns (*de facto* segregation). The 1885 amendment simply became the legislative basis which allowed the continuation of *de jure* segregation. For the next twenty-five years, those who advocated segregation in San Francisco would quote this amendment as the justification for preventing Chinese children from going to school with whites.

On March 18, 1885, Moulder reported passage of the bill to the board. He asked that the school site committee of the board provide the necessary accommodations for the one Chinese class that he said was all that was needed at first. Moulder praised San Francisco legislators for discarding their political differences to aid the passage of the legislation.[34]

Two weeks later, a joint sites and classification committee of the board noted that it had found a sufficient number of Chinese children desiring school facilities. The joint committee reported:

We have been offered a building on the corner of Jackson and Stone Streets for the monthly rental of $60. The building contains rooms sufficient for three classes, and a store which the Department can subrent for $25 per month, an offer having been made to the Committee. We recommended that the Committee on School Houses and Sites be authorized to rent the building and put it in proper condition for the accommodation of the children, and that the Committee on Classification be authorized to open the school and designate a teacher.[35]

Director Deane said that the Chinese consul had informed him that there would be nearly one thousand children who would eventually desire school advantages. This was because many children in private schools would go to the public classes when the school opened. Commenting on this information, Superintendent Moulder said that such an assertion was preposterous. He thought that there wouldn't be one hundred children in this situation.[36]

The most hostile expression toward the establishment of a Chinese School, however, was made by Mr. Culver, the director who first offered the resolution that led to the establishment of the Chinese classes. He asked anxiously if furniture and supplies would have to be given these classes. When he was told that such would be the case, he made a motion, which was turned down, to postpone the subject. He then asked to speak on "this Chinese question." He said he had made a mistake in offering the resolution that led to the establishment of the Chinese classes, and apologized to the citizens of San Francisco for his action. He felt that if the matter had been left as decided by Judge Maguire, it would have settled itself in time. In the course of his remarks, he said that the matter of Chinese in our public schools was a most momentous question:

A question of greater importance to our commonwealth than anything that has arisen in the history of our State, and if we have patriotism, if we have love for our fellowmen, the Caucasian race, if we have any regard for the 50,000 children that the sovereign voice of the people has placed in our charge for two years, we should cry "halt!" Let us consider the matter and see what is right. If we cannot avert, put off, postpone this danger, and not stand like stall-fed cattle to the end of our term, and then be led to the shambles and suffer an ignominious political death.[37]

Fortunately, a majority of the board felt they had had too much trouble already with the case and the report of the joint committee was adopted over Culver's suggestion.[38]

By April, 1885, a separate school still hadn't been established and the Chinese were impatient with the board's delaying tactics. On April 7, 1885, little Mamie Tape, accompanied by her attorneys, W. F. Gibson and another lawyer named Kellogg, went to Spring Valley Primary School and asked Principal Hurley to admit Tape to the eighth grade in accordance with the decision of the Supreme Court. The request was made on a writ of mandate directed to Hurley and issued by Judge Lawler. Superintendent Moulder, School Director English, and many others were present.

Principal Hurley refused to admit Mamie Tape on two grounds. She cited a rule of the San Francisco Board of Education that pupils had to present a certificate of vaccination from a reputable physician. Hurley demanded a certificate and this nonplussed the attorneys momentarily. They quickly recovered and argued that the writ superseded any ruling by the board and announced that they intended to ask the court to cite the school authorities for contempt.

Hurley then pursued a second approach. She pointed out a board policy of limiting class size to 60 pupils. The two eighth grade classes in Spring Valley already claimed 62 and 70 students, respectively, so Hurley said she was willing to register the Tape girl and place her on the waiting list. Superintendent Moulder promised Hurley that should proceedings for contempt be brought against her, he would try to protect her.[39]

The *Evening Bulletin* reflected the sentiment of the city school authorities:

While it is in the Tape girl's favor that she is unobjectionable as regards health, cleanliness and manner of dress, yet it is considered that her case is exceptional; that following her admission, other children would come who would be objectionable, and by their association drive from the schools the white children. The class to be formed on Jackson Street for Chinese exclusively is certainly the proper place for Chinese children.[40]

That same evening, the board held a special meeting. Moulder stated that he hoped prompt action would be taken to organize the Chinese class. He thought it probable that the Tape child had not been properly vaccinated, and that this would absolve the school district from responsibility. He also labeled as "cranks" Henry Ward Beecher, Rev. Dr. Talmage, Bob Ingersoll and others who had sharply criticized the school authorities for restraining Chinese from attending the public schools. Moulder defended his position this way:

It would not be benevolence to put that child in that school [Spring Valley Primary School] for a short time, then to be taken out into the Chinese School. It was not a question of race prejudice; it was a question of demoralization of one high race by a lower.[41]

A board committee recommended the appointment of Miss Thayer to the new Chinese class at the salary of $100 a month. Superintendent Moulder thought the salary too much, since he assumed there wouldn't be over fifteen pupils in the class. But directors Deane and Wentworth thought differently and said a teacher in Chinatown ought to be paid as much as any other. The superintendent said that while the law made the board educate the Chinese, no support was obtained from them. The report of the joint committee was adopted unanimously.[42]

Another motion was then made by director English to rent the building on the corner of Jackson and Stone streets for the Chinese School for a period not exceeding two years at a monthly rental of $60. Superintendent Moulder wanted to know if the building could be obtained for a shorter period. After debate, it was decided that a special committee would be empowered to form the Chinese class immediately, but to rent the building for no longer than a year. At the end of the meeting Superintendent Moulder predicted that the school would not last more than six months. He was of the opinion that the caste system among the

Chinese—a rich merchant would not allow his child to associate with that of a coolie laborer—would mean a lack of pupils.[43]

Frustrated that her daughter was thwarted from enrolling at Spring Valley School, Mrs. Tape wrote a long letter to the board. Her communication was read before the board on April 15. A portion of it reads:

> May you Mr. Moulder, never be persecuted like the way you have persecuted little Mamie Tape. Mamie Tape will never attend any of the Chinese Schools of your making! Never!!![44]

As far as can be ascertained, the board did not respond to Mrs. Tape's letter.

By the time Mamie Tape had all the necessary papers completed to enter Spring Valley School, the board had established the Chinese Primary School at Jackson and Powell streets. The date of the opening was April 13, 1885. Unlike the first school in 1859, this school was based upon legal foundation. But the Chinese were still the only racial group separated from the rest of the students in California. The *Evening Bulletin* gave a full-length report on this momentous event.

> Yesterday the first public school for the exclusive use of Chinese children was opened at the corner of Powell and Jackson Streets, in the rooms formerly occupied by the Morrow Guard. The rooms, which are rented for $40 per month, are situated over a grocery store and occupy the two stories above the ground floor. The school [class] room is on the second floor, the rooms on the floor above being at present set apart for play-rooms. Miss Rose Thayer, a bright teacher, who is well-known in the Department, has charge of the class, which now numbers six. The first pupils to appear yesterday morning were Frank and Mamie Tape, whose cases were taken before the Courts, resulting in the establishment of a public school for Chinese. The boy is six years old and the girl eight. Both children are bright, and talk English as well as most pupils at the public schools. They are dressed neatly in clothes like those worn by American children, and have none of the Chinese peculiarities in regard to the manner of wearing the hair. Frank has no queue, his black hair being allowed to grow as it was meant to do, and neatly trimmed. Mamie has the traditional braid of American children hanging down her back and tied with a ribbon. Soon after the school was called to order there was heard a tramping on the stairs, and four bright Chinese lads, two twelve years of age and two ten, politely doffed their hats when Miss Thayer appeared, and asked to be allowed to join the class. They were given seats, and at once began to manifest an interest in the studies given them, which cannot fail to make their

teacher enthusiastic in her work, if it continues. The Tape children have never been to school before, and they are, consequently, somewhat restless; but the four Chinese boys who wear their queues and distinctive style of clothing, having already been taught in mission schools, conducted themselves as well as any other children would do. All speak English fluently, and can read and write. They comply easily and naturally with the new method of teaching which they find in the public schools, and are seldom spoken to twice about anything. Their knowledge of English is unusually good, and the definitions of words which they give are surprisingly accurate and clearly original. In arithmetic they are very proficient, and in solving simple problems without the aid of slate, they are quick and correct. Miss Thayer has already found reason to believe that she will have no trouble in causing her class to take a high rank as to attainments. The four elder boys laughed when they were for the first time today initiated into the mode of rising from their seats and marching from the room at recess, but they fell into line at once and marched out like veterans of the public schools. Only Frank and Mamie Tape could not see the use of going as far as the door in line, and came trooping back to have a frolic. The boys are allowed to play in the rooms above, and from the clatter made it is evident that they are very active at play. Yesterday one of them was found hanging out of the window so far that there was danger that the class would be reduced to five; but no one has yet fallen to the sidewalk. The Tape children bring their roller skates, and indulge in skating during recess. Yesterday the Chinese Consul-General visited the school and was so pleased with its appearance and its teacher that he caused his interpreter to tell Miss Thayer that he regretted that he was not a child himself, that he might become a member of the class. As the new school will continue to be an object of great interest, it will have many visitors. Already Miss Thayer says that if she is expected to teach her pupils, friends of the school must not permit her to be interrupted. She has set apart Friday afternoons for visitors, and requests those who desire to visit the class to do so only on Friday afternoons. There was no increase in the class today, but it is expected that the classroom will be filled before long.[45]

After the initial enrollment of six children, three more were registered a few days later.[46] The attendance at the Chinese School seemed to be living up to Moulder's prediction. Only nine school-age children out of 561 went to the Chinese Primary School during that first year.[47]

The small attendance, however, only meant that the Chinese, unsure of the intentions of the capricious board of education, kept their children away from the public school.[48] The location of the school, outside the boundaries of Chinatown at Jackson and Powell, certainly didn't help the situation. Chinese parents, affronted by the strong opposition to public instruction of their children, sent them either to China to be educated,[49] or to private schools.[50] Consul Bee said he would try to remove this feeling of distrust. He thought it would not be long before there would be a class of twenty-five students.[51] The *Alta* did not agree with the Chinese consul:

A school has been established for Chinese children, but pupils are not forthcoming. The alleged eagerness of the San Francisco Chinese to have their children educated by the State is belied by the reluctance they now show to take advantage of the educational opportunities opened to them. Eastern sympathies have been invoked in times past for the Chinese of California because they were debarred from the advantages to which they now manifest so much indifference. If the establishment of this school has done nothing else, it has at least dissipated the myth of Chinese thirst for American learning.[52]

## The Anti-Chinese Movement Broadens to Anti-Asian

THE STRUGGLE FOR PUBLIC EDUCATION took place within the larger context of racial hostility against the Chinese. On March 20, 1886, the Anti-Chinese Non-Partisan Association held an imposing anti-coolie demonstration at the Metropolitan Temple in San Francisco. Speakers called attention to the failure of Congress and in particular the Exclusion Act in lessening Chinese competition to white laborers. The meeting ended with the following unanimously adopted resolutions:

Resolved, That the people of San Francisco in mass meeting assembled, heartily endorse the action of the convention held March 10th at Sacramento by the California Anti-Chinese Non-Partisan Association. We particularly endorse the boycotting resolution. We firmly believe that when a boycott has been established the Chinese question will have been solved, and,
    Resolved, That we pledge ourselves to give moral and financial support to the State Executive Committee.[53]

Three days later, prior to the adjournment of the school board, director Culver introduced anti-Chinese resolutions for the board to adopt. The resolutions were passed unanimously "amid much merriment," because board members expected to be in opposition gave in to the pressure of anti-Chinese opinion. Here was an example of outside anti-Chinese forces influencing school board resolutions. The resolution read:

Whereas, In this State an earnest and continued effort is being made by the Caucasian race to rid themselves of the Chinese element in our midst, whose presence here is a gigantic evil and productive of great wrong to the laboring men and women of the community, and if not checked will directly and most injuriously affect the future welfare of at least three-fourths of the children now in the public schools of this city, who of necessity must be the coming wage workers and whose welfare it is our duty to protect and advance in every way possible; and

Whereas, The press, the labor organizations, our representatives in Congress and the municipal governments of our cities and towns are doing all in their power to further this work and accomplish by peaceful ends the desired result; therefore be it

Resolved, That it is the sense of this Board that no principal, teacher or employee of the Public Schools Department shall employ, patronize, aid or encourage the Chinese in any way, but shall do all in their power to legally promote their removal from this coast and to discourage further immigration.[54]

A week later Superintendent Moulder issued the above resolution to all school principals and gratuitously added:

In these sentiments the Superintendent heartily concurs. They represent the feeling on this subject of the taxpayers of San Francisco by whose liberality and cheerful contributions our public schools are supported.

But independently of this consideration the duty which the teachers owe to the children committed to their charge should prompt them to active efforts to save the rising generation from contamination and pollution by a race reeking with the vices of the Orient, a race that knows neither truth, principle, modesty nor respect for our laws. The moral and physical ruin already wrought to our youth by contact with these people is fearful.

Let us exhaust all peaceful methods to stop its spread.[55]

After the Exclusion Act, Republicans and Democrats continued to try to outdo each other in enacting harsher measures against the Chinese.[56] On October 1, 1888, the Democrats held a large anti-Chinese meeting at Metropolitan Hall in San Francisco to celebrate the signing of the Scott Act, which barred Chinese laborers from entering the United States.[57] When the act went into effect, there were more than twenty thousand Chinese who had temporarily left the United States with certificates entitling them to return. However, six hundred of them were subsequently refused re-entry because their certificates were declared void. Some of them had families and property interests.[58]

In 1892, Congress passed the Geary Act, which suspended Chinese immigration for another ten years. This harsh measure practically stripped the Chinese of protection in the courts, denied bail in habeas corpus cases, required Chinese to obtain a certificate to remain in the United States, and made the burden of proof fall upon them if they were arrested without a certificate. The phrase "not a Chinaman's chance" was coined in this period, when the Supreme Court declared the Geary Act "constitutional" on the grounds of public interest and necessity.[59]

The harsh exclusion laws, accompanied by white hostility and violence, extended into the new century. These bitter experiences were etched into the minds of the Chinese and contributed to their isolation from white American culture.

By 1890, the gold cycle was completed and unemployed "natives" were in the cities clamoring for jobs they once refused.[60] The California State Legislature, on March 20, 1891, passed an act prohibiting Chinese from coming to California.[61] Beginning in 1893, terrorism and violence against Chinese broke out in rural California. For the first time in California, there was a real drop in the Chinese male population. Those who could afford the passage returned to China, while many others departed for the East Coast. Still others sought refuge in the crowded Chinese settlements of the large cities, from which, until the 1920s, it was impossible to venture without fear of being beaten.[62]

By 1895, secure in the knowledge that they were Chinese Americans, the Chinese formed the Native Sons of the Golden State (NSGS,同源會) with headquarters in San Francisco. This organization's purpose was to "do battle for the preservation of the rights of American citizens of Chinese ancestry and the willingness to challenge any discrimination that may arise because of race and color."[63] Eager to show that they were "native sons," they had wanted to be chartered members of the Native Sons of the Golden West (NSGW), but were denied permission by the parent body. Their enthusiasm undaunted, they simply changed "west" to "state."[64] NSGS was one of the first groups in Chinatown to have a predominantly American-born membership.[65]

After World War I, NSGS was renamed the Chinese-American Citizens Alliance (CACA) to reflect a national rather than state membership.[66] This group claimed America as their home and it was here they wanted to stay. Through this organization, the Chinese mounted a stronger legal effort to acquire their right to first-class citizenship.[67] Their struggles with the San Francisco School Board would occur in the 1920s and 1930s.

As federal exclusion laws were about to expire, San Francisco's Mayor Phelan organized an anti-Chinese convention on November 22, 1901, to support re-enactment of Chinese exclusion. The convention appointed a committee of five, headed by the mayor, to work for their cause in Washington.[68.] Five days before, Mayor Phelan said:

This is not a racial, nor merely an industrial question; it is an American question. Coolie immigration threatens the American standard of living.... If he [the American workingman] must compete with coolies he must come down to the coolie level and must dwell and rear his children in the fetid labyrinths of Globe theaters or dark depths of sub-cellars.[69]

Moreover, the increasing importance of the Chinese question in public discussions prompted President Roosevelt in 1901 to bring the matter officially to the attention of Congress in his first annual message:

With the sole exception of the farming interest, no one matter is of such vital moment to our whole people as the welfare of the wage-workers.... Not only must our labor be protected by the tariff, but it should also be protected so far as it is possible from the presence in this country of any laborers brought over by contract, or of those who, coming freely, yet represent a standard of living so depressed that they can undersell our men in the labor market and drag them to a lower level. I regard it as necessary, with this end in view, to re-enact immediately the law excluding Chinese laborers, and to strengthen it wherever necessary in order to make its enforcement entirely effective.[70]

The result was the Congressional Act of April 29, 1902, which extended existing Chinese exclusion laws.[71] But by 1910, the decrease of the Chinese population due to successive exclusion laws had been countered by an increase in the Japanese population in California. The sentiment of Californians shifted from a particular anti-Chinese[72] bias to a general anti-Asiatic one.[73] Governor Henry T. Gage in his first biennial message on January 7, 1901, voiced this feeling:

The people of California, from their experience in the past, and in view of their prominent seacoast with respect to the ports of the Orient, have reason to dread the immigration of Chinese and Japanese laborers into this State, a fear justly founded and shared in by the American workingmen of other States.[74]

# The Chinese Primary School
# from 1885 to 1900

By 1886, the Chinese Primary School had increased to 24 students.[75] One reason was that the school had been moved to 807 Stockton Street,[76] a safer and more convenient location. Distrust still existed, however, for the Chinese refused to give information to school authorities and hid their children from the census marshals.[77]

The progress of the Chinese Primary School was reported in the *Daily Morning Call:*

Thirty-eight scholars had enrolled at the school that was situated on Stockton Street between Clay and Sacramento Streets. Three of the pupils were girls. All the scholars regardless of age studied in one room. The multi-graded classroom required separate groupings in Reading and in other subjects. Most of the pupils understand no English at all when they enter the school, but the teacher stated that they quickly learn it as spoken.

All the pupils wear the garb of their nation at school, and when they talk to each other they speak in Chinese.

Miss Thayer said that until they are taught the necessity of silence, it is often hard to suppress the chattering of Chinese pupils while learning English.... [78]

Even as attendance increased, sketchy data from the superintendent's reports show more children were not attending school or were attending private schools (see Table 4).

Despite the fact that *de jure* segregation was firmly established at the Chinese Primary School, there were people who voiced their objection to segregated schooling. In 1886 a Reverend Baldwin spoke at length on education by race at the annual meeting of the National Educational Association. He said that the Chinese are a race worthy to be educated, but that it is not desirable that they should have special schools by themselves.[79]

Sketchy school reports show a gradual increase in Chinese male students beginning in 1887. Two teachers were needed from 1887 to 1889,[80] three teachers from 1893 to 1897,[81] and in 1898 five teachers were needed.[82]

According to the school census from 1885 to 1890, Chinese girls five to seventeen years old were as numerous as boys. As indicated in Table 4, girls outnumbered the boys in 1886 and 1888. However, while the reports did not indicate whether the girls were attending the Chinese Primary School, one newspaper did report that eight girls attended the school in 1898.[83] Presumably, Chinese parents continued the custom of keeping their daughters home, because they didn't think it worthwhile to educate them.[84]

But white children maintained the prejudicial attitudes im-

**TABLE 4**

**Attendance at the Chinese Primary School, 1885–1890**

| Year | Native-born Chinese 5–17 of age | School attendance (at any time during the school year) of Chinese children between the ages of 5 and 17 years | | | Page located in Superintendent's Annual Report |
|------|------|------|------|------|------|
| | | Public | Private only | None | |
| 1885 | 291 boys 270 girls 561 total | 9 | 154 | 398 | 106–107 |
| 1886* | 241 boys 332 girls 573 total | 24 | 122 | 294 | 60–61 |
| 1887 | 484 boys 383 girls 867 total | 51 | 457 | 359 | 26–27 |
| 1888 | 395 boys 398 girls 793 total | 166 | 142 | 485 | 86–87 |
| 1889 | 480 boys 361 girls 841 total | 122 | 648 | 71 | 12–13 |
| 1890 | 503 boys 404 girls 907 total | 62 | 372 | 473 | 24–25 |

*Horizontal figures do not add up to the total.

bued into them by their parents. In 1891, the superintendent was so impressed by the politeness of Jefferson School students that he cited in his report the children who formed "bands of mercy" and pledged "not to fight, not to abuse animals, and not to stone Chinamen."[85]

In one school report of this period, Superintendent John Swett used the term "Chinese uniformity." This wording appeared three times in his report and was used to convey the sense that Chinese did everything one way.[86]

It isn't clear exactly when the Chinese Primary School moved to the Clay Street address. The site was first mentioned in 1897 in the superintendent's report,[87] but the address had been cited in the *Call* in 1894.[88] No reason was given as to why the move was made. The increase from two to three teachers may have meant that the Stockton Street facility could have accommodated only two classes. If this was the reason, the Clay Street facility must have been used as early as 1893 to house the expanding number of classes at the Chinese Primary School.

A major incident of 1894 wasn't mentioned in the city school report. There was a decline in attendance and only two classes were needed instead of three. The board proposed economizing by relocating the Chinese School from Clay Street to the basement of the Commercial School on Powell Street between Clay and Sacramento streets.[89] The proposed savings amounted to $155 per month—including the decrease in rent and the elimination of one teacher.[90]

Property owners in the Commercial School neighborhood protested the move. They claimed it would tend to enlarge the Chinese quarter, which in turn would depreciate property values along Powell Street. Moreover, they charged that the school would be obnoxious to white children "forever afterward."[91] They stated that if any action were taken by the board, it should be toward depopulating Chinatown rather than enlarging it.[92]

E. J. Shattuck, one of the property owners, claimed that moving the school to that area would cause property values to go down 25 percent. The neighborhood had been extensively improved and property owners considered themselves more as Nob Hill dwellers than as neighbors of the Chinese quarter.[93] The *Chronicle* provided a detailed account of the board proceedings on the contemplated move:

Director Clinton moved that the petition be referred to a special committee and that action relative to the moving of the school from its present location on Clay Street be delayed until the committee should report.

Director Ames opposed delay, as the matter had already been fully investigated. He did not believe that the people of the neighborhood would ever become aware of the presence of the school.

Director Dunn said that it was proposed to have the Chinese enter the school by a side alley. It would not be a month before the pig-tailed Chinese would be strutting along Powell Street. Again, he did not like the idea of contaminating a school occupied by white children by placing Chinese in the building.

Director Rosewald thought that the proposed location would not be more objectionable than the present.

Director Clinton said that the white residents of Powell Street had the sense of smell, and it would be an outrage to locate a school of Chinese in their neighborhood.

Director Ames thought the reference to smell was sentimental and absurd.

The motion to refer and delay was lost by a vote of 5 to 4....

After a long string of motions and a jumble of parliamentary ruling, during which Dowling and Rosewald changed their votes, it was finally decided to postpone all work upon the approaches and entrance to the school building after the next meeting of the Board.[94]

Other newspapers gave different versions of the length of the delay and why the board decided to postpone action. The *Examiner* reported that the board deferred action for one month to give the residents of the district a chance to gather stronger opposition to the proposed change.[95] The *Call* reported that Dowling's motion was adopted as a compromise to appease taxpayers who had protested.[96]

With the board determined to move the Chinese pupils to the new location, protesters issued a circular to Powell Street residents asking them to put pressure upon board members not to force the relocation.[97]

Prior to the next board meeting, J. H. Culver, one of the board members against the Powell Street site, told the *Call:*

The place for a Chinese School is in Chinatown. If the present school is to be moved at all, it should be moved nearer to the heart of Chinatown.... If it were put to a ballot, 90 per cent of the voters of San Francisco would declare against the proposition. I do not believe there is one member of the new Board of Education who would not protest if it were proposed to establish a Chinese School next door to his residence. In the last two years, thousands of dollars have been extended in the erection of new buildings on Powell Street. The men who have invested their money there are entitled to some consideration.[98]

The *Call* concluded with J. T. M. Kelly, of 928 Sacramento Street, saying:

We have the signatures of 150 property-owners to a petition requesting the Board of Education not to convert the basement of the Commercial High School into a Chinese School. There is plenty of room in Chinatown for a Chinese School. The proposed change would merely extend the limits of Chinatown over our section of the city.

The Board of Education cannot defend the plan on the ground of economy, as we have offered to find a tenant who will take the property which it is proposed to convert into a Chinese School and pay $60 a month for it for a term of years.

The Commercial High School building was closed and condemned as unsafe for the occupancy of white children. I do not see how it can then be regarded as safe for Chinese children.…

The Chinese consul opposes the proposition. He declares that the proper place for a Chinese School is in Chinatown and declares that if the Chinese children are forced to attend a school in a white neighborhood, they will suffer from the attacks of the white children.[99]

The next day the *Call* followed up with an editorial on the Chinese School:

As there is here and there a Chinaman who pays taxes the city is under an obligation to provide schools for Chinese children. This is now done by the maintenance of a separate school. The cost of educating Chinese children is considerably more than the average for white children, but the city prefers to incur that extra expense rather than admit Chinese children into white schools. But the same disinclination to mix white children with Chinese should govern the location of the Chinese School. Why gather the Chinese children into a single building and then place that building in a locality occupied exclusively by white people? While the proper place for a Chinese School is not in the heart of Chinatown it should be within what are now recognized as Chinese limits.… Chinese children have a right to free instruction, but they certainly cannot expect the department to locate their school in the heart of a white neighborhood.[100]

The day before the board meeting, the storm of indignation among the Powell Street residents against "inoculating their district with Chinese" brought a committee of school directors, headed by President Hyde of the board, to meet with over twenty real-estate owners. The confrontation was reported in the *Call*:

President Hyde's statement was to the effect that they proposed to close the front entrance of the old Commercial School building on Powell Street, build a stairway up over the forty-five foot hill from Clay Street to the rear entrance of the building and then confine the Chinese pupils to two rooms, only allowing them to enter and depart from the building by the Clay Street way.

The citizens attacked the plan first on the ground that the School Directors would be violating the fire ordinances by building the stairway as proposed from Clay Street and tried to show the Directors that the old Commercial School building being situated in the midst of a lot of frame buildings if ever a fire broke out the little Chinese boys and girls would probably never reach the street down the long steep stairway.

Secondly, they denied that it would be a saving of $155 per month to the city to make the change because the city is only paying $60 per month for the building at 916 Clay Street and the owner of that building is willing to make such changes as will enable the directors to do away with a $95 a month teacher as well there as on Powell Street.

Thirdly, that in bringing Chinese up to that portion of the city the value of property in rents and taxes would diminish to an extent that would impoverish property-owners and cut down the taxes paid the city far below the savings, and in support of this representatives of the estate of Daegner, Mrs. Green owning $80,000 worth of property nearly all rented, T. Nunan and others stated that they had been notified by their tenants that as soon as a Chinese School was established in the old Commercial School building they, the tenants, would move out.

As a fourth and last proposition the property-owners declared that if Chinese were brought into their midst the diseases incident to the mode and manner of living in Chinatown would be spread broadcast among the white children in case of an epidemic, and they further urged that even the Chinese were against the removal and did not want their children sent up the proposed stairway and into the "ramshackle old building" known as Commercial Hall.[101]

After the board members left, two different points of view were expressed by the residents. One side said that if the neighborhood had to have Chinese, they wanted "to show the little Mongolians how to get out by a front entrance in case of fire." The other side stated that if the board members persisted, property-owners would carry the matter into the courts.[102]

On the night of the board meeting, a letter from Thomas D. Riordan was read regarding the relocation of the Chinese School. It was written at the request of the Chinese consul, who protested against moving the school. The consul said the Clay Street location was satisfactory and that the move could result in conflicts between American and Chinese boys. He mentioned the right of education according to state law and said the Powell Street site had been condemned as unsafe. The letter ended by stating that the city received nearly $8,000 from the state for educating the Chinese, but the expenses of the present school were only $2,800.[103] The matter was tabled and this action kept the Chinese School on Clay Street.[104] The *Chronicle* reported a higher figure of $3,840 spent on the school. It also reported on how the subject was tabled:

When the board sustained Director Dowling's move that the whole matter of the Chinese School be tabled, this action was greeted with applause from the lobby. Director Clinton made an effort to get the Chinese School question off the table. It appeared that the applause of the lobby, when the whole subject matter was tabled, was premature. The action of the board at a previous meeting in ordering the Chinese School removed from Clay Street to the Powell Street building still stands and the protest of the property owners against the establishing of such a nuisance in their midst was of no avail. Clinton's motion to take the subject from the table in order that justice might be done to the protesting American citizens was defeated.[105]

Director Clinton made one final attempt to erect a schoolhouse for the Chinese on a lot owned by the school department on Clay Street, but the motion was ruled out of order.[106] The tabling saved the board from having to rescind their original proposal to establish a school for Chinese on Powell Street. The "economy move" was never brought up again because attendance at the Chinese Primary School on Clay Street began to climb after 1894.

The course of study at the school was the same as that followed in the other primary schools of the city. Reading, writing, spelling and arithmetic were taught in the first grade. In the higher grades, language, geography, and history, including the early history of the United States and the biographies of Columbus, Washington, Franklin, etc., were studied.[107]

The teachers at the school said their pupils were "equally

bright, quick and tractable." The children "particularly excelled in drawing from models and sketches," and anything that "required an accurate and observing eye and imitative ability," but they were "slow to originate or to apply abstract rules to actual practice."[108]

One reporter described the pupils as quiet and exceedingly docile, showing a profound respect for their teachers. He reported that they received no report cards, but worked for the pleasure of learning. Arithmetic "was especially easy for them, but reading was their chief enjoyment."[109]

Another reporter contrasted their behavior at the Chinese language school with their behavior at the Chinese public school. In the latter, the Chinese children were as restless and mischievous as white children, but in the presence of their Chinese language instructors they were models of deportment and perseverance and paid the Chinese teachers the compliment of wearing long blue gowns.[110]

The average number of boys attending the Chinese Primary School in 1900 was 130. The first few Chinese pupils who finished all the grade levels at the Chinese School were initially allowed to attend the high schools of San Francisco. However, an attempt was made to compel Chinese pupils to remain at the Chinese Primary School, even though the school had no adequate high school course. When the Board of Education ordered the Chinese boys to quit the high schools, the Chinese daily papers threatened that the parents would take their children from the Chinese Primary School. This action would create chaos in the assignment of principals and teachers in the school department. The threat was serious enough for the board to withdraw its order.[111]

# Wong Him v. Callahan: Attempt to Enter Neighborhood School

ALTHOUGH THE CHINESE in San Francisco resided in Chinatown, some would have preferred to live outside the area but couldn't get housing elsewhere "at any price, no matter how wealthy they may be nor how quiet and clean."[112] The few who lived outside of Chinatown in this period attempted to send their children to the schools nearest their places of residence or places of work. Such was the case of Dr. Wong Him's daughter, Katie.[113] Though they lived at 115 Mason Street,[114] he wanted her to attend the Clement School located at Arguello and Point Lobos (now Geary) streets, in the Richmond district[115] — presumably near his office. Having regularly attended school since July 22, 1901,[116] Katie was notified by the acting principal Helen F. McFarland on March 1, 1902, that she could no longer attend the Clement School as she was of Chinese descent and must attend the Chinese Primary School in Chinatown at 920 Clay Street.[117]

The reason was the same as that used in 1885 to exclude Mamie Tape from the Spring Valley School. The school board cited Section 1662 of the Political Code of California to justify their action:

...and also to establish separate schools for children of Mongolian or Chinese descent. When such separate schools are established, Chinese or Mongolian children must not be admitted into any other schools.[118]

Dr. Wong Him filed a complaint in United States Circuit Court on June 18, 1902, and alleged that Section 1662 conflicted with the Fourteenth Amendment of the Constitution of the United States in that it denied equal protection of the laws to citizens of Chinese descent. The complaint asserted that Negroes (blacks), Indians, and Japanese were admitted into the public school and that no separate schools had been established in San Francisco for any race or nationality other than for children of Chinese parents. The complaint asked for an injunction restraining the Board of Education from excluding his daughter from the white schools until the case was adjudicated.[119]

On August 19, 1902, the principal, McFarland, testified that she admitted Katie because she thought Katie was a "nice little child,"[120] but that she told Katie she must go to the Chinese Primary School after she received a circular from Superintendent Webster calling attention to the code regarding the attendance of Chinese children.[121]

On November 29, Judge Seawell denied Dr. Wong Him's plea to compel the Board of Education to allow Katie to remain a pupil at the Clement School. The judge held that so long as the Board of Education provided a school expressly for children of her race, she must attend that school.[122] Dr. Wong Him objected on the grounds that legislating against his daughter's admission to the public schools was class legislation, and that, as he did not reside in the Chinese quarter, his child ought not to be compelled to attend school so far from home.[123]

On December 5, United States District Judge de Haven ruled that the state had the right to provide separate schools for children of different races, as long as it made no discrimination in the educational facilities they afforded. Dr. Wong Him had not claimed that the Chinese Primary School had fewer advantages than the Clement School. Judge de Haven said in referring to Wong Him's charge that the discrimination was based on the hatred of Chinese:

The validity of the statute [Section 1662] referred to does not depend upon the motive which may in fact have actuated the members of the Legislature in voting for its enactment. Upon such an inquiry the courts have no right to enter. If the law does not conflict with some constitutional limitation of the powers of the State Legislature it cannot be declared invalid.... When the schools are conducted under the same general rules, and the course of study is the same in one school as in the other, it cannot be said that pupils in either are deprived of the equal protection of the law in the matter of receiving an education.[124]

The attempt by Dr. Wong Him to have his child attend a school other than the Chinese Primary School was viewed by the judge as a plea similar to the unsuccessful pleas blacks had been making in the courts since the Civil War. The problem had been addressed in the case of *Plessy v. Ferguson*,[125] where the United States Supreme Court officially accepted the doctrine of separate but equal facilities. Thus, the Chinese Primary School in San Francisco was legally reaffirmed. Regardless of where they lived in San Francisco, Chinese children were assigned to the school in the heart of Chinatown.

Thoroughly dissatisfied with the school board's segregation policy, Chinese merchants, backed by the Chinese Six Companies, decided to petition the legislature to amend the school law to force the city to open its public schools to their children. They declared that the exclusion of their children from the public schools was not only unjust but at variance with the Constitution of the United States.[126]

One of the merchants, L. Lowe, said:

The present law is most unjust. It limits the Chinese children to the Chinese Public School, which is nothing but a primary institution.

Its highest grade is the sixth and with that a scholar's education, as far as the public schools go, is at an end. We Chinese are heavy taxpayers and we do not propose to put up with this state of affairs any longer. Why should we contribute to the support of the public schools from which the native-born children of Chinese parents are excluded? [127]

On February 19, 1903, the Chinese Six Companies issued thousands of circulars, which they posted on the street walls of Chinatown protesting the city's board of education. They stated that the taxes paid by the Chinese in 1901 entitled them to $28,000 in school privileges. They pointed out that only $6,900 was spent on the little Chinese School, so they wondered "what had become of the remaining $21,000?" [128]

To seek the change in the law, the Chinese asked Claudia White, a former Baptist missionary, [129] to go to Sacramento and present the Chinese protest to the legislature. Prior to her trip, she accompanied Tong Fay, a merchant's son, to the Board of Education where he told how the Chinese felt about being deprived of education. After hearing Tong's presentation, the board members told Miss White they were powerless to act under the law and advised her to get the legislature to act. [130]

The *Examiner* reported the following comments from board members about that law:

President Woodward of the Board of Education: "The law says that where special schools are provided for them, Indians, Mongolians and Chinese shall attend such special schools. The wording is a little queer, but there is no question as to the intent."

School Director Lawrence Walsh: "I am not only opposed to having the Chinese attend any school other than that specially provided for them, but I would also like to see the same rule applied, were it possible, to the Japanese. That is not possible now, since there is no Japanese school; but with the Chinese pupils, there is no reason why the law should not be carried out. I don't think the general intermingling of Chinese children with white pupils would prove to the advantage of the latter. The special school at 920 Clay is a well-equipped institution. It has five teachers and has done good work for thirteen years."

School Director C. W. Mark: "I believe in the law as it stands. We have a Chinese School, and the Chinese children should go there. I shall oppose anything different." [131]

Given the above attitudes, one can see why the San Francisco school board was not about to abolish the Chinese Primary

School, even though it would have been administratively easy to do, since the school was not a permanent structure. The attempt by the Chinese Six Companies to change Section 1662 of the Political Code of California did not meet with success.

## The Japanese Problem in the San Francisco Schools

WHEN THE 1891 *Annual Report* noted the presence of "Mongolian" children in the school system,[132] this meant Chinese and Japanese students. Whether the latter attended the Chinese Primary School could not be ascertained. But by 1893 the school board did pass a resolution that required Japanese pupils to attend the Chinese Primary School.[133] However, no supportive evidence could be found to indicate that the resolution was followed through.

Beginning in 1896, the increasing number of Japanese students overshadowed "the Chinese problem." The Japanese were attending the city's public schools rather than the Chinese Primary School and school superintendents from Babcock to Roncovieri required all school principals to list the Japanese children in their schools.[134] By the turn of the century, the requirement was to list both Japanese and Chinese children.[135] Evidently, Chinese living outside of Chinatown were sending their children to neighborhood schools. This practice of allowing Japanese and Chinese children into the city's public schools was allowed as long as white parents did not object and there were vacancies in the schools.

By 1905, however, the question of the large numbers of Japanese pupils in white schools was placed repeatedly before the school board. The board held a special meeting and decided that separate schools for the Chinese and Japanese pupils would be established, not only to relieve congestion, but "for the higher end that our children should not be placed in any position where their youthful impressions may be affected by association with pupils of the Mongolian race."[136]

According to Dolson, this openly proclaimed prejudice was politically profitable because board members and the superintendent owed their respective posts to the Union Labor Party, whose platform in 1901 called for continued segregation of all Asiatic children in the schools.[137] Besides, the mayor of San Francisco had been elected on a platform advocating separate schools.[138] Furthermore, the board had another ally in the newly formed Japanese and Korean Exclusion League whose purpose was "to work against all Oriental immigration." This organization warmly commended the board's action and urged that the educational authorities of other localities throughout the state and country take similar steps to protect the rights of American children against the "destructive influences of forced association with Mongolians."[139]

The separate Japanese public school did not materialize. The only real effort came when the board of education made an unsuccessful request to the board of supervisors for an appropriation to construct added facilities at the Chinese Primary School in order to house the Japanese pupils.[140]

Since the Chinese Primary School was intended for Chinese, Japanese students continued attending the public schools of San Francisco well into 1906. But foreshadowing what would eventually happen to the Japanese was board president Aaron Altmann's circular to school administrators:

We wish once more to direct your attention to the State Law, No. 1662 of the Political Code which excludes children of Mongolian descent from attending our schools. The Chinese Primary School at 916 Clay Street is the place to direct all Mongolian children. Under the State Law a special appropriation has been provided for that purpose and we must insist on its enforcement. Any child that may apply for enrollment or at present attends your school who can be designated under the head of "Mongolian" must be excluded, and in furtherance of this please direct them to apply at the Chinese School for enrollment. This applies to all Schools in the department whether of mixed pupils or exclusively girls or boys. We call on every principal in the department for active compliance with the provisions of the State Political Code and insist on its necessary enforcement.[141]

Altmann simply extended Section 1662 to include the Japanese pupils under the category of Mongolian children, but no action was taken on the matter until after the 1906 earthquake and fire.

# Contrasting Views of the Chinese Primary School

WHEN THE CHINESE PRIMARY SCHOOL opened in 1885, Rose Thayer was the principal. She held that post until 1904, when she got married and resigned from her position.[142] She was replaced by Cecilia Newhall.[143]

Principal Newhall wrote an article describing the Chinese School. She discussed the increase of students, the field trips taken by the classes outside of Chinatown and the school's Christmas festival. The school was trying to reach a goal of ten classes, because the board promised to erect a more suitable facility when that number was reached. Its greatest pride was the after-school departure:

No other school in the city can show such orderly departure from the building, each class passing two by two down the hill till the corner of the street is reached, then the pupils quietly disperse to their homes. The dismissal of the school has become one of the attractions of Chinatown, and admiring tourists and other pedestrians watch it with openly-expressed admiration.[144]

Two perennial problems confronted Newhall and her staff. One was the customary 10:30 A.M. breakfast hour of the Chinese that caused several hundreds of tardy reports at the end of each month.[145] This problem was solved by allowing the children to march home from school for their breakfast during their recess period. Thus, tardiness was reduced to a minimum.[146] The other problem was Chinese New Year. Scarcely a child attended school during the two-week celebration. The school solved this problem by joining in the festivities — the staff visited nearly two hundred families.

Solving these problems led Principal Newhall to conclude that her staff had gained the confidence of the Chinese residents, and that the Chinese Public School would become "one of the most attractive and ornamental on this coast, and a credit to the Public School Department of San Francisco."[147]

In contrast to Newhall's article was one written by Francis John Dyer. He expressed wonder that the Chinese Public School was even continuing, when support for it had been so half-hearted. According to Dyer only eight percent of the eligible children attended the school, which once was a proud mansion. The ambiguous status of the school was one of its peculiarities, he said. Another problem was what to do with the few students who had gone beyond the fifth grade, the highest grade at the school. Since the school department established the school to keep the Chinese apart from white students, Chinese students who were sixth-, seventh- and eighth-graders had to stay in the fifth grade and do the best they could. The board defended its segregation stance by saying that the Chinese boys who still wore their national dress were disinclined to go to other schools, where their "peculiar clothes and queues gave invitation to mischievous boys to torment them."[148]

The Chinese Primary School was in existence from 1885 until the 1906 earthquake. Although this public school was destroyed, the concept of a segregated school facility for the Chinese in San Francisco could not be obliterated. Out of the rubble came a more solid structure to separate the Chinese children from the rest of the student population.

# Chapter 5
# The Oriental Public School
（遠東學校）：
# Permanent Segregation
# 1906-1923

## The Anti-Asian Bias

ON APRIL 18, 1906, San Francisco was devastated by earthquake and fire. Chinatown was completely destroyed. While the Chinese took temporary refuge in the city's Portsmouth Square,[1] the mayor announced that the Chinese would not be allowed to build on their old sites.[2] It was said that Chinatown would be moved to Hunter's Point in the southeastern portion of the city near the slaughterhouses.[3] Indeed, the architect who submitted a comprehensive scheme for building a new San Francisco left Chinatown out, because he felt it was occupying a valuable section of the city.[4] These feelings reflected pre-earthquake sentiments, because even in 1902, city authorities had wanted to clean up the "plague-infected" Chinese quarter by "improving it out of existence."[5] Despite these anti-Chinese sentiments, Chinatown was rebuilt at its original site due to the fact that restrictive clauses in most property deeds barred the use or occupation of property by Chinese outside of Chinatown.

During the earthquake many of the city's vital statistical records were destroyed—particularly the birth records of Chinese American children. Recognizing the advantages of American citizenship, some of the immigrant Chinese claimed citizenship for themselves and their offspring by listing both real and fictitious children. The recording of fictitious citizen-children created a "slot" for new immigrants from China who could purchase the name and, if clever enough, enter the country as citizens. These "paper" sons and daughters were thus able to circumvent the discriminatory exclusion act.[6] San Francisco's Chinese quarter rose out of the ashes with a complement of "new" citizens and an opportunity to change the image of the "exotic but vice-ridden quarter" of San Francisco.

Before the earthquake, the school district had 76 school buildings, but the catastrophe destroyed 31, so only 45 remained.[7] Damages to the Chinese Primary School amounted to $52,000 and the estimated cost of rebuilding was $130,000.[8] The razing of the Chinese Primary School drove many Chinese families across the bay to Oakland where there were better school facilities.[9] For a brief period Chinese youngsters who remained in San Francisco were able to attend existing schools with students of other races.[10]

However, when a temporary Chinese School was opened in September in Chinatown, Superintendent Roncovieri discovered that enrollment was below expectations because so many Chinese had left the city.[11] Complicating the problem was the fact that Japanese students were occupying seats in the city's public schools that white parents felt belonged to their children. To appease white parents and increase attendance in Chinatown, the superintendent simply changed the name of the Chinese Primary School to the Oriental School.

On September 27, 1906, the name change became official through the following board resolution:

Resolved, That the school formerly known as the "Chinese Primary School," and located at 926 Clay Street, between Powell and Mason Streets, the same to be known hereafter as the "Oriental School."[12]

Two weeks later, a resolution was passed to bar Asian[13] children from access to the city's public schools:

Resolved, That in accordance with Article X, Section 1662 of the School Law of California, principals are hereby directed to send all Chinese, Japanese or Korean children to the Oriental Public School situated on the south side of Clay Street, between Powell and Mason Streets, on and after Monday, October 15, 1906.[14]

This resolution and the March 13, 1907, resolution provided the only references to Korean children in the San Francisco school system. Data from the school district's archives indicate that Korean children began entering the city's public schools around the turn of the century.

This incident nearly precipitated an international crisis as China and Japan protested the board's action.[15] The situation was alleviated when the school board and the mayor were invited by President Roosevelt to Washington, D.C., where a compromise was shaped. If the city's school authorities would allow the Japanese children back into the public schools, then the national government would attempt "to restrict Japanese immigrants of the coolie class."[16]

Thus, on March 13, 1907, the following resolution was passed:

Resolved and Ordered, That the following resolution adopted by the Board of Education on the 11th day of October, 1906, be and the same is hereby repealed excepting in so far as it applies to Chinese and Korean children....

Resolved, That: Section 1—Children of all alien races who speak the English language, in order to determine the proper grade to which they may be entitled to be enrolled must first be examined as to their educational qualifications by the principal of the school where the application for enrollment shall have been made.

Section 2: That no child of alien birth over the ages of 9, 10, 11, 12, 13, 14, 15, 16 years shall be enrolled in any of the 1st, 2nd, 3rd, 4th, 5th, 6th, 7th or 8th grades, respectively.

Section 3: If said alien children shall be found deficient in the elements of the English language, or unable to attend the grades mentioned in Section 2 by reason of the restrictions mentioned therein, such children shall be enrolled in special schools or in special classes established exclusively for such children as and in the manner the Board of Education shall deem proper and most expedient.[17]

Children of all alien races with English deficiencies were assigned to Hancock, Washington Irving, Garfield, Washington Grammar (for boys), Jean Parker (for girls), and Oriental schools. Those with more advanced qualifications were assigned to ungraded classes at five other schools.[18] The school district for the first time formally recognized its non-English-speaking student population. Also, the practice of allowing Japanese adults to sit with white children in the elementary schools was abolished.

Roosevelt's intervention prodded the board to reclassify Japanese as "Malayans" and not "Mongolians,"[19] a nomenclature that enabled them to attend neighborhood schools instead of the Oriental School. It was a bitter pill for white San Franciscans to swallow, and some parents withdrew their children from public schools. However, as private tuition was high, most eventually returned to the "Mongolized schools," as they were derisively termed by white citizens.[20]

Superintendent Roncovieri claimed he had no idea that trying to segregate the city's Asian children was going to cause such a furor:

We had no conception when we endeavored to enforce this rule that it would cause any national commotion. It was purely a local regulation for the good of San Francisco children, whose parents urged us to action and which was much easier to enforce after the fire than before.[21]

At the time of the earthquake, there were nearly two thousand Asian schoolchildren in San Francisco.[22] Had half this number attended the renamed and rehabilitated Oriental School, space would have been a problem, for the school could hold only four hundred pupils.[23] When the order went out to segregate the Asian students, Roncovieri and the board had no plans in the event of an overflow of students.[24] Roncovieri, indicating his anti-Asian bias, said on one occasion, "The Asiatic must understand now and for all time that he cannot insist on a personal association of his children with those of the white race."[25]

In 1905, upon learning that several janitors in the public schools were employing Japanese to assist them in their duties, Roncovieri issued the following directive to the principals:

You are hereby directed to notify janitors that under no circumstances will this condition of affairs be allowed to continue. No person of Asiatic descent will be permitted to serve in the employ of this Department, and any infraction of this ruling will be visited by the summary discharge of the offender. . . .[26]

At the 1906 San Diego Convention of school superintendents, Roncovieri was unsuccessful in getting the group's approval of a resolution favoring separate schools for Chinese, Japanese, and Koreans.[27]

Although these instances of Roncovieri's anti-Asian stance occurred during his early years in office, his racist attitude set the tone of discriminatory treatment towards Asians in general and Chinese in particular within the school system during his continuous tenure as school superintendent from 1906 to 1923.[28]

# Circumventing the Oriental School

BY 1908, as attendance increased at the Oriental School, the school board added more classes.[29] Although Chinese students weren't allowed into other public schools, attempts were made to circumvent the regulation.

The first attempt was made by three Chinese girls under the care of Donaldina Cameron, the founder and director of Cameron House, a center for homeless Chinese girls in San Francisco Chinatown. Cameron's three teenage wards attended school in Oakland because of San Francisco's strict observance of the school law. Stating that the trip to Oakland was unsafe for her girls, and that the Oriental School was unsuitable,[30] Miss Cameron tried to enroll them at Denman School in San Francisco. The principal, however, refused to register the girls and sent them home.[31]

Cameron petitioned the city attorney to find an exception to the rule, but the latter's opinion strengthened the board's anti-Chinese position. He said that place of birth had no bearing on the classification of Chinese as Mongolians,[32] and that the board of education had the discretionary power to establish separate schools: "So in this case it is discretionary with your board whether you admit these children to the public schools or provide separate schools of equal and adequate standing," he said.[33] The school board's policy stood and the three girls "whose offense was that they happened to be born in America of Chinese parents were denied their rightful education."[34]

A few months later, the San Francisco school board ejected three daughters of Soo Hoo Fong and seven other Chinese girls from Jean Parker Girls School to comply with Section 1662 of the school law. A few girls had been sent to Jean Parker because of crowded conditions at the Oriental School.[35] Others were at Jean Parker because their parents objected to them attending the crowded Oriental School with Chinese boys, but the board viewed these moves as temporary.[36]

After a special class was established for Chinese girls, the board ordered the principal at Jean Parker School to transfer the girls out of the school.[37] Soo Hoo Fong, a Chinese merchant, hired a law firm to prevent the removal of his daughters, claiming he and his family were American-born citizens. His attorneys threatened legal complications,[38] but when the girls were ordered back to the Oriental School, the attorneys did not press their threats.[39] They presumably knew that two months earlier, the city attorney's opinion had favored the board. Furthermore, the decision two years earlier concerning the Japanese had shown that San Francisco was in compliance with the state law.

As to Soo Hoo Fong's claim to American citizenship, Leffing-well, the school board secretary, said, "It makes no difference whether the Fong family were natives of the United States for ten generations back, they still remain Mongolian and come under the state law affecting the attendance of Mongolians at the public schools."[40] School board member David Oliver, Jr., spoke in the board's defense:

We have endeavored at all times to meet the conditions as they have arisen. We have endeavored to arrange the matter to meet with the demands of those who are laboring for the moral welfare of the Chinese girls. But the law of the State is very plain, and in the absence of any other law to guide us, the members of the Board of Education must act according to the law. Accordingly we have acted as we have thought best for the welfare of the children concerned. We have provided a separate class for the Chinese girls and until some legal process is brought to bear upon us, we shall pay no matter to the communication sent from the attorneys.[41]

In a third attempt to circumvent the Oriental School, three Chinese boys told the principal of the school, Mrs. Newhall, that they were leaving San Francisco and going across the bay to Berkeley. The principal supplied them with a letter of introduction, but instead of going to Berkeley, they applied at Hearst Grammar School in San Francisco. The boys were denied admission, but they did attend Crocker School in the city for a day before the school authorities caught up with them and sent them back to the Oriental School.[42] The boys' addresses were 2600 Jackson Street and 1371 Masonic Avenue,[43] both beyond the "Chinatown limits."

After these three nonproductive attempts to bypass the Oriental School, the Chinese appealed to the national government to amend Section 1662. On February 9, 1909, the Chinese Six Companies sent a telegram to President Roosevelt protesting the inequitable treatment accorded to the Chinese in America. They cited California's discriminatory school laws as an example of educational discrimination. They pleaded with the nation's chief executive to side with them in their protest:

We ask of you to enter a strong protest against the present school laws of California which discriminate against Chinese children, whether citizens or aliens, and we respectfully ask you to assist us in taking these laws into the courts to test their constitutionality....[44]

Curiously, the message was sent directly to President Roosevelt and did not go through the office of the Imperial Chinese consul-general, Hsu Ben Chen, who disclaimed all knowledge of it.[45] No evidence was found that President Roosevelt responded to their plea or that help was forthcoming from the federal government. In fact, San Francisco was given even more authority to segregate the Chinese in the city's public schools when the California legislature amended and approved Section 1662 on April 14, 1909:

The governing body of the school district shall have power to exclude children of filthy or vicious habits, or children suffering from contagious or infectious diseases, and also to establish separate schools for Indian children and for children of Chinese or Mongolian descent. When such separate schools are established, Indian, Mongolian or Chinese children must not be admitted into any other school.[46]

Even before the plea to President Roosevelt, an attempt was made to destroy the Oriental School by fire. Principal Newhall asserted that the fire was set by vagrants who loitered about the school, in retaliation for being driven away by the police.[47] The identity of the arsonist was never determined.[48] One could speculate that mounting frustrations over the board's segregated school policy might have driven the Chinese to respond in anger by setting the school on fire. If the Oriental School had been destroyed, the school board would by law have been forced to admit the Chinese temporarily into the public schools of San Francisco. It remains an undocumented but fascinating speculation.

# Homer Craig and the Farmers' Union of California

THE PRESENCE OF Asian laborers in California's fields and orchards became a problem to a segment of the agricultural community, and on March 20, 1910, Homer Craig, chairman of the San Jose branch of the Farmers' Educational and Cooperative

Union of America, was appointed to investigate labor conditions in the prune orchards of the valley. Craig appeared before the Asiatic Exclusion League and told them of his plan to replace Asian laborers. By timing school vacations with the fruit harvest, white schoolchildren could be hired in their place. He said he had the approval of school superintendents Roncovieri of San Francisco and McClymonds of Oakland.[49]

Labor leaders in San Francisco and Superintendent Roncovieri promised the Farmers' Union their assistance,[50] and by the fall Craig's plan was broadened to include entire white families. Educators throughout the state endorsed the plan and it was scheduled to be put before the state legislature in January.[51]

One of the opponents to Craig's plan was State Labor Commissioner J. D. MacKenzie, who reported that the orchards and vineyards "needed Oriental labor, because there weren't enough white laborers."[52]

Craig next asked a special committee of the board of supervisors to recommend that the board of education make summer vacation coincide with the harvest. In so doing, "the estimated two million dollars given yearly to aliens employed in harvesting the crops would be given to native-born Americans needing money for their families."[53] Craig's position was looked upon with favor by Roncovieri and the school board.[54]

A week later, Craig told the board of supervisors, "The fruit industry of this State needs this white help, and it must have it. If we can't get it, the floodgates may have to be opened to Asiatic labor."[55] The supervisors acted favorably on the resolution and the matter was referred to the city's board of education.[56]

The *Daily Morning Call*'s editorial was supportive of Craig's plan: "This readjustment of the vacation period would relieve the fruit growers from their dependence on Asiatic labor for gathering the crop."[57]

Before the school board voted on postponing summer vacation from July to August, it made an inquiry whether parents and children would take advantage of the opportunity. A circular was sent out emphasizing the improvement in health and knowledge available to the children. No mention was made of the displacement of Asian laborers.[58] In fact, even the *Chinese World* made no mention of the anti-Asian motive for the change.[59]

But after the information was collected from the parents, the board of education decided not to change summer vacation, because the board wouldn't allow students to do the work unless they were accompanied by their parents. The board did decide, however, that children who spent their vacations in the orchards would not lose credits, provided they reported immediately to their teachers upon getting back from the country. Special classes were to be arranged for the latecomers to catch up with their school work.[60]

The intention of replacing Asian laborers with white schoolchildren ended limply with a set of resolutions by Homer Craig and the Farmers' Union of California commending Superintendent Alfred Roncovieri for his part in adjusting the school vacations to coincide with the fruitpicking season in central California.[61]

## Oriental School: From Temporary to Permanent Structure

FOR MANY OLD-TIMERS in Chinatown, their proudest memory was when Dr. Sun Yat-sen came to San Francisco in 1910 to gather support for a revolutionary party.[62] When the Republic of China was founded in 1911, both the immigrants and first-generation American-born Chinese turned their thoughts to serving the newborn republic.[63] One of their first acts of liberation was the removing of their queues, long a symbol of Manchu domination over the Chinese. In San Francisco's Chinatown, there were four barber shops that advertised the cutting of queues.[64] It has been estimated that by this time only one of six students was still wearing this symbol of oppression.[65] Some students, wanting to adopt the Western style, had removed their queues as early as 1909.[66] A few, like Frank Tape, had cut off their queues in the late 1800s.

As the queue was a symbol of inferiority in China, so the temporary structure that housed the Chinese students was an ever-present reminder of racial discrimination in San Francisco. Many Chinese hoped the school would be torn down.[67] The idea of tearing down the Oriental School was first expressed by the Reverend John Hood Laughlin and later by two Chinese American writers.[68] Laughlin wrote:

...But fortunately, for our contention, the Chinese School building in San Francisco is a flimsy wooden shack, scarcely fit now to house the pupils. The question of erecting a substantial structure must soon face our city government. How opportune, therefore, to reconsider the whole matter, and, perchance, let the shack decay, build no substitute, thus satisfy the State law, and delight the hearts of a worthy people by treating them as we treat the rest of the world.[69]

This message went unheeded as the school board began their plans for a permanent Oriental school structure.

As early as 1908 the city architect outlined school plans which included a permanent Oriental School structure—an eight-room school at a cost of $80,000 at Clay and Powell streets.[70] Six months later, he recommended that the school be built on a lot on the west side of Powell Street between Washington and Jackson streets. The board took his recommendation under advisement.[71] No reason was given for the change in location.

In the interval between the architect's plan and his recommendation, an investigative committee cited dangerous conditions in the two-story temporary Oriental School:

The Oriental School is built on a small lot, which gives no adequate yard space. It is the one instance of a shack school two stories in height, and a need exists for more doors from some of the classrooms to facilitate rapid exit in case of fire. The hardships and danger from these two sources will be enhanced by the erection of a building on the adjoining property.[72]

In 1909 the city health officer, Dr. Brodrick, complained to the board of education about unsanitary conditions at the Oriental School and asked that the basement of the school be enclosed.[73] This complaint was often repeated in board meetings.[74]

The school board did make contact with the Chinese consulate-general[75] and Mr. R. O. Park of the Chinese Six Companies[76] to consider their views concerning a new Oriental public school. The location being contemplated was reported in the *Municipal Record* on October 28, 1909, as being on Powell Street near Clay.

But in 1912, the board of education asked the board of supervisors to purchase the lot on Washington Street west of Stockton Street for building the Oriental school.[77] No reason was given as to why the board did not stay with the Powell Street location. This action by the board came just six days before a petition was signed by several hundred Chinese, Japanese, and other residents asking for the speedy construction of a new Oriental school.[78]

Three weeks later, the supervisors still had not purchased the Washington Street site. The school officials urged the city attorney to aid them to hasten the process.[79]

Complicating the matter was J. S. Churchill's offer to sell his lot on Powell Street adjacent to the existing Oriental School.[80] To make matters worse, members of the board of education and an advisory committee of architects had visited the proposed site on Washington Street and said that the lot, while advantageous in some ways, was situated on the slope of the hill and made the building of the foundations and the necessary retaining wall extremely expensive. The school board wanted the supervisors to defer action on the lot. If the proceedings were delayed, an effort was to be made to secure another site.[81]

The supervisors postponed the purchase and were told by architects that the city owned a sizable school lot on Powell Street near Clay. This lot was for sale and less than a block away from the proposed site and Churchill's vacant lot. The Powell Street location was desirable from a building standpoint.[82] The public buildings committee of the supervisors expressed surprise that the board of education had not spoken about the Powell Street lot. The school authorities had considered using the Powell Street lot for another school, and did not feel disposed to locate the Chinese and Japanese school on Powell Street.[83]

As indicated in Chapter 4, the board had protected the Powell Street owners from encroachment by Chinese as early as 1894. This renewed threat stirred up a large delegation of white property owners and residents of Washington Street to protest the board's proposed site on the south side of Washington Street between Powell and Stockton streets.[84]

J. H. Condit, the spokesman for the protesting committee and a teacher for twenty-five years, declared that for half a century the west line of Stockton Street fixed the western boundary of the Chinese quarter, and that if the school were erected on the site, property values would decrease 50 percent. He further stated that a school on Washington Street would aggravate the race war existing between white and Chinese schoolboys.[85] Others asserted that the presence of Chinese would be disastrous to the business interests of the area.[86]

President d'Ancona of the school board informed the delegation that the site had not been purchased, although the board had voted to buy the property and the mayor's signature was all that was necessary to complete the deal for the land. Dr. d'Ancona was appointed a committee of one to explain the objections of the property owners to Mayor Rolph, who had five days in which to sign or veto the action of the supervisors.[87]

The mayor did sign the order to purchase the Washington Street lot, and J. H. Condit and the protestors brought their objections to the board. Supervisor Bancroft of the building committee pointed out to the property owners that plans for the building were already being prepared.[88] But when Bancroft made a motion that the school building be erected on the site, it failed on a vote of eight to eight and the matter was referred back to the board of education.[89]

At the next school board meeting, Condit and the residents in the neighborhood of the Oriental School proposed a lot on Clay Street east of Stockton Street as a possible site for the new school.[90]

At the following board meeting, representatives of the North Beach Promotion Association and the Powell Street District Improvement Association reported their efforts to change the location of the school. The board informed them that the matter was in the hands of the buildings and grounds committee.[91]

Other attempts were made by Condit and his delegation to locate the school on Grant Avenue[92] and on the east side of Stockton Street south of Clay.[93]

The perseverance of the residents in the neighborhood of the Oriental School effectively forestalled board action temporarily. Meanwhile, the constantly increasing enrollment at the school forced the board to rent two rooms from the Chinese Six Companies at $15 per month each, for the use of fifth, sixth, seventh, and eighth grade boys.[94] By early 1913, the school board unanimously passed the following resolution:

That the Board of Public Works be requested to prepare plans and specifications for the Oriental School as follows:
Classrooms 14–16 as the lot can best be utilized, manual training room, domestic science room, auditorium.[95]

At its next meeting, director James C. Power proposed a resolution that was rejected by the board:

Whereas: Children attending schools at present located in shack buildings are subjected to more or less inconvenience thereby and
Whereas: This Board should do everything possible to relieve these conditions at the earliest possible date so that said children will not be obliged to spend another winter in such shack buildings,
Resolved: That the Board of Public Works be and is hereby requested to expedite the plans for and construction of the following 1908 bond issue school buildings:
Cooper, Washington Irving, Marshall, Oriental, LeConte.[96]

The problem was that these five remaining schools were the last to be built from 1908 school bonds. The building and grounds committee of the school board reported that the supervisors would not build the schools with a deficit in sight and suggested that the $26,750 set aside for the equipment of eight schools, or that the building of the Le Conte School, at a cost of $55,750, be held up to meet the deficit.[97]

On April 23, Sallie J. Jones, chairperson of the building committee of the board, submitted a plan to delete the equipment money and build all the schools except Le Conte. Three days later, the school board adopted the plan[98]

But in May, the proposal to build the remaining schools except Le Conte was defeated by the board of supervisors. This happened in spite of the fact that the supervisors' own building and finance committees had approved transfer of the money.[99] Supporters of the Le Conte School claimed that their school was badly needed and that other schools' estimates had gone up. They did not think it was fair to deprive the Le Conte district in order to pay the excess cost of the other schools.[100]

At its next meeting, the school board, after debate, reaffirmed its original position of not building Le Conte in order to build the other four schools.[101]

At the next supervisors' meeting, Andrew J. Gallagher blamed the Oriental School for the lack of funds for Le Conte School, but he failed in getting the board to reverse their rescinding of the Le Conte appropriation.[102] Chairman Bancroft of the building committee stated that the Le Conte School would cost $19,000 more than the first estimate, and that the Oriental, Cooper, and Washington Irving schools were more urgently needed. He declared that $3 million would be needed within the next three years for school construction.[103] The initial resolution authorizing the construction of the new Oriental school was passed at this meeting.[104] As it turned out, a delay of over six months would occur prior to actual construction of the school.

With other schools also being held up, the school board passed a resolution urging the board of supervisors and the board of public works to commence construction at the earliest possible date.[105] Meanwhile, Supervisor Gallagher, at a Union Labor Party meeting, declared that his fellow supervisors were not trustworthy and did not recognize the needs of the people. He said there was a need for more labor supervisors on the board.[106]

At that same meeting, Charles A. Meinert, one of the speakers, declared his anti-Asian stance:

San Francisco will never stand to be Orientalized. But that is what some of the present Board of Supervisors are endeavoring to do. They have taken money that was intended for a school for our white children and have given it to an Oriental School....[107]

Is San Francisco to become a second Tokyo or Hong Kong? Are we to be ruled by these yellow people with the sanction of our own city officials? California as a whole has let the world know that we do not solicit Orientals, but San Francisco, through the Board of Supervisors, has officially installed them in our business life.[108]

Meinert also deplored the attitude of some of the supervisors toward Japanese and Chinese laundries, declaring that the Orientals were depriving white women of work.[109]

On November 4, 1913, in a letter to the school board, Mr. K. Owyong, consul-general for China, expressed appreciation that work would soon begin on the new school. He suggested a roof playground be built in case no additional grounds could be purchased. The board told him that his suggestion was provided for in the plan.[110]

By December, city architects had requested the supervisors to set aside funds for the school.[111] But a delay occurred when Supervisor Gallagher cited a mistake in the resolution, locating the school at 929 Clay Street instead of Washington Street.[112]

At a January meeting, the location was corrected and the board, over the objection of Supervisor Gallagher and the North Beach Promotion Association, authorized the expenditure of $120,000 for the building of the Oriental School and fixed the site on Washington Street between Stockton and Powell.[113]

George Skaller of the North Beach Promotion Association suggested that a better site was on Sacramento Street between Stockton Street and Grant Avenue.[114] He contended that it was inadvisable to place the school near the Washington Grammar School (on Washington and Mason streets), as there had been warfare between the boys of the two schools and the killing of a white boy. He further stated that the Washington Grammar and Jean Parker schools were crowded and that the Washington Street lot could be utilized for building another school for white children.[115]

Supervisor Bancroft said that the objections had been carefully considered by the board of education and city architects. They had agreed that the Washington Street location was best for the Oriental School. There would be greater objections to any other site that could be bought, and there was no money available for purchasing another lot. Bancroft thought that the construction should be ordered without further delay.[116]

Four days later, the Civic League of Improvements communicated to the North Beach Promotion Association their endorsement of the latter's protest against the location of the school on Washington Street near Powell.[117]

At the next board of supervisors meeting, the five labor supervisors bitterly fought for two hours over the increase in construction costs of the Oriental School.[118] Supervisor Gallagher tried to delay action to remedy the injustice to Le Conte.[119] Supervisor Powers introduced an amendment limiting the cost of the Oriental School to $90,000, but it was defeated.[120] Finally, the board of supervisors (13–4) reaffirmed the school site on Washington between Stockton and Powell.[121] Of the five labor supervisors, only Powers voted for the ordinance as passed.[122] The board then authorized the board of public works to advertise for bids for the construction of the Oriental School on the approved site.[123] Two months later the school board unanimously adopted the following resolution:

Resolved: That the plans for the Oriental School in accordance with pencil sketches adopted by the Board of Education July 23rd, 1913, be and are hereby approved.[124]

By April, contracts were awarded by the board of public works. The lowest bid was by Elmer Carlson, to construct the Oriental School for $87,285.[125] Since this figure was below the $120,800 allocation authorized by the board of supervisors, the latter notified the school board that the surplus amount would be transferred back to the school bond fund.[126]

By 1915, the alumni of the Oriental School, along with the Chinese Native Sons of the Golden State and the Chinese Six Companies, prepared to donate gifts in anticipation of the newly constructed building.[127]

On October 20, 1915, at 2 P.M., under the auspices of the North Beach Promotion Association, the Oriental School was formally dedicated.[128] Mayor Rolph, members of the board of education, Superintendent Alfred Roncovieri, and the teachers of the Oriental School met with Consul-General S. C. Shii and other prominent local Chinese to lay the cornerstone of the completed structure "where young China will hereafter be educated."[129] The program included remarks from the above persons and music was provided by the Oriental School pupils and the Chinese Six Companies band.[130]

Remarks by the consul-general were published in *Chung Sai Yat Po* (Chinese Western Daily). It was his wish that the city school authorities would be rid of their prejudicial attitudes toward Chinese and that Chinese students would not be restricted to the Oriental School, but that they would have access to the city's public schools like other ethnic groups.[131]

The debate over a location extended construction of the Oriental School to seven years. It was San Francisco's decision to provide the state-mandated education in a segregated school—a continuation of a historical prejudice begun in 1859.

## Criticisms of the Oriental School

BEFORE 1915, the economic situation of many Chinese parents required that their children assist them in financial support. These children didn't stay long in school and those with two or three years of study were looked upon with awe. Some of the parents of the first Oriental School graduates had photographs suitable for framing taken of their children's diplomas. After putting the original in the safe, photographic copies were sent to China to be placed in the village temples, and banquets were held both here and abroad.[132] From 1907 through 1915, at least 94 students graduated from the Oriental School, according to newspapers of the period.[133]

In 1917, the United States Commissioner of Education made a study of the San Francisco school system. In considering the question of "Americanizing the foreigner," the report focused upon the Oriental School and pointed out three areas of concern. First, the school had no official records as to the students' birthplaces. The investigator had to do a hand count in each of fifteen classrooms and found almost half of the students were born in China and the rest in the continental United States. Second, the school presented a striking lack of course-of-study adjustment to meet the special needs of the pupils. With a racially homogeneous group, the investigator felt the school had an unusual opportunity for course-of-study adjustment along racial lines. Third, many of the pupils did not speak English, yet the course of study they followed, according to the statement of the principal of the school, was the regular course prepared for the elementary schools of San Francisco. The investigator found it difficult to see how the regular course of study could be covered satisfactorily when the language handicap weighed so heavily upon these foreign children. What brought the matter up was the investigator's witnessing of the salute to the flag and oath of allegiance to the United States:

This salute was performed in such a perfunctory fashion that it was absolutely impossible to catch a word that was uttered. An effort was made to ascertain what this ceremony meant. The teacher was asked to indicate her best pupil, and the question was put to him. In this particular case no reply at all was forthcoming, and it is extremely doubtful if he understood the English. Various other pupils were asked the same question with only slightly more favorable results on the linguistic side, but no more satisfactory replies were received as to the substance of the question.[134]

Criticizing the Oriental School from a Chinese point of view was Mary Bo-Tze Lee in her master's thesis, "Problems of the Segregated School for Asiatics in San Francisco." One of Lee's charges against the Oriental School was the placing of older immigrant students with younger native-born Chinese children. Further, since the students came from Chinese-speaking homes, the English spoken in the school was often deficient. The small numbers of Chinese who did go on to non-segregated high schools experienced difficulties because of the lack of exposure to American ways and the absence of language models other than teachers.[135]

Lee also criticized the Oriental School for having very few social contacts with other American public schools, making it difficult for friendship to develop between Chinese and Americans. She questioned the efficacy of a segregated school that reinforced alienation caused by residential separation.[136]

Lee recommended the following changes for the Oriental School:

1. Equalize the cost per capita for all schools. At present the Chinese children's cost per capita was $10.00 less than the average school.
2. Hire specially trained teachers who are sympathetic and have an understanding of the cultural and linguistic needs of the Chinese.

3. Group children by ability to meet the needs of the slower children and the mentally gifted.
4. Rules should be made to compel the use of English during school hours.[137]

The recommendations were reminiscent of San Francisco school superintendent John Pelton's proposal made fifty years earlier for hiring a teacher for Chinatown who spoke English and Chinese. None of their ideas came to fruition—either as policy decisions or administrative procedures. It would take another fifty years before reform was mandated by federal law in *Lau v. Nichols.*

# Initial Admittance to Neighborhood Schools

HOW DID CHINESE CHILDREN who were not graduates of the Oriental School enter their neighborhood schools? One way was through school principals who, on their own initiative, admitted Chinese, as long as white parents did not object. Also noteworthy was the fact that Chinese students might be mistaken for Japanese.[138]

It was recorded by Lee that as early as 1903 some Chinese families living outside of the Chinatown district sent their children to schools other than the Chinese Primary School.[139] Dyer reported that in 1904 Chinese were attending the Clement Grammar School at Jones and Clay streets.[140] The following year two Chinese girls graduated from the Jean Parker Girls School at Broadway and Powell Street.[141]

*East/West,* a Chinese American weekly newspaper, reported the following incident that took place in 1905. Since the Chinese Primary School only went up to the sixth grade, four of its graduates were the first Chinese boys to enroll at Washington Grammar School (for boys) at Washington and Mason streets. To encourage academic excellence, the school had monthly examinations. The results of the tests determined seating assignments. It so happened that the first four seats were occupied by the Chinese Primary School graduates. White parents complained to the teacher that the reason the Chinese gained the first four seats was because they exchanged answers in their own language. The parents suggested that the teacher separate the Chinese students at the next examination. This was done, but the results still awarded them the first four seats. Unwilling to stop at this point, the parents complained to the board of education, and the four Chinese boys were sent to different schools. One of the boys, a student named Leong, was sent to Clement School where he lost a fight in the yard concerning his queue and resolved not to wear it anymore. As to the other three boys, no mention was made as to their school assignments.[142]

Lee found that in 1918, a seventeen-year-old Chinese boy sought admission to a school near his home and was told that he could enroll if he claimed to be Japanese. He refused to do so, was rejected by the principal, and had to attend a private school. However, a year later, he reapplied to the same school and was admitted without having to mention his nationality.[143]

Another incident mentioned by Lee concerned a Chinese girl who had moved far from Chinatown. The board of education said that she had to continue to attend the Oriental School, but when she by right demanded carfare for traveling to and from school, the board backed down. Thus, she was allowed to enter an American public school.[144]

Lee cited one more case: The children of a wealthy Chinese merchant living in one of the city's finest residential districts tried to enter a school near their home. They were refused and forced to return to study at the Oriental School. Later they tried another public school near their home and were allowed to enter in spite of the fact that they were known to be Chinese.[145]

The initial entry of Chinese students into the city's elementary schools occurred at the turn of the twentieth century. The board of education's unwritten policy was to allow Chinese children who lived outside of the Chinese quarter to go to neighborhood schools as long as white parents did not object. If white parents complained of the presence of Chinese children in their schools, the school board would resort to Section 1662 as the legal basis to enforce segregation.

By the end of World War I, the imagined Chinese threat to white Americans evaporated. Even the most rabid demagogue could not keep alive the flames of hatred. Although prejudice against the Chinese was still widespread, hostile acts against them decreased considerably.[146]

Educational discrimination against Chinese continued, however. By 1921, Section 1662 of the California school code was amended as follows to include the segregation of Indians and Japanese:

The governing body of the school district shall have power to exclude children of filthy or vicious habits, or children suffering from contagious or infectious diseases, and also to establish separate schools for Indian children and for children of Chinese, Japanese or Mongolian parentage. When such separate schools are established, Indian children or children of Chinese, Japanese, or Mongolian parentage must not be admitted into any other schools.[147]

There was no evidence that this anti-Asian amendment made any impact on San Francisco's educational treatment of its Japanese population. For the Chinese, Section 1662 was a continual reminder of their educational status in California. This amendment would remain in the state school code for the next twenty-five years.

# Chapter 6
# The Transitional Years 1922–1940

## The Oriental School Renamed Commodore Stockton School

AN IMPORTANT ARTICLE describing the new Chinatown appeared in the *Chronicle* on January 18, 1922. Written by Dr. Ng Poon Chew, editor of *Chung Sai Yat Po*, the article described the fast disappearance of the customs which so characterized the old Chinatown as a quaint and mysterious quarter for visitors to San Francisco:

After the republic was established in China, the spirit of independence and democracy contributed its vigorous influence toward the rapid displacement of old manners of life and thought among the Chinese residents here. Take it all in all, the Chinatown of today is not the Chinatown of the bygone days. The spirit of change, of evolution and revolution in the thoughts of the people of the world has taken a strong hold upon the Chinese. They are carried along upon the wave of the changing sea of modernism in spite of their ultra conservatism, which had characterized almost everything Chinese.[1]

In his article, he listed many changes that had taken place. The skullcaps and traditional raiment had given way to closely cropped hair, smart American clothes and Boy Scout khaki uniforms. Chinese games had been replaced by American games and the children paraded around with wooden guns and the American flag. The Chinese children preferred speaking in English and had a mastery of American slang.

Instead of being sheltered at home, Chinese girls became independent and self-assertive women who dressed in the latest fashion. Courtship had replaced arranged marriages and the young men and women were taking the initiative in choosing their partners.

Young people were eager for a first-rate education and many were able to achieve a college degree. They were ambitious, patriotic to the extreme, and dedicated to the responsibilities of American citizenship. In speech, thought, and action, Ng found them highly assimilated, with nothing distinctly Chinese about them except their complexion.

Finally, he observed a spiritual change in the Chinese community, which included eight Protestant churches, a large Catholic mission, an active YMCA, an equally booming YWCA, and many popular social clubs. To those who lamented the passing of the old culture, Dr. Ng assured them that the change was better in the long run.[2]

The new Oriental School couldn't continue to house the growing number of Chinese students during the early 1920s. Concerned over the crowded conditions, the Native Sons of the Golden State sent two representatives to discuss the problem with Cecilia Newhall, the principal of the Oriental School.[3] With Section 1662 recently amended to include separate schools for Japanese children, the only alternative seemed to be to conduct half-day classes at the Oriental School. The Native Sons opposed this move and favored an increase in the facilities at the Oriental School.[4] The principal of the Oriental School wrote to the mayor suggesting the purchase of land adjoining the school.[5]

Finally, the school board approved renting property in the neighborhood of the Oriental School to accommodate the overflow of pupils, pending issuance of a school bond.[6] Since the bond wouldn't go before the voters until late November, the board had to do something to relieve congestion. So, on August 23, 1922, the Oriental School was allowed to form a new class.[7] This solution was short-lived.

Three months later, the North Beach Promotion Association proposed that the lots adjoining the Oriental School be bought and that new buildings be erected there.[8]

An annex to the Oriental School had been proposed as early as April 18, 1922, when the school board presented construction plans to the board of supervisors.[9] By September, Principal Newhall had given the school board the names of purchasers of a lot on the west side of the school.[10]

Part of the building program of the school board included the construction of Portola School and the North Beach Primary

School as well as the Oriental School Annex. Apparently there were so many difficulties in building the Portola School that it delayed the construction of the other two schools. But by October most of Portola's problems had been cleared away, so the school board proceeded rapidly with the building of all three schools.[11]

In order to rehabilitate the schools of San Francisco, a bond issue had to be passed by the voters in the city. Mayor Rolph and the board of education made an appeal to the people concerning the educational plight of the city.[12] There were 233 classrooms housed in temporary wooden buildings, 17 old school buildings built between 1868 and 1890, new land for new buildings to be secured, 13 schools unfit for winter use, and a dozen schools with leaks in their buildings. The last three categories applied to the Oriental School.

When the bond issue was approved, the Oriental School Annex, the Portola School and the North Beach School were at the top of the list of schools to be built.[13] The preliminary plans by the city architect for all three schools were approved by the board on January 2, 1923. The North Beach Primary School was to be named Francisco Primary School and the Oriental School Annex was to be erected opposite the present school.[14]

Contracts were awarded by the board of public works in April.[15] Construction of the Oriental School Annex went smoothly, although the purchase of the land took several weeks and did delay construction.[16]

While the annex was being constructed, the board added another teacher[17] to the Oriental School because of the large enrollment—more than 900 in daily attendance, according to one newspaper report.[18] The additional teacher served only until March, 1924, when the principal announced that, because of the lack of accommodations, the Oriental School would be conducting half-day sessions until the completion of the annex.[19]

On April 21, 1924, the Oriental School Annex was formally opened for instruction,[20] and the crowded conditions were temporarily relieved.

From its opening in 1915 the Oriental School had predominantly Chinese students. Members of the Native Sons felt that the name Oriental School denoted discriminatory treatment. They had their English secretary check with an attorney to determine the legal process to change the name of the school to Harding School in memory of President Warren Harding.[21] Once the process was established, representatives of the Native Sons sought out parents of schoolchildren at the Oriental School to sign the petition for the name change.[22]

By February, the Native Sons sent its communication to the school board for the change of name. It was signed by Lester B. Fong. The board said they would give the matter consideration.[23]

A week later, the school board received from the North Beach Promotion Association an endorsement of the Native Sons' effort to change the name of the Oriental School to Harding School.[24] The board resolved to change the name, but said that the board members would make a suitable selection.[25] It was made on April 1, 1924, and the school and annex were named Commodore Stockton

...in honor of Commodore Stockton, who at the time California asserted her independence from Mexico, and upon the first organization of a Civil Government in California, ordered that the proceeds of the confiscation of the enemy's property or of property which escheated to the existing Government for want of an owner, should be appropriated to the construction of school houses and for the employment of teachers and the support of a free school. The first school house was built in San Francisco by the first free school organization and put in operation by the funds thus escheated by Commodore Stockton.[26]

A week later the school board received an acknowledgment of appreciation from the Native Sons for the new name.

# Attempts to Segregate
# at the Secondary Level

TWO YEARS AFTER Francisco Primary School began operation in the North Beach district (adjacent to Chinatown), the superintendent recommended that the school be reorganized as a junior high school. Clubs and associations interested in the Francisco School were invited to discuss the superintendent's recommendation,[27] and two weeks later Francisco was changed to a secondary school.[28]

At the time of reorganization, the "neighborhood school" system was still a citywide practice, but it did not apply to Chinatown. In fact, board minutes specifically named Commodore

Stockton School as an exception to the neighborhood school regulation.[29] Attendance at junior high schools for Chinese students was still determined by race and the Native Sons insisted that this discriminatory practice should not be extended to the secondary level.

As the school district geared up for Francisco's room use[30] and assignment of teachers,[31] it was apparent that the school's reorganization did not include the admission of Chinese students. Concerned that all schools, except Commodore Stockton, had been notified to send their seventh and eighth graders to Francisco Junior High, the Native Sons, along with the North Beach Promotion Association, appealed to the board of education to include the Chinese children from Commodore Stockton in its plan.[32]

Just prior to the school board's finalizing of the plan for Francisco Junior High School, the Native Sons appealed to the board to "make such changes and transfers as may be necessary to afford the students of the Commodore Stockton School equal advantages at the Francisco Junior High School with the students of other schools."[33]

This appeal had enough weight to influence the school board members to give consideration to the Chinese students at Commodore Stockton. The board decided that "all pupils [in the Beach District] now in grades 6B to 8A, inclusive, be transferred to the Francisco Junior High School, with the exception of the pupils now in 6B and 7A in the Commodore Stockton School who will be accommodated as soon as additional space is provided at the Francisco Junior High School."[34]

A week later the Native Sons' efforts were supported by the Northern Federation of Civic Organizations, a group of clubs located in the northern part of San Francisco, who asked that Francisco accommodate the seventh and eighth grade pupils of Commodore Stockton.[35]

By August the board of education did act on this matter:

Resolved: That all seventh grade pupils of the Commodore Stockton School be and they are hereby ordered transferred to the Francisco Junior High School; effective August 26, 1925.[36]

No sooner had school begun in the fall than parents of white pupils began registering complaints with the Central Council of Civic Organizations. The problem was that Chinese pupils of the Commodore Stockton School were being graduated into Francisco in such numbers that white students withdrew from the new school and were attending schools outside the neigborhood.

To relieve the situation, two suggestions were made at the Central Council meeting. One plan was to add junior high classes to Commodore Stockton School. The other plan was to erect a junior high school in the Chinese quarter.[37] Either plan would have meant the segregation of Chinese from white students above the elementary school level.

The idea of a separate junior high school for the Chinese gained momentum and, in February, members of the Native Sons made plans to protest to the school board against the segregated school concept.[38]

Meanwhile, Chinese newspaper publisher Dr. Ng Poon Chew and some Chinese students from Francisco attended the February 5th meeting of the Central Council of Civic Clubs. A bitter argument took place when the executive committee tried to appoint a committee to investigate segregating the Chinese pupils. Dr. Frank J. Fischer, who had been an instructor in the public schools for thirty years and who at this time taught at Francisco, fought against any consideration of the proposal. He said that the subject was out of order unless representatives from the North Beach district brought up the question. With the matter open for discussion, Fischer attacked the proposal on the grounds that it was "illegal, un-American, unfair and unjust," and pointed out the many "advantages to be gained by Oriental children by their association with other races in the schools."[39]

Dr. Ng Poon Chew addressed the council and commented upon the progress the world had made in the area of human rights. He mentioned that during World War I, Chinese and American youths fought side by side. Prejudice exists because Chinese and other children are not allowed to go to school together. His experience of buying a home in Oakland was used to strengthen his argument. Oakland residents did not want him to live in their neighborhood. However, Ng purchased a house and moved into his new residence. Social interaction with his neighbors gradually reduced their suspicions toward him. He then asked the audience to look at the Chinese students and judge if it was reasonable to set up a separate school for them. His presentation was greeted with applause.[40]

The meeting ended before a committee could be named to report upon the "means and wisdom of segregation."[41] The proposal was to move the Chinese children now attending Francisco

Junior High School to vacant rooms in the Washington Grammar School.[42]

The Chinese consul-general also protested the establishment of a separate school. He claimed that some of the civic organizations in the city and most of the Chinatown organizations had registered their extreme displeasure over this contemplated move. He asked the Central Council of Civic Clubs not to endorse the segregated school concept that would be proposed by a delegation of North Beach residents at the February 19th meeting of the Northern Federation of Civic Organizations.[43] When the proposal was made at the meeting, Fischer opposed it on the basis that it deprived the Chinese of their civil rights. He stated that Chinese students in his class never interrupted the studies of white students, and that the school department could not afford to build a new school. Dr. Ng spoke in support of Fischer at the meeting, as did Mr. Fung, an officer of the Native Sons.[44]

A lively debate occurred when the Italians of North Beach spoke for the separate school. They denied that their proposal had anything to do with race prejudice or that the Chinese were of a lower status. As parents they wanted to protect their children's character and their academic progress. They said that since Commodore Stockton School had over 160 vacant seats, Chinese students of junior high age should continue their schooling at Commodore Stockton.[45]

This last statement was challenged by a representative of the Chinese Young Women's Christian Association. She claimed that there were no empty chairs at Commodore Stockton, that enrollment was up to capacity, and that the school was conducting half-day sessions.[46] After the debate, the chairman asked the Northern Federation members as to the next course of action. The majority wanted another hearing on the subject.[47]

A committee on segregating the Chinese pupils attending Francisco Junior High School was formed two weeks later. Their report was to be discussed at the next meeting of the Central Council of Civic Clubs.[48] In that meeting, according to *Chung Sai Yat Po*, both Stanford University's president, Dr. Jordan, and the principal of Francisco Junior High School opposed segregating the Chinese students. The latter said that the Chinese pupils pursued their studies with diligence. He pointed out that of the 1100 students at Francisco, there were only 190 Chinese students. All the students got along well and no parents had complained to him about the Chinese in the school. Only those of a lower social class, he maintained, would advocate segregation.[49] The only Chinese who spoke was Fung, of the Native Sons. He said that the establishment of a separate school for Chinese was illegal and unreasonable.[50] No action was taken at this meeting. The question would be brought up again at another time.[51]

The longest debate took place on March 19, 1926, when the Northern Federation of Civic and Improvement Clubs considered the recommendation that Chinese schoolchildren be removed from the Francisco Junior High School as a preliminary move to the segregation of all Chinese schoolchildren in the city.[52] The segregationists, led by Harry Hutton, ex-police commissioner of San Francisco, accused the integrationists of packing the meeting. Heated denials and counter-accusations were made by opponents of the proposal, led by Dr. Frank Fischer.[53]

The proponents of segregation claimed that Section 1662 of the political code governing school segregation was being violated. Those opposed claimed that "inasmuch as there was no junior high school for Orientals, there had been no violation of the code since the maintenance of adequate school facilities for Orientals was obligatory by law."[54]

The major issue for the proponents was that the presence of 190 Chinese children at Francisco Junior High School had forced 240 other students of this school to be removed to classrooms in the Washington Grammar School.[55] The motion to segregate the Chinese pupils was voted down after Dr. Frank Fischer declared that the meeting was in the nature of a judicial tribunal and that all interested parties were entitled to a hearing.[56]

Meanwhile, the Chinese Chamber of Commerce appealed to the San Francisco Chamber of Commerce for help. The communication contained the following passage:

There are over 100 Chinese students studying at Francisco Junior High School located in the North Beach section of the city. The situation up to this point has always been calm and stable. Of late, some of the residents in that section of the city are advocating to bar our Chinese students from going to Francisco and are recommending a separate Chinese School. This kind of activity is most unreasonable, unfair and inconsistent with a republican form of government. As one examines the Chinese situation at Francisco, most of the students are American-born and are children of the members of our organization: thus they are free subjects entitled to equality of treatment, etc. Discriminatory treatment must not be allowed. As some of the children's fathers are members of your organization, so some of the Chinese children's fathers are members of our organization. In fact, some of us are members of both organizations. The Chinese Chamber of Commerce cannot but oppose the move to segregate our children. Your organization has always been generous, ethical, and brave in your endeavors. We hope that you will join us in this struggle to rid this prejudice. However you handle the problem would be most appreciated.[57]

After six months of heated discussion in the North Beach district, the Chinese problem at Francisco was not resolved. The squabble was then taken up by the board of education. Opposing the segregation plan was the North Beach Promotion Association. They communicated the following concerns to the board:[58]

1. That such segregation would militate against good citizenship as it would evoke resentment in native-born citizens
2. Would cause economic waste
3. That the association of the two races would prove mutually beneficial
4. That fifty years experience has shown that association of the two races in the schools of California has resulted in no undesirable results.

Moreover, Dr. Frank Fischer transmitted a 400-signature petition to the board requesting that the Chinese children now in the Francisco Junior High School be retained there. He also pointed out that the opposing side had secured only 200 signatures.[59]

The proponents of segregating the Chinese used the neighborhood school concept rather than race prejudice against the Chinese as the basis for separation. This can be seen in the following communication to the school board from the Italian Federation of California:

1. That steps be taken to allow the students living nearby the Francisco Junior High School to attend said school instead of more distant schools, and that in case it were deemed necessary to send elementary students to Francisco, preference be given to such of those students who live in the neighborhood of the school.
2. That it has been reported that children of the 7th and 8th grades who should rightly go to the Commodore Stockton School are permitted (against regulations and in violation of the third paragraph of Section 1662 of the Political Code) to attend classes at the Francisco Junior High School, thereby causing students who should rightly go to said school to be sent to more distant schools. That the organization cannot refrain from presenting the above facts although it does not favor or encourage any question of race.[60]

In the debate before the school board, James Herman, Dr. A. S. Musante, J. F. Kelly of the Central Council of Civic Clubs, and Stephen Malatesta of the North Beach Improvement Association argued against the enrollment of Chinese at Francisco. Herman stated that he had a petition signed by 351 parents of children now attending the Francisco Junior High School protesting the enrollment of Chinese pupils. He said that including only the first six grades in the elementary school was in violation of the law, which, he said, stipulated grades one through eight in elementary schools. If Chinese children were not excluded from Francisco, he said that it should be discontinued as a junior high school.[61] White parents in North Beach were angry that their children could not attend Francisco, their neighborhood school. Unfortunately this concern blinded them to the larger issue: the integration of Chinese into the public schools.

It must be explained that prior to the junior high school reorganization, the city's elementary schools went from the first to the eighth grade. By designing a junior high school system, the school district opened up the segregated school question at the secondary level. Since the Chinese in the city could not be housed in one site, a segregated junior high for Chinese was out of the question.

The board's response to the proponents of segregation reflected a lack of historical knowledge as to the educational treatment of the Chinese in San Francisco. The delegation was informed that if the board had established a Chinese school, it was not with the thought in mind that the school be a segregated school, but rather with the idea of enabling the children to attend a nearby school. After the discussion the question revolved around two points:

1. The production of the original resolution establishing a Chinese School, which the Board's secretary could not locate.
2. The request of the delegation to be informed as to what action the Board of Education would take, if the resolution was found.[62]

The original resolution establishing a Chinese School was found and reported at the next board meeting. Members of the board of education were told that the Commodore Stockton School was formerly called the Oriental School and established as a segregated school.[63]

This information strengthened the argument of the segregationists. On June 28, Herman, Malatesta, and Dr. Andrew Musante, president of the Golden Gate Valley Improvement Association, went to the Board of Education and argued that under the board's 1906 resolution segregating Chinese children, seventh and eighth graders couldn't be removed from Commodore Stockton School.[64] They objected to the instruction of some 280 Chinese children at Francisco[65] and contended that Chinatown was becoming so thickly populated that a separate school would soon be necessary to care for the Chinese.[66]

The acting president of the educational body, Daniel F. Murphy, declared that such a proposition was against the very principles of the United States Constitution.[67] School director Dohrmann suggested that in the absence of the superintendent the matter await his return.[68]

The pressure by the North Beach delegation on the school board to erect a separate Oriental School at the junior high level failed. The reason was based more on economics than on consideration for the Chinese children. As reported in the *Examiner:*

The school board invited the delegation [favoring segregation] to propound its ideas in writing, promising consideration of them, but declared it seemed impossible to erect enough junior high schools for the city at large, without considering the needs of special classes.[69]

Tackling the segregated school law at the state level was Chinatown's civil-rights organization—the Native Sons of the Golden State. On July 7, 1926, its executive council decided to give its endorsement only to those political candidates who would assist its members in abolishing Section 1662 of the state school code. All branches of the Native Sons in California were notified of this decision.[70] Although this organization was not successful in changing the law, it represented another effort by the Chinese to rid California of segregated schooling.

This incident showed the efforts of the Chinese community and their friends to have Chinese children attend nonsegregated schools. They had already gained access to the city's high schools in the early 1920s.Though discriminatory housing regulations would limit their attendance only to Francisco Junior High School over the next twenty years, the fact that establishment of a separate junior high school in the Chinese quarter was averted was a major victory. Having gained the right to attend secondary schools outside of Chinatown, it would be only a matter of time before all elementary schools in the city would be opened to Chinese children. By the late 1920s, the elementary school barrier was broken and Chinese children were no longer confined to Commodore Stockton School.

The school in 1929 reached a peak enrollment of 1500 children.[71] It was impossible to house the city's Chinese in one school. Since Chinese students were walking in a northerly direction to Francisco Junior High School, the first elementary schools opened to Chinese were Jean Parker and Washington Irving, schools near the border of Chinatown.[72]

With the city's public schools opening up to the Chinese, Commodore Stockton changed from a segregated school by law and policy (*de jure* segregation) to a segregated school by geographic location (*de facto* segregation). This subtle change shifted the responsibility of educational discrimination in San Francisco from the school authorities to residential patterns, even though Section 1662 of the school code was re-codified in 1929 into the following sections:

3.3 The governing body of the school district shall have power to establish separate schools for Indian children and for children of Chinese, Japanese or Mongolian parentage.

3.4 When separate schools are established for Indian children or children of Chinese, Japanese or Mongolian parentage, such Indian children or children of Chinese, Japanese or Mongolian parentage must not be admitted into any other school.[73]

# Pioneering Chinese Teachers

AS CHINESE STUDENTS were confined to Commodore Stockton School, so too were the pioneering Chinese teachers in San Francisco. They entered the teaching profession in the late 1920s — Alice Fong in 1926, Katherine Chan in 1928, and Suey Ng in 1930. These three were all Americans of Chinese descent, did not attend public schools in San Francisco, and were the only Chinese teachers throughout the 1930s. They were tireless workers, and their main task was to work with the school's Chinese-speaking population.

**Alice Fong.** Alice Fong was born in 1905 in Nevada County, California. She attended school in Vallejo, California. With the encouragement of a Red Cross leader, Mrs. Morgan Jones, she began her teaching preparations at San Francisco State Teacher's

College (now called San Francisco State University). Her hopes were dimmed when the president of the college advised her not to go into teaching. In her words the conversation went thus:[74]

President: Don't go into teaching. Why go into it when they can't use your talents. You know you'll never be hired.

Alice Fong: Yes I know. But I won't be teaching here. I'm going to help my people in China.

Under these circumstances she was admitted to the college's teacher training program. During her preparation at San Francisco State, Cecilia Newhall, the principal of the Oriental School since 1905, retired and was replaced by Anna T. Croughwell.[75]

With a change of principalship and the concentration of Chinese students at Commodore Stockton, the Native Sons of the Golden State went to bat for Alice Fong to be Commodore Stockton's first Chinese teacher.[76]

According to Fong, Anna Croughwell, although unable to handle the situation, was honest enough to say so.[77] The principal approached the college president and said, "If you have a Chinese teacher, you'd better send her to me because I have had this job for a whole term and wasn't able to run the school."[78] As Fong was about to graduate from State College, the president said to her, "You don't have to worry anymore. A job is waiting for you at Commodore."[79]

Before going to Commodore Stockton, Fong went through the teacher interviewing process of the school district. The one question that stayed in her mind during her oral interview was, "How do you dream at night?" Reflecting on that question during the interview with this writer, Fong believed it to be a deceptive question. She felt the interviewing panel was fearful she might speak Chinese in the classroom. They had hoped that her response would be that she had her dreams in Chinese, so they could have used the answer as an excuse not to hire her.[80]

Fong successfully went through the normal procedures of teacher hiring and was assigned to Commodore Stockton as a "swing teacher." Later on she became a teacher/clerk. These titles meant that she was the school's counselor, clerk, nurse, translator, parent-teacher liaison, and administrator all rolled up into one. Her services to the school and to the community were summarized this way:

In every respect Miss Fong is most capable, industrious, progressive, tactful, diplomatic, displaying good common sense and judgment. She is invaluable in the position that she holds as Swing Teacher. She has the good will and confidence of the community she serves. She is an indispensable link in tying up the school with the community.[81]

**Katherine Chan.** Very little is known of Katherine Chan. She was born in 1889 in Los Angeles, where she attended public schools and taught from 1920 to 1928. Her teaching assignment in Los Angeles was to teach in a Japanese school. In the words of the assistant superintendent of the Los Angeles City School, "It was a delicate task to place her in a Japanese School but she made the adjustment admirably."[82]

She attended the University of California at Berkeley to do her postgraduate work and decided to continue her teaching career in San Francisco. Her ethnicity was noted by those who wrote letters of recommendations for her:

...she has the best qualities of her race.[83]

...and being a Chinese will do wonderful work with children of her race.[84]

Her assignment at Commodore Stockton School was the kindergarten class, where she would remain until retirement in 1952.[85]

**Suey Ng.** Although born in San Francisco, Suey Ng's public schooling took place in Sonora, California. He graduated from the University of California at Berkeley with a secondary teaching credential. His professors at the university alluded to his racial background and the parameters of his teaching occupation:

Suey Yuen Ng is a very pleasant Chinese boy with a good command of English.[86]

Mr. Suey Ng is admirably qualified to teach upper division English either in Chinese schools in California or in China.[87]

With his secondary training, the school authorities in San Francisco could have placed him at Francisco Junior High School, but assigned him instead to Commodore Stockton School to "aid the principal in the many ways that only an Oriental could do."[88] His task was "to do for the Chinese boys what the Chinese woman teacher [Alice Fong] had been doing so successfully for the Chinese girls for some time."[89]

Angry about being assigned to an elementary school, he complained and didn't get along with the school's staff.[90] In spite of this, Principal Croughwell had this to say about him:

In contacting the community Mr. Ng has rendered a most valuable service. He has been most unselfish in his devotion to his people and their needs. He has given many hours after school to work connected with the school interests.[91]

In 1931 Suey Ng asked the deputy superintendent in charge of personnel if Francisco Junior High School could use him in situations involving absentee students from Chinese-speaking homes. The deputy superintendent wrote a letter of inquiry to the principal of Francisco:

It seems to me that there might be quite a future in your section of the city for the right sort of a Chinese young man.... Possibly it might be best to start out with giving him one or two cases and try him out before discussing with him any sort of a definite program. If his work appears to you to be of distinct benefit, he might be given more important assignments.[92]

The next day the deputy superintendent wrote to Suey Ng that he had already notified the school's principal and that the latter would get in touch with him by phone.[93]

The principal's reply to the deputy superintendent's idea was that it would be an unwise move to inject a young Chinese into the attendance situation. The reason was that Mr. Sweeney, a police officer, had been doing the attendance work and had the cooperation of the entire Chinatown police squad. In the principal's words:

I doubt very much whether any Chinese could handle the situation as well as he does. The Chinese respect our police and the injection of a young man of their own race would at once cause jealousy and disagreements. For this reason I have not written to Mr. Ng nor shall I do so unless I receive further directions from you.[94]

More than a week passed by with no communication forthcoming from the principal to Ng. Since Ng had received notification from the deputy superintendent that the principal would call, he decided to make contact with the administrator at Francisco. Ng's call was timely, for the principal was writing a formal letter to the assistant director of personnel dated March 20, 1931.

He inserted the following handwritten remarks: "Mr. Ng has just called and we will put him on the trail of some of our slow pupils."[95] Ng immediately wrote a letter to the assistant director of personnel informing him of his conversation with Francisco's principal:

Today I had the pleasure of interviewing Mr. Rhodes [the principal], who informed me that inasmuch as Officer Sweeney's efficient work is harmonizing with his present attendance program, it would be foolish for me to interfere with it. He does, however, want me to do some counseling work for his school. I shall begin to do this next Wednesday, when Mr. Rhodes hands me the necessary information.[96]

Apparently there was a misunderstanding between the assistant director and the principal of Francisco regarding the services of Ng. To clear up the matter, the assistant director drafted the following memo to Francisco's principal:

I fear you misunderstood what I had in mind in suggesting that Mr. Ng see you, or perhaps I did not make my purpose clear.

The motive that actuated my letter was the hope that Mr. Ng, being a Chinese and speaking the language, might be of some assistance to you outside of the regular channels. I certainly had no intention of even intimating that I expected you to make use of him. If you feel that his services would be embarrassing to you, or to Mr. Sweeney, do not hesitate to tell him so. If you feel that you do not care to tell him, please drop me a note and I will be glad to help you out.[97]

The deputy superintendent wrote to the California Board of Education to grant Ng an emergency credential so that he could work as a Supervisor of Attendance with the Chinese,[98] but the records do not show that the state granted him the emergency credential.

In the meantime, Suey Ng worked at Commodore Stockton as an opportunity class teacher from 1930 to 1939. He also volunteered at Francisco. Like Alice Fong, his duties went beyond the normal teaching assignments, as noted in his evaluation:

In this school, Mr. Ng has done an outstanding piece of work in contacting the parents of truant children, in investigating home conditions of neglected children, of children difficult to understand in their attitude toward school and their schoolmates, and of children whose shoes are in a deplorable condition.

All of the above cases have been handled by Mr. Ng wisely and tactfully. Many hours of time after school have been spent by him in this type of work. In helping this school to progress quietly, peacefully, efficiently and to serve the best interests of the Chinese Community so that its influence for good might be felt, Mr. Ng's splendid work has been no small factor.[99]

His volunteer work at Francisco eventually paid off. In 1939 the school had a change of administration and was ready to accept a Chinese teacher onto its staff. Since he was on the junior high teacher eligibility list in dramatics and English, the deputy superintendent transferred him to Francisco "to provide for instruction for the large numbers of Chinese pupils who enter Francisco with very low reading ability."[100]

Questions must have been raised regarding a Chinese teacher teaching outside of Chinatown. Ng remained there more due to the heavy concentration of Chinese students than because of his qualifications, as can be seen from the following:

Keep him here at Francisco by all means. This school is now over 65% Chinese. The incoming L7 class is 70% Chinese. He is invaluable. I wonder now that we ever got along without him. His class work in English is excellent.[101]

As Alice Fong bridged the school with the community at Commodore Stockton, Suey Ng did the same at Francisco.

Mr. Ng has done more to build up an interest in our PTA [Parent-Teacher Association] and an understanding on the part of our Chinese parents than all the rest of us combined.[102]

Suey Ng stayed at Francisco until 1947. From that time until 1963 he taught English to Chinese-speaking adults in San Francisco. These classes were known as Americanization and citizenship classes. According to an interview with his son, Jerry Ng, teaching in San Francisco was not a happy experience for Suey Ng. Although he scored high on the teacher examination, he was bitter that he wasn't given school assignments commensurate with his training, and that the school district never granted him tenure, which would have meant job security. He advised his son not to go into teaching because politics influenced the hiring process. Moreover, the take-home pay wasn't adequate given all the extra work he had to do outside of teaching—especially as disciplinarian for the Chinese students at Francisco. "It was no picnic in those days," he told his son.[103]

THE ABOVE PIONEERING TEACHERS—Alice Fong, Katherine Chan, and Suey Ng—served under the principalship of Anna Croughwell at Commodore Stockton School. Their main teaching responsibility was to the non-English-speaking children in the school. The net effect of this was that Commodore Stockton's English-speaking Chinese children were kept in the domain of white teachers. It would take another ten years before a Chinese teacher was allowed to teach English-speaking children at Commodore.

By the 1930s, although the young people in Chinatown were native-born Americans and college educated, failure to find employment in occupations for which they had been trained disillusioned many of them. This generation of young people suffered from the traditional prejudice of white society against Chinese workers. Since it was difficult for them to seek careers outside of Chinatown, some sought escape from the situation by going to China to seek outlets for their skills. Other Chinese Americans swallowed their bitterness and learned to cope and survive within the Chinese community.[104] The narrowness of vocational channels can be seen by the fact that there were only three Chinese teachers employed throughout the 1930s.

Research did not yield any data on the number of Chinese graduates with teaching credentials during this period. What could be gathered was that Chinese American students in San Francisco weren't encouraged to choose teaching as a career. Those who did obtain teaching credentials were advised to seek jobs in Hawaii or China.[105]

The burning question regarding employment during the 1930s was whether one's future was in China or in America. This controversy was heatedly contested by college students and was reported in the *Chinese Digest*, a weekly newspaper that catered to a growing English-reading population in America's Chinatowns.[106]

# The Last Gasps of the Segregationists

IN 1933 the board education wanted to "earthquake proof" some of the schools in the city—among them Commodore Stockton School.[107] The original building, built in 1915, was to be closed for six months and its 350 primary grade pupils shifted to the Commodore Stockton Annex for half-day attendance.[108] Somehow 350 seventh and eighth graders were still attending Commodore instead of Francisco.[109] They would be housed in nearby buildings in the neighborhood. The board rented the facilities of Nom Kue, a Chinese language school on Sacramento Street; Cumberland Presbyterian Mission on Jackson Street; and True Sunshine Mission on Clay Street during the period of repair.[110]

Washington Grammar School, located one and a half blocks away from Commodore Stockton, was originally one of the schools to be earthquake-proofed.[111] The board considered closing the school because of its close proximity to Commodore Stockton and the fact that it wasn't operating as a grammar school, but as an ungraded school. This question led to a last-ditch effort by Stephen Malatesta, president of the Columbus Civic Club, to ask the board of education to repair Washington Grammar School so it could be used to prevent Oriental children from attending schools in the North Beach district.[112]

The main issue was over Chinese students attending Francisco, but also a factor were Chinese children attending elementary schools outside of Chinatown in the late 1920s and early 1930s. Schools such as Jean Parker and Washington Irving were the first "Caucasian schools" opened to Chinese. These schools bordered Chinatown and the North Beach district. From the evidence available, it can be surmised that a smattering of Chinese children were even attending Garfield, Hancock, and Sarah B. Cooper—schools that were also located in the heart of the North Beach district. This Asian presence led some of the residents to propose salvaging the Washington Grammar School to keep the Chinese students closer to Chinatown.

The segregation proposal was strongly opposed by members of the Chinese community. Attorney Kenneth L. Fung, appearing for the Chinese-American Citizens Alliance, said to the school board:

Segregation does not make for good American citizenship. Our children, born here, should be given American training comparable with that of other American students and should not be subjected to a humiliation which would only breed discontent. This would start a prejudice against our children.[113]

Dr. Chester Lee, past commander of Cathay Post of the American Legion, declared, "The only way our children can become good American citizens is to mingle with American people."[114] The Chinese-American Citizens Alliance protested in writing that such a proposal was "un-American, discriminatory, unwise and unnecessary in that it would engender a feeling of resentment in the hearts of these children, 90 percent of them citizens of the United States."[115]

Both Fung and Lee left the board meeting with assurances from school board members and the superintendent that no segregation of pupils was contemplated for the future development of Washington Grammar School.[116]

A week later the North End Improvement Association, a civic club in the North Beach district, went on record against the proposal to segregate the Chinese pupils in the old Washington School building and called the board's attention to the following facts:

1. The children whom this action would affect are, almost without exception, native-born, many of them representing the third generation of native-born Americans. This is the only land they have ever known. To deny their Americanism is to place them in the position of a man without a country. To ostracize them in the manner proposed would be to deny them those equal rights and that equal opportunity that is guaranteed by our institutions.

2. Those who have taught children of Chinese descent are unanimous in their testimony that they are in general, industrious, obedient, and respectful of authority, and that, as an example to the rest of their classmates, their presence is an advantage; and

3. The Washington School building has been condemned as dangerous and unfit for use. If it is unfit for children of Caucasian birth, it is unfit for children of Chinese descent. Be it further

Resolved, That this association hereby respectfully urges upon the Board of Education the summary rejection of this un-American proposition.[117]

After a stiff fight by the above organizations, the board of education voted down the segregation proposal.

One final attempt at segregation was made in March 1935. Over a flimsy pretext regarding a pregnant white girl at Francisco Junior High School, a civic club went so far as to appear before the mayor of San Francisco to claim that a Chinese boy was responsible for the act and demand segregation in no uncertain terms. The Chinese-American Citizens Alliance protested in favor of the moral and legal rights of the Chinese children attending the school, and immediately requested the juvenile court authorities to launch an impartial investigation. The investigation absolved the Chinese from any blame, and the segregationists were silenced.[118] After this incident, public voicing of segregating the Chinese students in San Francisco terminated.

# Chapter 7

# The Breakthrough Years 1941–1959

## The New Image

THE 1940s were marked by an improved racial attitude towards Chinese by the general society. The pivotal event was World War II. Americans were impressed with China's heroic struggles against Japanese aggression.[1] With the arrival of Madame Chiang Kai-shek to the United States in 1943, the negative images of Chinese as heathens and aliens were transformed into positive ones. The Chinese were now considered fiercely democratic, friendly, and the natural allies of the United States.[2]

In San Francisco, the board of education declared March 18, 1943, a minimum school day "to enable the schools of this Department to join in the city's reception to the wife of the Generalissimo of China."[3]

Madame Chiang's arrival was delayed a week, and when she arrived on March 25, the board permitted Chinatown's children to be away from school all day and the remaining schoolchildren to be on a minimum day.[4] San Francisco's school personnel were impressed with her poise, knowledge, and use of English.[5] The editor of the *Chinese Press* quoted her:

We know that anything any Chinese does well in the United States—we at home shall share in his credit, and vice versa.... Every Chinese in the United States must win the respect of the community in which he lives ... must participate fully ... in the community.[6]

With China as an ally of the United States, Madame Chiang used her influence to lobby congressmen to do away with discriminatory immigration laws. Partly as a gesture to improve relations with China, Congress repealed the humiliating exclusion laws in 1943.[7] Under the Magnuson Bill, Chinese were permitted to be naturalized and granted an annual quota of 105 immigrants to the United States.[8]

The labor shortage in the United States during the war, coupled with the new Chinese American image, paved the way for Americans of Chinese descent to gain employment in many industries, corporations, and government agencies which had previously been closed to them.[9] However, some educated Chinese avoided the white world and voluntarily remained in Chinatown.[10]

After a restrictive state code was lifted in 1947, Chinese began buying homes outside Chinatown in the Richmond and Sunset districts of San Francisco.[11] Some of the older established families spilled over into adjoining communities such as Oakland, Berkeley, and Richmond.[12] Still, there were others who were reluctant to move because of society's prejudice and rebuffs in renting an apartment or buying a home.[13]

After World War II, new immigrants and younger Chinese Americans were spared the harsh discrimination of earlier generations. Nevertheless, the Chinese were still subject to slurs such as "Chinks" and "Ching Chong Chinaman."

Rights taken for granted by other Americans were finally acquired by the Chinese. Acceptance in the United States coupled with the civil strife in China led many of the older generation to give up their sojourner mentality. Moreover, a broader Chinese American leadership formed that was versatile in English, at home with American customs, and familiar with the democratic process. They had developed a civic consciousness that made Chinatown an integral part of the city. As stated by one of its spokesmen, Lim P. Lee:

No longer can Chinatown be considered as a separate unit from San Francisco's civic life. No longer do we live—or want to live—in social isolation. Whatever affects the city, Chinatown is ready to assume its responsibilities.[14]

During World War II, students contributed to the war effort by collecting scrap metal,[15] and the Cathay Club, composed of Chinese students, at Girls High School sponsored a war-bond rally during the celebration of Chinese New Year.[16] Other students salvaged waste paper,[17] made toys for children of wartorn lands,[18] or bought war bonds and stamps.[19] Some overseas students had the tenacity to create a victory garden in a former refuse dump on a steep bank in back of Washington Irving School Annex. Commenting on this fact, a reporter wrote glowingly, "A look at that garden will give you an idea why nobody will ever defeat the Chinese."[20]

Cementing the postwar Chinese American image was a full-page coverage of a flag-raising in the *San Francisco News*. The copy read:

San Francisco, city of many nationalities, can count her Chinese-Americans among her most industrious citizens. With the largest Chinese community in the nation, she has found the Chinese among the foremost in civic programs and answering the many appeals and campaigns for aid that make up a part of the life of a major city. Young Chinese-Americans pay honest allegiance to this nation, but remember the Chinese culture and study the Chinese language and customs in several schools. Typical of young Chinese-Americans are Arlene Kwock and Weyman Lew shown raising the Flag of their allegiance at Commodore Stockton School.[21]

The post–World War II image of Chinese as Americans also saw the end of formal *de jure* segregation in public education. In 1947, Superintendent of Public Schools Dr. Herbert C. Clish was informed that the cornerstone of Commodore Stockton School still read "Oriental School." He ordered the old named buffed out immediately.[22] That same year, a court decision declared that students of Mexican ancestry could not be put into segregated schools without legislative support.[23] This case focused attention on the issue of school segregation and on the state statutes that permitted such practices. The legislature finally repealed the section pertaining to racial segregation from the California Education Code,[24] and on June 14, 1947, Governor Earl Warren signed the repeal into law.[25] This ended California's *de jure* segregation and the policy of permitting local school districts to establish separate schools for non-white children. For the Chinese in San Francisco, their struggles with the city school board over segregated schooling came to a close.

*De facto* segregation still occurred in San Francisco through "neighborhood schools." Anyone who wanted to avoid racial integration could move into "better neighborhoods," because gerrymandering of housing patterns was used by the board to determine school boundaries.[26]

# Acquiring Play Space

PLAY SPACE AT Commodore Stockton School has always been minimal. Two weeks after the opening of Commodore Stockton Annex (1924) the school board received a communication from the board of supervisors' education and playground committee to consider acquiring more land to be used for additional play space for that school.[27]

It took nearly a year before the school board requested that the board of supervisors purchase additional area at the southeastern side of the school.[28] However, the supervisors filed the request away for more than a year. In June 1926, the school board made another appeal to the supervisors to expedite the play-area purchase.[29]

The school board's short-term solution was a small addition to the boys' yard on the southwestern side of the school.[30] A longer-range solution involved acquiring a larger property on the southeastern side of the school. This was accomplished through an exchange of the district's old Lowell High School, a cash payment of $5,000,[31] and the organizational efforts of the Chinese community and their friends.

The depression during the 1930s may have been a major deterrent to solving the play-space problem at Commodore Stockton. The issue seemed to have been placed on the back burner and didn't surface again until the 1940s. By then the need for a playground was more than a school problem—it was a community problem.

On March 18, 1941, George K. Jue, chairman of the Chinatown Improvement Association, asked the board of education for a new playground for Chinatown. He suggested that "sufficient land adjacent to the Commodore Stockton School property be purchased and converted into a playground to be used not only as a school yard during school hours, but also as a public playground after school hours under the supervision of the recreation commission."[32]

A petition had been distributed throughout the city that cited the fact that there were more than six thousand children in the Chinatown area for whom playground facilities of less than one acre were available. This congestion created a high tuberculosis rate among the Chinese children, and delinquency, though less prevalent, was nonetheless serious.[33] Describing the Chinatown area as congested and neglected, an editorial in the *Call Bulletin* was of the opinion that:

The petition for a playground is ... of utmost urgency. It can hardly be conceived that the responsible authorities of San Francisco will fail to see the necessity of the proposed project, or will brook any unnecessary delay in making it available as promptly as possible where such facilities are so sorely needed.[34]

On April 8, 1941, a large delegation from Chinatown made their case before the board of education. The speakers were Dr. Theodore Lee and George Jue of the Chinatown Improvement Association, Father C. A. Donovan and Father Bradley of Old St. Mary's Church, and Dr. Margaret Chung. They said that the school yard of 0.6 of an acre was inadequate for the district's 17,000 adults and 6,000 children.[35] The physical properties committee of the board was directed to confer with the recreation commission to determine if a joint program could be worked out. Furthermore, Superintendent Nourse called to the board's attention the urgent need for the expansion of the Commodore Stockton School's yard and recommended that it be considered in the 1941–42 budget.[36] According to the *Call Bulletin*, a long list of civic organizations and leaders endorsed the playground proposal.[37]

At the end of the month, Superintendent Nourse reported to the board that the recreation commission would meet and decide what action they would be willing to take in furnishing equipment, if the school board was to enlarge the present yard at Commodore Stockton School.[38] The project began to move in August:

Resolved: That the City's Director of Property, Mr. Joseph J. Phillips, be hereby requested to negotiate for the purchase, or the acquirement by exchange of School Department property, of a site, approximately 90 feet by 137 feet 6 inches, on Washington St. adjoining the Commodore Stockton School site on the east, and to report findings to the Board for its recommended action thereon. The above resolution was duly seconded and was carried by the unanimous vote of the Commissioners present.

The Secretary was directed to advise the correspondents sending endorsements of the above project (three organizations hereinabove named) of action taken this day; also to similarly advise the Chinatown Improvement Association.[39]

For some reason, the board amended the size of the lot from 90 feet to 64 feet 1¾ inches on Washington Street. It further directed the Director of Property to take an option on the acquisition.

Resolved: That the Director of Property be also requested to take an option on the acquisition of the remainder of the Fifty-Vara lot at the southwest corner of Stockton and Washington Streets, and to report to the Board of Education his findings in the above matter for further action of this Board.[40]

By late August a work order was issued to acquire additional land adjoining the Commodore Stockton School. Money accrued from the sale of school properties was to purchase the property in Chinatown.[41] Eminent domain proceedings against the property owners on Washington Street were authorized near the end of the year.[42] Some legalities over condemnation were encountered but they were smoothed out and the city attorney proceeded with the condemnation of property on the east side of the school.[43] Unfortunately, wording in both the December 2, 1941, and January 13, 1942, resolutions made condemnation proceedings temporarily inoperative, but the issue was straightened out in the February meeting.[44]

As the play space adjoining the school began to materialize, the Chinatown Improvement Association requested that there be a two-level structure—an enclosure at street level (cafeteria, showers, play space) and an open playground at the level of and adjoining the present school yard. The executive secretary for this organization was Alice Fong Yu.[45]

Appearing before the board on the same matter were Miss Susie J. Convery, principal of the Commodore Stockton School, and George K. Jue of the Chinatown Improvement Association.[46] Their request was referred to the board's physical properties committee for investigation to provide additional play space in Chinatown.[47]

Four years would go by and still the condemnation proceedings were not completed. The Chinatown Improvement Association communicated to the board the importance of the immediate construction of this project. Associate Superintendent Brady stated that the school playground was a priority item on the list of improvements to be made as soon as materials were available.[48] The last obstacle toward the acquisition of the play space was removed by May 1946:

Resolved: That the Director of Real Estate be requested to negotiate for the sale and immediate removal of the brick buildings located on the property east of the Commodore Stockton School, 64' 1¾" facing Washington Street, which property is now owned by the school department.[49]

The board of education authorized the bureau of architecture to prepare plans and specifications and to call for bids for the development of the play area at the Commodore Stockton School— 64' 1¾" by 137' 6" immediately east of the present main school building.[50]

Wellnitz and DeNarde, the lowest bidder, was approved to do the general construction of the southeast yard.[51] Their bid was $32,514.00.[52] The sale of old school property would bring in no less than $32,400 to acquire property in Chinatown adjoining the school.[53] Although the two figures nearly matched, acquiring property was one thing and building a playground was another. It wasn't indicated how the board of education proposed to fund the construction of the playground, but the original estimate was $100,000.[54] From this standpoint the request by the Chinatown Improvement Association to add a cafeteria and showers was not an unreasonable one. The play space adjoining Commodore Stockton School was completed in 1949. It solved the recreational problem of the school but not that of the community.[55]

One organization that played a significant role in acquiring play space was Commodore Stockton School's Parent-Teacher Association (PTA). Organized in 1944, this PTA had just as difficult a time gaining acceptance from its parent body as did the Chinese in San Francisco in getting their children into public schools. Having little organizational experience, the Chinese were willing to learn how to structure the association.[56] After a couple of preliminary meetings, they became an integral part of the city's Second District, Congress of Parents and Teachers.[57]

During the first year of operation they recruited two hundred members. Meetings were informal and interpreters were there to translate for those who did not speak English. Topics covered were nutrition, proper clothing, dental health, etc.

Besides implementing a hot-lunch program, Commodore's PTA worked toward three goals: more play space for children, improved health conditions, and better housing.[58]

The district PTA participated in the installation of the Commodore PTA's officers and conducted classes on PTA rules and

procedures.[59] Commodore sent their officers to district meetings, and at one of those meetings Commodore's PTA president,
June Tom, overheard the following conversation between one of
the PTA mothers and Doris Lavazano, PTA president of Garfield
School:

*PTA Member:* Oh, I'd never go down to Chinatown at night. I'd be
so scared—all those tong wars and opium dens—

*Doris Lavazano:* I'm not afraid. I walk through there every night on
my way home to Telegraph Hill. Chinatown is safer than any other
area. The Chinese mind their own business.[60]

June Tom's reaction to the incident:

It was scary being the only Chinese attending the District PTA.
Doris was the only one that I knew there. You know how terrible you
feel when you hear something like that? I felt grateful to Doris because, after all, there's somebody who stuck up for the Chinese
people. Of course I've never seen those things [tong wars, opium
dens]. It might have happened before my time. It must have been the
Gold Rush days [laughter]. Anyway they must have listened to the
series on radio about the Chinese—if that's all they hear, they would
be scared to come down. In some ways you can't blame them. We
[Commodore Stockton PTA] spent a lot of time and money bringing
in different people [西人] into Chinatown so that they will know
that it's not like what they hear on the radio—it's not like that at all.
So gradually they started coming into Chinatown and we'd take
them to lunch and a tour. That broke the ice for the Caucasian
people to come to Chinatown. 'Cause they live out in the Avenues
and they have never come into Chinatown—so they hear the stories
on the radio in those days and, so well, they have a different view of
Chinatown. Now that I've gone out to the District meetings, they've
seen me—well, I'm just like anybody else. So we did pave the way
for the other Chinese mothers to integrate. And we did it by inviting
other PTA members to come to Chinatown. We spent a lot of time
and money—we put Commodore Stockton School on the map.[61]

Commodore Stockton's PTA was actively involved in securing
the Chinese Recreation Center located on Washington and
Mason streets, the site of the old Washington Grammar School.
Commented June Tom:

We didn't have enough recreation for the people in Chinatown and
we needed the recreation. There used to be an old empty storeroom
or brickhouse on Washington and Mason streets. We wanted the
Board to use that property for a playground. We had to get a petition

to get the property. Did you know that a lot of Chinese that owned their homes up there objected to it [the playground]; and then up there the rich ladies of Nob Hill objected too—God! Then we had all those organizations in Chinatown who were assigned different blocks to get signatures for the petition. They were supposed to do it. But who ended up doing it all—Commodore's PTA! So at the dedication of the Recreation Center who got all the credit? Everybody but us!! [Laughter.] That's okay. As long as we got it, that's the main thing—isn't that right?[62]

Another major project of Commodore's PTA was helping to secure the southeastern yard for the school. Quoting June Tom:

Remember we didn't have the yard on the other side? Well, Joseph Alioto was on the board of education then. He didn't want to spend the money on a yard for us. He never even looked at how much play space we had for all the students. He kept saying you have to have one Catholic [representative], one labor [representative], one like that. He said the Catholic schools don't have enough play space so why should we. But we saw all the schools have a lot [of play space]—all depend, you know what I mean? Other schools, they yell for it and they get it you know. And so we needed more space because we have a lot of students. And how could we all play in this dinky little yard, you ask me. So we asked him to buy the two empty spaces right down there—the dyeing and cleaning works ran by the Japanese. It was empty for the longest time. After the war [World War II], they didn't come back. So we went to the board to ask them to buy it but Alioto was the one that objected. So then his term ended—good thing his term ended. So then George Johns, the labor man came in. So we talked to him and then the board okayed it. So we bought the lot and finally we have a larger yard to play in. You gotta holler too! [She laughed at this point in the interview.][63]

Controversy over the use of firecrackers arose between Commodore Stockton's PTA and the district PTA. The latter decided that firecrackers were a nuisance and asked the city's police chief to stringently enforce the anti-firecracker ordinance. The chief's reply was read at the district meeting. He pledged "every effort to abate the meaningless and extremely dangerous practice of shooting firecrackers as a means of celebrating festive occasions."[64]

Mrs. Earl Louie, president of Commodore Stockton PTA, immediately protested both the district's action and the police chief's reply as a threat to religious freedom because the lighting of firecrackers during Chinese New Year celebrated a religious ceremony.[65]

At the district's next meeting, Commodore's PTA used a similar defense for the use of firecrackers in Chinatown.[66] They cited PTA policy forbidding interference with the religious customs of its members.

Mrs. Earl Louie said her group particularly objected because the issue was not referred to their group as the persons most familiar with the background of the situation. Commodore's PTA urged that action be taken to regulate rather than forbid the use of fireworks. The district PTA responded by saying the incident was a misunderstanding and that a PTA committee would meet with Commodore Stockton the following week to work out a satisfactory solution.[67]

As far as can be determined, the minutes of the Commodore Stockton PTA were thrown out as part of a general clean-up effort. The organization ended in the late 1960s, when Chinese American parents at Commodore Stockton began moving into other parts of the city and were being replaced by large numbers of working immigrant parents who could not attend meetings. Also, there wasn't a common language between the parents who remained and the new immigrants. Since regular meetings were required by the district PTA for affiliation, the connection to the parent group had to be dropped.[68]

While it was in existence, this local PTA played a significant role by inviting district PTA members and school personnel to Commodore Stockton to familiarize them with the school and the community. They fought to retain their community's religious customs and assisted in the struggle for more play and recreational space for Chinatown.

# The Influx of Overseas Chinese Students

DURING WORLD WAR II the Chinese in America showed their loyalty by bearing arms. There were other powerful incentives to enlist in the armed forces. China was being invaded by Japan in 1937, and furthermore, if one served in the military, it would take less time to acquire American citizenship.[69] Moreover, the disproportionate ratio of Chinese women to Chinese men in America[70] led the eligible bachelors to marry in China while serving as GIs in the American armed forces.

Bearing arms for America and possessing American citizenship did not exempt the Chinese GIs from harsh immigration laws. After the war ended, they couldn't bring their families to the United States until the enactment of the War Brides Act in 1946.[71] By the time the act expired in 1948, 5,634 wives had been brought to the port of San Francisco from China. Many of these women settled in Chinatown.[72] This act and subsequent congressional measures brought a steady influx of non-English-speaking students into the San Francisco public schools in the late 1940s and early 1950s.

The influx of Chinese immigrant students swelled steadily as China established a new government in 1949. With the outbreak of the Korean War and the subsequent fears by the Chinese GIs for their children's future across the sea, immigration to America increased.[73] These events contributed to a change in the perception of Chinese from a positive image to one of being considered the "enemy" by society at large.[74]

During the Korean War, for instance, the Chinese feared that if the war extended to mainland China, the Chinese in America might be interned as the Japanese Americans had been during World War II.[75]

When the new immigrants first arrived in San Francisco, the younger students as well as the war brides were sent to Washington Irving School. The older students went to Francisco Junior High School and Galileo High School.[76] The placement of some of these students into the secondary schools brought their living conditions to the attention of the staff. Not only were many of these students attending school all day, they were working eight to ten hours a day, seven days a week, for low pay. They arrived at school in the morning, often dead tired from their work the previous night. Some of them even slept in school all day. Upon inquiry, the students told the teachers that they had to work in order to pay back the passage fare.[77]

In 1953, Bruce G. Barber, Director of Immigration and Naturalization, reported to School Superintendent Herbert C. Clish that some Chinese students had entered the country illegally and were virtual slaves to their sponsors. Up to that time, forty cases of fraudulent entry had been recorded. This charge was reported in the *Call Bulletin*, and the writer felt this was a method used by Chinatown tongs to recruit teenage "junior hatchetmen."[78]

Six months later the charge of illegal entry was repeated by immigration officials, school officials, and a Chinatown leader. They reported that in some cases, Chinese high school students were virtually indentured servants as they worked long hours after school to pay off "sponsors." By falsely claiming blood kinship, these aliens reportedly paid from $2,000 to $3,000 to enter the United States as a citizen's "son" or "daughter." The students usually listed their guardian as an "uncle," who, on further probing, was found to have only a vague family connection with the youth.[79]

Regarding many of these newcomers, Dr. Edward H. Redford, assistant superintendent for secondary education, said: "I don't know how to describe them. They work half the night in laundries or sewing shops, apparently because they owe money to somebody who brought them here."[80]

Laurence Childers, principal at Francisco Junior High School, said: "Some Chinese have named a laundry or restaurant as their guardian."[81] Added one Chinatown leader: "There is no doubt that these youngsters are actually engaged in a kind of servitude. Some of these youngsters constitute a rowdy element in Chinatown, beating up other children and occasionally assaulting tourists."[82]

Bruce G. Barber summed up the situation: "The only way the problem will ever be licked is by the full cooperation from Chinatown. The solution must originate there."[83] Dr. Edward Redford initiated a China-born teenage committee to assist the new students. He expressed concern over how these students survived after school:

We could keep them off the streets during the school day, but heaven only knows what they were going home to—if they had homes at all, that is. Reports were numerous that the older boys were sleeping in flop houses, in homes of "friends," or—a stock answer, "I'm staying with my uncle." Also most of the boys were in bondage for their passage over, and were working late hours without work permits in unsupervised Chinatown industries.[84]

A school survey revealed that more than 50 percent of the immigrant Chinese children had after-school jobs. School personnel were convinced that many of these pupils far exceeded the twenty-hour maximum work week provided by child labor laws for children under 18 years old.[85]

Whether their entry was legal or illegal, the immigrant students compounded an old problem for the educational authorities in San Francisco. The presence in Chinatown of non- and limited-English-speaking children had always been a problem, but since discriminatory immigration laws kept the Chinese population small, these students could be isolated and the problem controlled. It was a common occurrence that Chinese children in Chinatown would begin their schooling with little or no English background and acquire some fluency by the time they left high school. With the additional arrival of 1,600 war brides and 1,500 immigrant boys and girls within a seven-year period (1948–1955),[86] teaching the Chinese-speaking population in English put a huge burden upon the teaching staff in the "Chinatown schools."[87]

The influx caught the secondary schools unprepared for the newcomers. Said Laurence Childers:

It got so that when we heard a ship whistle in the bay, we'd cringe. There were 88 in the first bunch we got at school here—and we simply didn't know what to do with them. They couldn't speak English. We didn't know what schooling they had. We didn't know where they were living. They were shy and homesick, some of them; and at first there was a definite anti-social feeling about them. The first graduation class was strictly a social graduation. They were 16 years old and had to be pushed on to high school. It was up to Galileo to take over from there.[88]

In the beginning Galileo High School fashioned the following program for the recent arrivals from Canton: the students were introduced to the American way of life and given the three "Rs" (reading, writing, and arithmetic) before they were enrolled in regular courses—including American history, English, geography, manual training, physical education, and mathematics.[89]

Washington Irving School held orientation classes for the war brides and took them on tours in the city so they were able to find their way around and learn the English names.[90]

By 1952, the task was to make "good Americans" out of the new arrivals. A special class started in the elementary schools called an "Opportunity Class," where pupils would learn how to speak and write in English and become oriented to life in America so that they could later join the regular grades.[91] In the junior high and high schools, classes for the immigrant youths were called "Americanization classes."[92] These were special classes in English, geography, and citizenship.[93]

Regarding the Americanization program, Superintendent Herbert C. Clish criticized the $500 per student cost of the program as "an extra burden on the taxpayer." Said Clish, "We want the Chinese who are legally in the United States but we cannot afford to accept those who are not."[94]

At first Chinatown was able to absorb the initial onslaught of newcomers. But by 1952, social problems began to become manifest. The lack of a normal home life, limited recreational outlets, and the language barrier set the immigrant students apart not only from white youths but from American-born Chinese.[95]

By 1954 Chinatown itself was being oversaturated by newcomers with social problems.[96] These issues weren't addressed initially by outside society, because Chinatown had a reputation for caring for its own people[97] and having little or no delinquency.[98] Moreover, the high academic achievement of Chinese students had been constantly in the news, particularly since World War II. Consequently, San Francisco channeled its energies and resources to the other districts while the problems in Chinatown continued to fester.

For the next twenty years (1948–1968) San Francisco "solved" the problem of the "English-handicapped" students by placing them in Opportunity classes in the elementary schools or in the Americanization department in the secondary schools. It was a sink-or-swim approach. The psychological and social cost to the individual in achieving some kind of English mastery was not taken into account, let alone the community divisiveness it engendered between young and old and between new immigrant and the American-born. This local problem in San Francisco would become a national concern in the 1970s as other linguistic minorities experienced the same inadequate educational treatment.

## Struggling into the Profession

AFTER WORLD WAR II, a teacher shortage, the lessening of racial hostility and the influence of fair-minded educators resulted in the increased hiring of Chinese American teachers into the San Francisco school system, which can be seen in the following tables compiled from the school district's personnel cards, retirement records, and microfilm data, as well as from interviews with Chinese American teachers employed before 1960.

Figure 1 shows that 71 Chinese American teachers were appointed between 1926 and 1959. Of the 71, 80 percent were hired in the 1950s, showing that teaching had finally become an option in choosing a career.

Figures 2 and 3 show that three times as many female Chinese American teachers as male teachers and two and a half times as many elementary teachers as secondary teachers were hired. Female teachers outnumbered male teachers by a ratio of sixteen to one in elementary schools (Figure 4). However, there were twice as many male teachers as female teachers at the secondary level (Figure 5).

In 1978, Chinese American teachers were interviewed for this study. One female teacher, Jannie Wu, commented on the highly competitive and selective nature of the teaching profession:

Although math was basically my most diffiicult subject, I majored in it because I knew it was the only way to get a secondary school teaching job.... If I majored in a field that was more to my bent like language, counseling, even elementary teaching, then the competition for jobs would be so great that I'd be better off to pick something else; that would be just like the same reason why a lot of Chinese fellows majored in engineering.

Men have generally thought of elementary school teaching as non-academic and have felt that the "real teaching" occurs at the secondary level. The few Chinese men who did aspire to be elementary-school teachers were rejected because of their deficiencies in speaking standard English. This proficiency requirement applied also to Chinese women, and will be discussed in more detail later.

Three teachers explained that it was job discrimination against women in the employment field that led so many Chinese American women to fall back upon elementary school teaching for work in the 1950s.

I really didn't choose teaching. Occupations were very limited to Chinese women.
*— Rosemary Fong*

I worked for an export-import company as a claims adjuster. It didn't work out because they discriminated against women.
*— Peggy Wing*

After I graduated from Cal Berkeley, I looked for a job in merchandising. All the stores in San Francisco would not interview a Chi-

FIGURE 1

Chinese American Teachers Employed in San Francisco,
1926-1959

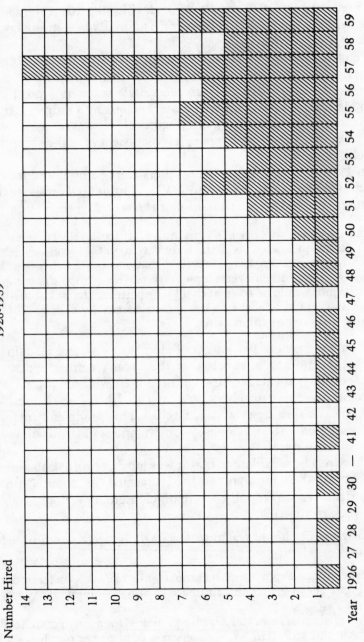

Total = 71 Teachers

FIGURE 2

Male and Female Chinese American Teachers Employed in San Francisco,
1926-1959

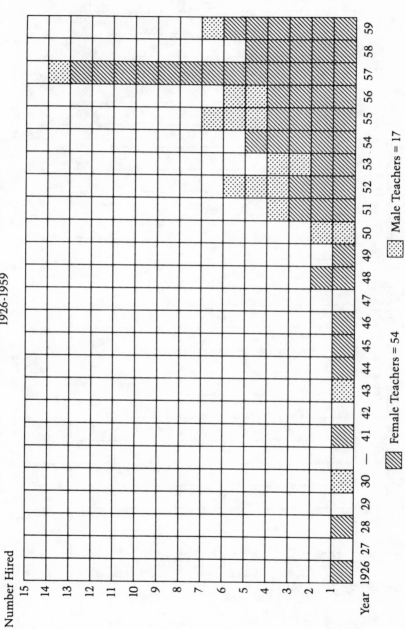

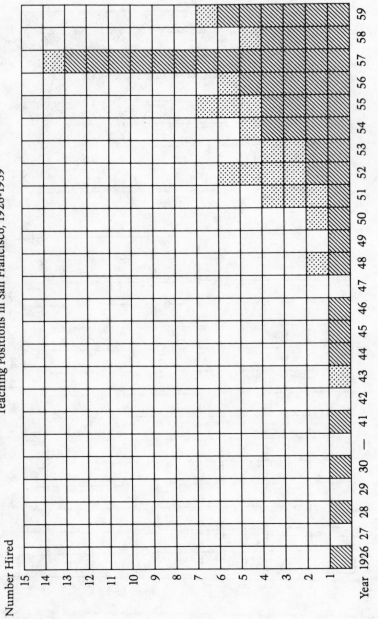

FIGURE 3

Chinese American Teachers Appointed to Elementary and Secondary
Teaching Positions in San Francisco, 1926-1959

FIGURE 4

Male and Female Chinese American Teachers Appointed
to Elementary Schools in San Francisco, 1926-1959

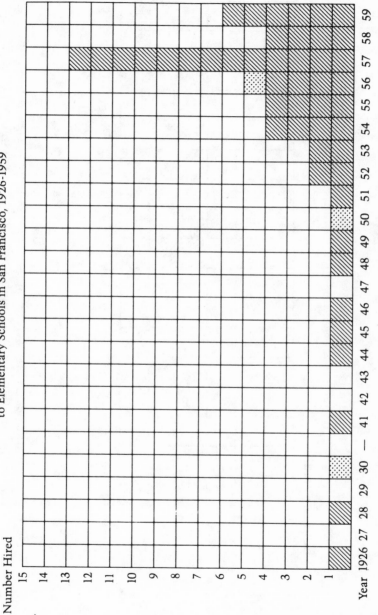

FIGURE 5

Male and Female Chinese American Teachers Appointed
to Secondary Schools in San Francisco, 1943-1959

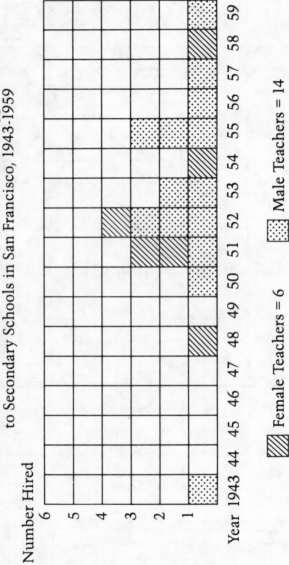

Note: Most of the secondary school appointments were assigned to junior high schools. Only two men had high school teaching assignments during this period; one in 1955 and one in 1956. No woman had a high school appointment.

nese.... So entering elementary teaching was not by choice; it was a means of earning a living.

*—Patricia Lum*

As can be seen in Figure 5, the school district began hiring secondary teachers in 1943. What was significant was that between 1948 and 1953, more than three-fourths of the junior high school teachers hired were assigned to Francisco. This means that the influx of new immigrants spurred the hiring of about half the Chinese American secondary teachers hired in San Francisco between 1943 and 1959. Thus, the pattern for secondary schools mirrored the earlier hiring pattern for Commodore Stockton Elementary School—Chinese American teachers were employed to instruct Chinese-speaking students.

A handful of elementary teachers were teaching in schools outside Chinatown in the 1940s and three junior high school teachers were teaching outside of Francisco in the early 1950s. These, however, were the exceptions to the general assignment practice for Chinese American teachers.

Of the 71 Chinese American teachers hired during the years 1926–1959, 27, or about 38 percent, left the school district. Moreover, 75 percent of those who left were hired between 1955 and 1959. This meant that a little more than half of the Chinese American teachers hired between 1955 and 1959 left the district.

While granting that the normal attrition was due to maternities, deaths, moving out of San Francisco, induction into the armed services, etc., resignations due to tough assignments and "old guard administrators" were also factors, as can be seen by comments made by these teachers in the interviews for this study:

Lots of beginning teachers started out at real rough schools. After the first year, they've had it; they quit. Marriage or moving away were secondary reasons. The primary reason for quitting was the rough assignment. You're lucky to get into a good school like I did. I was fortunate to get some of the breaks that others didn't.

*—Agnes Chan*

My girlfriend Diana taught outside of Chinatown. She was under this principal who was very strict—very particular about this and that. Diana found it so hard that she quit after two or three years. She just couldn't take it anymore. They were just too picky. And then Betty who started with me. She was very bright and she ended up with a high score on her test. But she had this principal in Chinatown to work with. Betty would go to school with sleeveless dresses and they'd complain about that—her skirt was too short and all that—every little thing they'd complain about.        —*Susan Chang*

We all knew that if we got hired that we would be put into the toughest positions.        —*Sandra Gin*

During my probation, I had the toughest principal in the city. She was well known for sending men to the foreign legions. But we got along fine because I did what I was told to do.

—*Name withheld by request*

As Chinatown expanded northward and westward, so Chinese children were attending schools such as Jean Parker, Washington Irving, Hancock, Sarah B. Cooper, Garfield, Spring Valley, Redding, and Sherman. Eventually these schools were called "Chinatown schools" because of the preponderance of Chinese students. The map that follows shows the location of these schools in San Francisco.

The placement of Chinese American teachers into each of these schools is pertinent to this study. A series of tables has been compiled regarding each of the "Chinatown schools." Information on student enrollment came from the school district's Bureau of Research Records; information on number of teachers per year and by school came from the certificated payroll records; and sources of the approximate percentages of Chinese students in the "Chinatown schools" are indicated at the bottom of each table.

The data indicate that all the Chinatown schools had an unofficial placement quota of Chinese American teachers, despite increasing numbers of Chinese students during this time period (1939–1959). Commodore Stockton's table, for example, shows that the school maintained a quota of three Chinese American teachers until 1954. The district hired three Chinese American teachers and placed them at Commodore Stockton in the late 1920s, but they didn't hire even one Chinese American teacher throughout the 1930s. Table 5 clearly shows that Commodore Stockton had a quota of three Chinese American teachers for almost a quarter of a century (1930–1954). This school, with its heavy concentration of Chinese students, could have used more Chinese American teachers to bridge the language-cultural gap at the school. From 1941 to 1955, San Francisco hired twenty Chinese American teachers for the elementary school division (Figure 4), but they were assigned to other schools. Some of them could have been used wisely at Commodore, but the three-teacher quota was maintained.

# FIGURE 6

## Location of "Chinatown Schools"

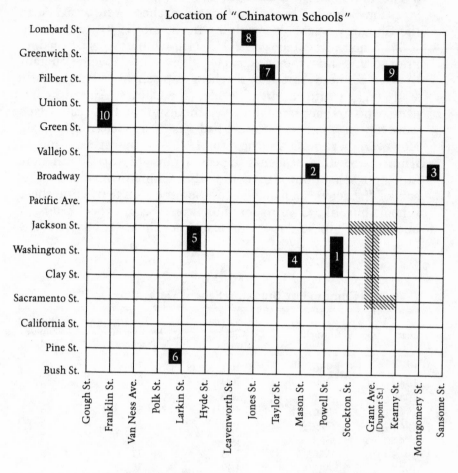

1. Commodore Stockton
2. Jean Parker
3. Washington Irving
4. Washington Grammar
5. Spring Valley
6. Redding
7. Hancock
8. Sarah B. Cooper
9. Garfield
10. Sherman

▨▨▨ San Francisco Chinatown in 1853

NOTE: Washington Irving since 1978 has been the School for Business and Commerce. Hancock School was changed to the Chinatown/North Beach Community College Center in 1981. Sarah B. Cooper has been rebuilt and is scheduled to be back in operation in 1983 as the Yick Wo School.

The tables show that, with the exception of Commodore Stockton School, Chinese American teachers were assigned to the Chinatown schools beginning in the late 1940s to the mid-1950s. Their placement coincided with Chinatown's expansion. Prior to this time, the principals in these schools were reluctant to place Chinese American teachers into schools where a white staff taught white children. Besides, the Chinese American students who first appeared in these schools in the 1930s and 1940s were few in number and most had a fair knowledge of English. However, beginning in the late 1940s, a new generation of Chinese-speaking students appeared not only at Commodore Stockton School but also at the other Chinatown schools. The school district began placing Chinese American teachers at these schools but, like Commodore Stockton, these schools had their quotas of Chinese American teachers. Thus, strictly limiting

### TABLE 5
### Commodore Stockton School Data, 1939–1959

| Year | Enrollment | Percentage of Chinese Students | Total Number of Teachers | Number of Chinese Teachers |
|------|-----------|-------------------------------|-------------------------|---------------------------|
| 1939 | 956 | 100* | 30 | 2 |
| 1940 | 959 | 100 | 30 | 2 |
| 1941 | 951 | 100 | 31 | 2 |
| 1942 | 836 | 100 | 31 | 3 |
| 1943 | 729 | 100 | 26 | 3 |
| 1944 | 665 | 100 | 23 | 3 |
| 1945 | 655 | 100 | 22 | 3 |
| 1946 | 632 | 100 | 22 | 3 |
| 1947 | 649 | 100 | 22 | 3 |
| 1948 | 684 | 100 | 21 | 3 |
| 1949 | 686 | 100 | 23 | 3 |
| 1950 | 675 | 100 | 23 | 3 |
| 1951 | 668 | 100 | 22 | 3 |
| 1952 | 662 | 100 | 22 | 3 |
| 1953 | 670 | 100 | 23 | 3 |
| 1954 | 558 | 100 | 27 | 3 |
| 1955 | 886 | 100 | 26 | 4 |
| 1956 | 835 | 100 | 27 | 5 |
| 1957 | 1065 | 100 | 36 | 5 |
| 1958 | 1201 | 100 | 39 | 6 |
| 1959 | 1247 | 100 | 40 | 4 |

* The location of this school in the heart of present-day Chinatown meant that most, if not all, of the students were Chinese.

Chinese American teachers according to the number of Chinese-speaking children led to a token representation.

These quotas in the Chinatown schools meant that additional Chinese American teachers had to be assigned to non-Chinatown schools in the late 1950s. This reflected a change in the hiring practice of the school district since 1926. But by this time, Chinatown schools were sought-after posts and schools in many other sections of the city were considered less desirable. From henceforth, Chinese American teachers who wanted a Chinatown assignment had to be "proven teachers" before getting the assignment, according to Sandra Gin, who told this writer:

.... We all knew there was a Chinese hiring quota. If by some small

### TABLE 6
### Jean Parker School Data, 1939–1959

| Year | Enrollment | Percentage of Chinese Students | Total Number of Teachers | Number of Chinese Teachers |
|------|-----------|-------------------------------|--------------------------|----------------------------|
| 1939 | 650 | ... | 21 | 0 |
| 1940 | 596 | ... | 21 | 0 |
| 1941 | 537 | ... | 21 | 0 |
| 1942 | 475 | ... | 19 | 0 |
| 1943 | 421 | ... | 17 | 0 |
| 1944 | 372 | ... | 16 | 0 |
| 1945 | 407 | 50* | 15 | 0 |
| 1946 | 372 | ... | 13 | 0 |
| 1947 | 375 | 75† | 12 | 0 |
| 1948 | 401 | ... | 15 | 0 |
| 1949 | 412 | 70‡ | 16 | 0 |
| 1950 | 422 | ... | 16 | 0 |
| 1951 | 377 | ... | 13 | 1 |
| 1952 | 368 | ... | 14 | 1 |
| 1953 | 450 | ... | 16 | 1 |
| 1954 | 409 | 90# | 19 | 1 |
| 1955 | 676 | ... | 21 | 2 |
| 1956 | 682 | ... | 22 | 2 |
| 1957 | 686 | ... | 22 | 3 |
| 1958 | 698 | ... | 23 | 3 |
| 1959 | 711 | ... | 22 | 3 |

*Interview with Louise Look, June 7, 1978.
†Interview with Darlene Wong, June 12, 1978.
‡Interview with Victor Rossi, former vice principal of Jean Parker, April 20, 1979.
#Dust jacket to *China Gold* by Theresa A. Sparks (Fresno, Calif.: Academy Library Guild, 1954), a biography of the family of Alice Fong, Commodore Stockton's first Chinese American teacher. Sparks was a former teacher at Jean Parker School.

chance we were hired, the initial assignment would likely be in a tough situation; so most of my friends didn't bother to apply in San Francisco. Also, I have several teacher friends who are very fantastic, creative teachers, who started out working in this city school district but are now teaching in other districts. This kind of talent was lost in San Francisco because it was not a supportive system. You had to either prove yourself to be tough by surviving in your assignment or you resigned. The downtown office didn't care whether you survived or not. This was especially true for minority teachers. The better schools in San Francisco like in the Avenues (Richmond and Sunset districts) had very few, if any, minority teachers. We knew when we were hired where we were likely to end up. This was something that we expected. I feel the fact that I was a minority had something to do with my being placed at a real tough school. As for

## TABLE 7
### Washington Irving School Data, 1939–1959

| Year | Enrollment | Percentage of Chinese Students | Total Number of Teachers | Number of Chinese Teachers |
|------|-----------|-------------------------------|--------------------------|----------------------------|
| 1939 | 581 | ... | 22 | 0 |
| 1940 | 559 | ... | 22 | 0 |
| 1941 | 507 | ... | 22 | 0 |
| 1942 | 421 | ... | 20 | 0 |
| 1943 | 340 | 25* | 19 | 0 |
| 1944 | 293 | ... | 16 | 0 |
| 1945 | 268 | ... | 12 | 0 |
| 1946 | 272 | ... | 11 | 0 |
| 1947 | 358 | ... | 14 | 0 |
| 1948 | 454 | ... | 18 | 0 |
| 1949 | 428 | 45† | 17 | 1 |
| 1950 | 377 | ... | 17 | 1 |
| 1951 | 368 | 50‡ | 11 | 0 |
| 1952 | 262 | ... | 11 | 0 |
| 1953 | 247 | ... | 11 | 0 |
| 1954 | 218 | ... | 12 | 1 |
| 1955 | 357 | ... | 13 | 1 |
| 1956 | 412 | ... | 14 | 1 |
| 1957 | 513 | ... | 15 | 1 |
| 1958 | 487 | 80# | 16 | 1 |
| 1959 | ... | ... | 16 | 1 |

*Interview with Rosemary Chan, May 9, 1979.
†Interview with Victor Rossi, former vice principal of Washington Irving, April 20, 1979.
‡Interview with Caesar Orsini, former teacher at Washington Irving as well as former principal of Commodore Stockton, May 24, 1978.
#Interview with Marian Hom, March 5, 1980.

my initial teaching experience—after days of coming home in tears and sheer frustration—I finally sat down and said, "I'm not going to let a bunch of kids push me around after working this hard." That determination was the only thing that kept me going. It was just sheer stubbornness on my part to want to stay and develop my teaching skills. I stayed at that tough school for three years. By the time I left that school for Chinatown, I knew that I could control a classroom of children but I didn't necessarily know whether I could teach a regular curriculum since most of the students I had worked with could not read well enough to do grade level work.

THIS NEXT SECTION explores the perceptions of Chinese American teachers by those in the educational profession—teacher training institutions, master teachers, interviewing panels, school administrators, central office personnel, etc., during the 1940s and 1950s. In all, 42 Chinese American teachers were contacted, with 31 granting interviews and 18 giving permission to

## TABLE 8
### Spring Valley School Data, 1939–1959

| Year | Enrollment | Percentage of Chinese Students | Total Number of Teachers | Number of Chinese Teachers |
|------|-----------|-------------------------------|-------------------------|---------------------------|
| 1939 | 329 | ... | 13 | 0 |
| 1940 | 293 | ... | 12 | 0 |
| 1941 | 285 | ... | 12 | 0 |
| 1942 | 269 | ... | 11 | 0 |
| 1943 | 247 | ... | 10 | 0 |
| 1944 | 239 | ... | 10 | 0 |
| 1945 | 283 | ... | 10 | 0 |
| 1946 | 265 | ... | 8 | 0 |
| 1947 | 274 | ... | 8 | 0 |
| 1948 | 275 | ... | 8 | 0 |
| 1949 | 297 | ... | 10 | 0 |
| 1950 | 343 | ... | 9 | 0 |
| 1951 | 347 | ... | 12 | 0 |
| 1952 | 386 | ... | 13 | 0 |
| 1953 | 446 | ... | 16 | 0 |
| 1954 | 398 | ... | 18 | 0 |
| 1955 | 661 | ... | 23 | 0 |
| 1956 | 778 | ... | 24 | .5† |
| 1957 | 777 | 100* | 26 | 0 |
| 1958 | 753 | ... | 24 | 0 |
| 1959 | 786 | ... | 25 | 0 |

*Interview with Sandra Gin, June 16, 1978.
†Bernice Chin served at this school from March 15, 1956, to the end of the school term.

review their personnel files.[99] From these 18 teachers, as well as records of the 27 teachers who were hired before 1960 but left the San Francisco school system, came the following information as to how Chinese American teachers were perceived by the educational system. The information is divided into seven categories, with those perceptions mentioned most often listed first. Names of commentators and reviewers are not mentioned in order to protect the confidentiality of the files.

## 1. Cooperation

AS A GROUP, the 45 Chinese American teachers were consistently viewed as cooperative. Nearly three-fourths of the remarks showed that they were more than cooperative:

She is cheerful, cooperative to the end and always dependable.

—*Master teacher, 1945*

### TABLE 9
### Garfield School Data, 1939–1959

| Year | Enrollment | Percentage of Chinese Students | Total Number of Teachers | Number of Chinese Teachers |
|---|---|---|---|---|
| 1939 | 385 | ... | 15 | 0 |
| 1940 | 375 | ... | 16 | 0 |
| 1941 | 347 | ... | 13 | 0 |
| 1942 | 315 | ... | 13 | 0 |
| 1943 | 305 | ... | 14 | 0 |
| 1944 | 302 | ... | 16 | 0 |
| 1945 | 382 | ... | 15 | 0 |
| 1946 | 360 | ... | 13 | 0 |
| 1947 | 375 | ... | 15 | 0 |
| 1948 | 412 | ... | 12 | 0 |
| 1949 | 350 | ... | 13 | 0 |
| 1950 | 309 | ... | 12 | 0 |
| 1951 | 322 | ... | 12 | 0 |
| 1952 | 297 | ... | 11 | 0 |
| 1953 | 313 | ... | 11 | 0 |
| 1954 | 268 | ... | 14 | 1 |
| 1955 | 498 | ... | 16 | 1 |
| 1956 | 549 | ... | 17 | 1 |
| 1957 | 521 | over 50* | 17 | 2 |
| 1958 | 535 | ... | 18 | 1 |
| 1959 | 576 | 80–90† | 19 | 1 |

* Interview with Peggy Wing, June 17, 1978.
† Interview with May Louie, May 14, 1979.

Enthusiastic cooperation.
*—Principal, 1949*

She is alert to any suggestions... and is cooperative and painstaking.
*—Department chairman, 1952*

His dependability at all times had made him one of the principal's loyal helpers.
*—Principal, 1953*

For the first two weeks... she conducted her class in the cramped quarters of our library. She never complained...
*—Principal, date not indicated*

Cooperative... always willing to assume more than her share.
*—Principal, 1958*

One possible explanation for the malleability of Chinese American teachers employed by the school district is their small numbers. Since no substantial hiring of Chinese American teachers occurred until the late 1950s, those already hired had to "toe

## TABLE 10
### Redding School Data, 1939–1959

| Year | Enrollment | Percentage of Chinese Students | Total Number of Teachers | Number of Chinese Teachers |
|------|-----------|-------------------------------|--------------------------|----------------------------|
| 1939 | 359 | ... | 14 | 0 |
| 1940 | 345 | ... | 13 | 0 |
| 1941 | 401 | ... | 13 | 0 |
| 1942 | 492 | ... | 16 | 0 |
| 1943 | 471 | ... | 18 | 0 |
| 1944 | 297 | ... | 12 | 0 |
| 1945 | 359 | ... | 11 | 0 |
| 1946 | 396 | ... | 12 | 0 |
| 1947 | 399 | ... | 13 | 0 |
| 1948 | 409 | ... | 13 | 0 |
| 1949 | 393 | ... | 14 | 0 |
| 1950 | 384 | ... | 13 | 0 |
| 1951 | 379 | ... | 13 | 1 |
| 1952 | 425 | ... | 15 | 0 |
| 1953 | 433 | 35* | 15 | 1 |
| 1954 | 347 | ... | 15 | 1 |
| 1955 | 424 | ... | 13 | 1 |
| 1956 | 408 | 50* | 14 | 1 |
| 1957 | 462 | ... | 15 | 1 |
| 1958 | 520 | ... | 16 | 2 |
| 1959 | 515 | ... | 16 | 2 |

*Interview with Agnes Chan, May 31 1979

the line" in order to keep their jobs. The older ones who were employed were often, for self-protection, driven to prevent the younger ones from entering the field of teaching:

In the early '50s, when the pay was about $2,700 a year—thank goodness things were cheaper then—I remember I needed a part-time job to help make ends meet. I spoke to the principals of the Evening Division [Community College and the Unified School District were one district then] in Chinatown—Galileo, Marina, Pacific Heights—very discouraging. One principal asked me to talk to Suey Ng, who was teaching night school at Commodore Stockton. He had about fifty students in his class. I think, like today, a teacher wants a big class, so that if some drop out, he would still have enough to maintain his job. Anyway, I called Suey, and I remember well his reply to my inquiry about the chances of getting in as a night school teacher. "Don't come to visit my class... What are you trying to do?

### TABLE 11
### Hancock School Data, 1939–1959

| Year | Enrollment | Percentage of Chinese Students | Total Number of Teachers | Number of Chinese Teachers |
|------|-----------|-------------------------------|-------------------------|---------------------------|
| 1939 | 331 | ... | 14 | 0 |
| 1940 | 334 | ... | 14 | 0 |
| 1941 | 243 | ... | 13 | 0 |
| 1942 | 223 | ... | 13 | 0 |
| 1943 | 220 | ... | 13 | 0 |
| 1944 | 229 | ... | 12 | 0 |
| 1945 | 194 | ... | 12 | 0 |
| 1946 | 109 | ... | 12 | 0 |
| 1947 | 116 | ... | 12 | 0 |
| 1948 | 187 | ... | 10 | 0 |
| 1949 | 173 | ... | 10 | 0 |
| 1950 | 197 | ... | 9 | 0 |
| 1951 | 201 | ... | 9 | 0 |
| 1952 | 187 | ... | 9 | 0 |
| 1953 | 221 | ... | 12 | 0 |
| 1954 | 210 | ... | 11 | 0 |
| 1955 | 221 | 25* | 13 | 0 |
| 1956 | 273 | ... | 15 | 0 |
| 1957 | 350 | ... | 15 | 0 |
| 1958 | 387 | ... | 15 | 0 |
| 1959 | 415 | ... | 16 | 0 |

*Interview with Victor Rossi, former principal of Hancock School, April 20, 1979.

You know how hard it is for a Chinese to get into the system. If we divide up my class, soon nobody will have a job." Later I did get in as registrar in the evening at Commodore Stockton.

*—Wellington Chew*[100]

## 2. Conscientious and Hard-Working

Closely linked with cooperation was the perception that Chinese teachers were conscientious and hard-working. Sixty-four percent of the Chinese American teachers were perceived this way:

Far beyond the usual expectations.          *—Master teacher, 1951*

...willingness to work hard and to be guided.

*—Department chairman, 1952*

I have never had a student who did as much as she has...

*—Master teacher, 1954*

### TABLE 12
### Sarah B. Cooper School Data, 1939–1959

| Year | Enrollment | Percentage of Chinese Students | Total Number of Teachers | Number of Chinese Teachers |
|------|-----------|-------------------------------|--------------------------|----------------------------|
| 1939 | 224 | ... | 10 | 0 |
| 1940 | 181 | ... | 10 | 0 |
| 1941 | 213 | ... | 10 | 0 |
| 1942 | 195 | ... | 10 | 0 |
| 1943 | 179 | ... | 9 | 0 |
| 1944 | 155 | ... | 9 | 0 |
| 1945 | 237 | ... | 11 | 0 |
| 1946 | 261 | ... | 9 | 0 |
| 1947 | 259 | ... | 9 | 0 |
| 1948 | 301 | ... | 9 | 0 |
| 1949 | 280 | ... | 10 | 0 |
| 1950 | 251 | ... | 9 | 0 |
| 1951 | 255 | ... | 9 | 0 |
| 1952 | 259 | ... | 10 | 0 |
| 1953 | 350 | ... | 11 | 0 |
| 1954 | 245 | ... | 12 | 0 |
| 1955 | 451 | 25* | 13 | 1 |
| 1956 | 437 | ... | 13 | 1 |
| 1957 | 415 | ... | 12 | 3 |
| 1958 | 432 | ... | 13 | 2 |
| 1959 | 412 | ... | 13 | 2 |

*Interview with Victor Rossi, former principal of Sarah B. Cooper School, April 20, 1979.

She made the highest score in her class. She was never tardy and had a perfect attendance record.
*—Instructor in education, 1956*

Most conscientious, working innumerable hours in planning her room environment and class program.
*—Principal, 1958*

A few comments provided clues that perhaps their conscientiousness was not task-oriented but approval-oriented:

Most conscientious of our student teachers... extremely anxious to please.
*—Supervisor, 1950*

Anxious to please, gives long and extra hours to her tasks, painstaking in her plans and works diligently.
*—Master teacher, 1951*

...seeks criticism but also seeks reassurance.
*—Supervisor of student teaching, 1955*

## TABLE 13
### Sherman School Data, 1939–1959

| Year | Enrollment | Percentage of Chinese Students | Total Number of Teachers | Number of Chinese Teachers |
|------|-----------|-------------------------------|--------------------------|----------------------------|
| 1939 | 382 | ... | 18 | 0 |
| 1940 | 368 | ... | 17 | 0 |
| 1941 | 410 | ... | 18 | 0 |
| 1942 | 424 | ... | 17 | 0 |
| 1943 | 366 | ... | 17 | 0 |
| 1944 | 320 | ... | 18 | 0 |
| 1945 | 380 | ... | 15 | 0 |
| 1946 | 363 | ... | 14 | 0 |
| 1947 | 366 | ... | 15 | 0 |
| 1948 | 401 | ... | 14 | 0 |
| 1949 | 377 | ... | 15 | 0 |
| 1950 | 379 | ... | 14 | 0 |
| 1951 | 377 | ... | 13 | 0 |
| 1952 | 333 | ... | 13 | 0 |
| 1953 | 351 | ... | 14 | 0 |
| 1954 | 334 | ... | 16 | 1 |
| 1955 | 446 | ... | 20 | 0 |
| 1956 | 580 | ... | 23 | 0 |
| 1957 | 539 | ... | 21 | 0 |
| 1958 | 665 | 20* | 26 | 0 |
| 1959 | 830 | ... | 29 | 0 |

*Interview with Franklin Hom, March 5, 1980.

## 3. Quiet

Sixty-two percent of the Chinese American teachers were perceived to be quiet by their evaluators. This characteristic was linked to their personalities as well as to good classroom management.

He delivers the goods all the time, quietly and effectively.
*—Principal, 1945*

...quiet and unpretentious demeanor. *—Teacher, 1953*

But the quietness was more often linked to being reserved than to possessing confidence. The quality of being silent was seen as getting in the way of positive action. Note the following comments:

Rather reserved questioning manner. *—Principal, 1956*

She was a quiet and diligent student, one really never gets to know, whose grade mark was good, but is ever in the background of the class. *—Assistant professor of education, 1956*

Unlike so many Orientals, she has sparkle and personality.
*—Master teacher, 1957*

In group situations she takes an active part rather than being passive which is characteristic of many of our Oriental students.
*—Director of supervised teaching, 1957*

She has a pleasant personality but needs to show more animation and initiative. *—Principal, 1958*

His quiet, unobtrusive manner belies his ability and possibilities.
*—Colleague, no date.*

## 4. English Language Deficiency

Information is not known on the rejection rate due to "language deficiencies" of Chinese American students wanting to major in education or of Chinese American graduates with teaching credentials wanting to teach in San Francisco. However, speech courses were required of Chinese American students at San Francisco State College (now University) majoring in elementary education, because they spoke English with a Chinese accent. Indeed, information from the personnel files indicates that there were two major hurdles or screening processes for Chinese Americans who wanted to become elementary school teachers—

one was the university's oral screening procedures and the other was the oral interviews for teacher applicants conducted by the San Francisco school district. The number of Chinese American candidates turned down by these two procedures could not be determined. Of those who were accepted, 37 percent had remarks made regarding their speech. Comments from these two institutional sources are seen below:

### From the teacher-training institutions:

...speaks both English and Cantonese. There remains some speech mannerisms as well as gestures which suggest another time and culture. In some situations I can see that these characteristics might be of some disadvantage to him.

*—Supervisor, 1955*

His speech difficulty, due to his Oriental background will, I feel, be overcome. He is conscious of this defect and desirous of greater perfection.

*—Principal, 1955*

...should be placed in a school where she will not feel at a disadvantage because of her bilingual Oriental background.

*—Supervisor, 1955*

She is a vivacious, alert, intelligent young woman with no trace of foreign accent.

*—Assistant professor, 1956*

State College asked her to work on her speech which is a bit inclined to be "sing-song." This, I believe, she was trying to improve in the speech clinic.... However her speech pattern may be one that cannot be improved.

*—Dean, 1959*

### From the school district's interviewing panels:

...very slight accent, weak expression, indistinct, slurring....

*—Interviewing panel, 1952*

...definite accent, voice monotonous, nondescript pronunciation.

*—Central office supervisor, 1952*

Language handicap, poor enunciation and pronunciation, definite or slight accent, weak expression.

*—Interviewing panel, 1956*

Once over these two hurdles, the candidates were accepted into the teaching profession. Rarely were they subjected to further language scrutiny. This, however, was not true for the first Chinese American teachers who taught outside of Chinatown.

Not particularly suited to this district on account of language difficulty.

*—Principal, 1944*

Alta Harris who was the district's supervisor in 1942 came along to observe me during my second semester as a long term substitute in a 100% all-white school. It was an unannounced visitation. Mrs. Harris arrived prim, proper, and fashionably attired. She sat in the back of my third grade classroom which served as a science lab previously. Nothing escaped the observant vision nor auditory system of Alta Harris. She gave me a beautiful evaluation. Everything was excellent except for the overcoming of my foreign language accent in my speech. That suggestion left me most sensitive about my speech pattern and accent. From thereon I became very self-conscious when I made any oral expression. Of course, after so many years and near retirement, I established self-confidence and had this "licked."

—*Nora Lim, 1978 interview*

I took a sabbatical leave[101] sometime after I was at Le Conte School. When I reported to the school board at the end of my sabbatical for my coming assignment, the assistant superintendent asked me what was my choice of school. I said I'd like to teach in Chinatown as I have not had the opportunity to do so and I feel I can really help the children there. Well, the answer from the superintendent was, "No, I don't think you should go back to Chinatown because being born and raised there... you all have that Chinatown accent. We don't want you to teach the children there and perpetuate that kind of English." I thought to myself, "Gee, do I really speak with such a noticeable accent?"

—*Rosemary Chan, 1978 interview*

One final remark needs to be made regarding English language deficiencies. Although the evidence was found in only one instance, there may very well be a relationship between being quiet and one's degree of English fluency, as one's way of getting into the teaching profession—particularly for Chinese Americans who were born and/or raised in San Francisco's Chinatown. This can be seen in the following comment:

... hesitancy in participating in class discussions. She rarely if ever contributed. It wasn't until well along in the semester that I realized that she has a speech difficulty which may in part explain her reluctance to participate.

—*Associate professor, 1957*

### 5. Ethnicity

Thirty-one percent of the comments dealt with their ethnicity. Although there were more females than males in the school district, comments about the men's ethnicity were more frequent than those about women:

... should be retained here because of his race in this school of predominantly Chinese.

—*Principal, 1949*

May I also say that since he is of the Oriental race, there would be no finer person that I know anywhere who can, by his very presence, represent the finest ideals of American democracy in any community.
— *Counselor, 1951*

He is a perfect example of the "American Dream," the boy who, against all odds has made something of himself. His family was poor: he had to postpone education in order to support his mother, brothers, and sisters. Many of his stories dealt with the conflict between the ancient Chinese work of his home and the new American world of which he wished to become a part.
— *University professor, 1953*

He...is of Chinese extraction and finds no difficulty in handling normal secondary Physical Education classes.
— *Professor, 1957*

Significantly, some of the ethnic comments alluded to the practice of racial discrimination by the educational profession:

I feel convinced that he will succeed in any school situation where an intelligent, cooperative American-born Chinese is acceptable.
— *Position unstated, 1951*

I believe she will be a very good teacher. Any school administrator who has the courage to depart from the Caucasion tradition will be well rewarded.
— *Assistant professor, 1951*

He has a personality and manner somewhat different from that of the many people of his race whom I have known (I refer to the students). Not only is he of a somewhat larger build than the average, but he has a friendly, natural smile and manner much more Occidental than Oriental. I mention this because I do not know whether or not this question might arise in connection with placement. This man would fit into any school system.
— *University professor, 1952*

## 6. Culture

Twenty-eight percent of the comments dealt with this aspect. As Chinese American male teachers were perceived as "ethnics," Chinese American female teachers were perceived to possess culture. Culture as defined by the comments seemed to indicate a person of refinement, a good upbringing, discriminating taste, and a dedication to the art of teaching. There were no indications from the comments that culture had any implications of stereotyping Chinese American female teachers or that it carried negative connotations.

In only one case was their ethnicity noted: "The applicant is a cultured Chinese gentle woman" (director, 1940). Also in only one case was culture perceived as related to a given group of people and that it had potential educational value in a pluralistic society: "...she brings to teaching a rich Chinese cultural background. She should make a real contribution to inter-racial relations" (supervisor, 1956).

## 7. Interpreters of Americanism

Very few (only six percent), but significant comments were made regarding the teaching role of Chinese Americans at the secondary level. The Americanization program was developed by the school district for "language-handicapped" youngsters. With a steady influx of Chinese immigrant students to the secondary schools (Francisco Junior High and Galileo High), Chinese American teachers were assigned to these schools to help the newcomers adapt. For example, one principal in 1952 commented upon a Chinese American teacher as follows: "He has done much to adjust our students, recently from China, into the American school system."

Chinese American teachers in the Americanization program were perceived as a positive force by providing a smooth transition for the Chinese-speaking students. A principal in 1950 said a Chinese American teacher was "exceptional in the interpretation of American ideals." Another principal commented in 1957 that another teacher had "an enthusiastic influence in developing American ideals."

But Chinese American teachers also had a negative influence. They helped perpetuate a system unresponsive to the needs of culturally different students. It was the students who had to do the adapting and not the school system. For example, principals in 1951 and 1955, respectively, cited Chinese American teachers for being "very helpful in 'breaking in' new students from China in our junior Americanization groups" and getting students "to advance into regular groups."

LET US NOW EXAMINE the teachers' responses when interviewed about their most unforgettable experience in entering into the teaching profession. Mentioned most often in this respect were linguistic and racial discrimination. Over fifty percent of the respondents mentioned each of these two aspects.

### Discrimination by Language

Of the teachers who cited English language requirements, a little over fifty percent pointed to the school district and the others mentioned the teacher training institutions as the obstacles to their careers. The following are some of the comments made in the interviews with this writer:

I talked to a lot of people who couldn't get into San Francisco and had their teaching credentials. Couldn't remember their names or how many—just a vague impression. The question they always asked them was "Don't you have an accent? You're Chinese." You're Chinese per se, you have an accent even before you open your mouth. They asked candidates what you are doing about your speech. Are you taking any speech class? Very demeaning, condescending kind of a question. Maybe a great deal has to do with people in power. In those days the supervisor had a great deal of power—like Hogan, Harris and all those. They did the interview and they decided who will be hired. If they were unconsciously prejudiced, very few minorities could get in. This is over-generalizing it but you have to be Catholic, you have to be white and then you're in the majority. They sort of controlled the jobs in those days.

—*Wellington Chew*

I graduated from Cal with a teaching credential but then I got married. After my children were in school I went back to State to get some units because my credential had lapsed. That's where I met prejudice a lot more than Cal. After being a housewife for five years and with a credential already, I had this very traumatic experience. I was told by this professor in the Education Department that I would never pass to get my credential: and even if I passed, my language would keep me back. I needed speech courses and if I passed that, I would never be hired because I am an Asian. He said that to me in the presence of another professor. The other professor looked a little embarrassed. He did not say anything in defense. I was really devastated. I went ahead anyway. I needed to get my credential to get back to work.

—*Mildred Hom*

The panel members sit real close to you, eyeball to eyeball you know. They ask you different questions and they want to hear your accent. That's what they're looking for and it makes you more nervous and your accent would come out. That's what they want to hear, they'll get it.

—*Susan Chang*

At one point in time I had to take an oral exam at State College. I don't remember but I think they were screening for the speech lab or something. And I always remembered this one comment, "You don't have an accent." They said it with such a surprise that I thought, "Gee, I'm supposed to have one!" I was kind of surprised myself that I didn't have one! I didn't know I was supposed to. But .that's the only thing I remembered.

—*Roberta Lai*

I had this speech teacher at State College. I took a test and he said I had everything wrong with my speech—from not knowing how to

say the "r" as in relative, not pronouncing the end of letters, everything that you could say was wrong with the Chinese. So I took a
speech class. Nobody corrected me; but each time I took it, they
would say, "You sound like a Chinese." When it was time to take the
credential's speech test, my speech teacher said, "You will never
pass the English test; you could never pass the speech test." He not
only told me, he told most of the Chinese.... A lot of the students
went out crying because we were into our third year at State College. That really upset us.

—Anita Wing

The strict language requirement applied even to Chinese
Americans born and raised outside of San Francisco's Chinatown:

Before you were admitted into the teacher-training program you had
to take a speech test. The speech teacher there was a very prejudiced
person. In his thinking all Chinese had a speech impediment—you
know, like an accent or something like that. I was told that he had
flunked all the other Chinese who were trying to get their credentials. That was probably one of the bad things at that time at State.
Most of the Chinese could not pass the speech test to get the credential because the teacher was a very biased person....I passed the
speech test because he had to answer a phone call during my examination. By the time he returned, the other two members on the
panel had already passed me. Even if the speech teacher had examined me, I would have challenged him if he had heard any accent
because I wasn't reared here. I was reared up in Seattle with all the
Caucasians. So I didn't have this Chinese accent. No way did I have
it. In fact I can hardly speak Chinese.

—Agnes Chan

I was interviewed by three members of the staff at the downtown
office. I was told that I had a special kind of accent. I don't remember
what type of accent and where my problems were in that I didn't
speak English very clearly. They mentioned certain sounds like "r"
and I don't remember what. One of the interviewers said, "I know
Miss Low that you're trying to speak very clearly and distinctly and
you're overcoming your accent." I said yes at the time because I *was*
trying very hard to speak very clearly and distinctly. Then after the
interview I thought it over and I think what they were referring to
was they had assumed I was either an immigrant Chinese or I had
grown up in San Francisco and I have these particular kinds of accents. But they may have mistaken my mid-Western Minnesotan
accent—I don't know which. But the interview went very well. I
could tell they were very pleased.

—Lily Low

Chinese American teachers most scrutinized were those born
and/or raised in San Francisco's Chinatown. Speaking English

with a "Chinatown accent," three-fourths of those teachers interviewed mentioned criticisms of their speech pattern. The fact that many of these same teachers were also students at Commodore Stockton School elicited the following comments, which provide the study with a descriptive picture of the early education at that school:

I think I can say this, maybe I'm criticizing the system. Here I am a product of the San Francisco Unified Schools. I was very disappointed—here I went through twelve years of schooling and my English was so poor. When I say poor—sure I'm bilingual—never was I ever told that my speech for example like final *l*'s were dropped. I had to wait until I went into training as a teacher, then I started learning these skills. I was never told the third person, first person— I learned my grammar when I started taking French and Spanish or when I started teaching Chinese and ESL [English as a Second Language]. In other words, as far as the public school, I was never sat down and said, "Hey, the final *l* is like hall—not haw!" ... I had one bad experience in the second grade at Commodore. I remembered I was kept in during recess time because I couldn't pronounce a certain word. This teacher really shook the hell out of me. I couldn't even remember her name. I wasn't trying to be stubborn—I just didn't know the difference. I think she was trying to to get me to make the "th" sound. Of course in my excitement I forgot and slopped over the sound.... And when I went to Francisco—same thing—nobody ever called my speech to my attention.

*—Wilbur Woo*

They were very, very strict at Commodore. We weren't allowed to talk in the hallways, in the classrooms, and all the teachers had their very favorite students. I guess you'd call them teacher's pets. And usually these were the ones who spoke better English or probably their parents were American-born or you could even say the very bright ones.

*—Anita Wing*

We had Miss Holland as our instructor in our 5th and 6th grade at Commodore. She really did an excellent job. She knew what we lacked and she did a lot of oral reading to us and we had to do a lot more oral work with her. The other teachers, it was paper and pencil—everyone did the same thing. But she stood out in my mind.... Most of the teachers penalized us for speaking our home language. If they caught us speaking Chinese to each other, even during our recess time, we were penalized—our privilege taken away. But I imagined it was because they wanted us to use our English more. But then it was very difficult because we had no pattern or model to follow; so we had the accent. All of us were speaking the same way so how can we learn. I accepted the taking away of privileges. It's because of our upbringing more than anything else—we accepted it. In fact, as I recalled, there were no problems in the classrooms. I remember one of the teachers would just turn red and we were just as still as still can be.

*—Mildred Hom*

This emphasis upon respect and obedience toward authorities and rules rather than upon education continued throughout the 1940s when this writer was a student at Commodore Stockton. The quiet classroom implied students attentive to their studies and teachers maintaining good discipline. Memorization of facts was more important than creative thinking, and secondary language skills (reading and writing) were more important than primary language skills (listening and speaking). Consequently, Chinese American students who grew up in this environment demonstrated less initiative and less verbal fluency, and tended to be followers rather than leaders. Comments (again made in 1978 interviews) from Chinese American teachers who taught in the Chinatown schools in the late 1950s and early 1960s supported this writer's recollection:

Chinatown schools had an interesting mix of teachers. There were basically three types. First, the seasoned Chinese teachers who had supposedly proven themselves elsewhere and were then allowed to go there and teach. This group approximated 10% of the faculty. Second, there were some Caucasian teachers who were on their third assignment and if they couldn't make it in Chinatown, they couldn't make it anywhere. Third, old-timers that started out there in the beginning and never left until retirement. This group constituted almost half the faculty.... The one lingering feeling I had after having taught the kids in Chinatown—the one thing I probably have to be thankful for—is that I was fortunate I wasn't brought up and educated in Chinatown. The educational climate was—it might not be true now because many of the older teachers having retired—one which knocked into you the sense of obedience. I don't think you can develop leadership qualities if you insist on obedience from your students. Initiative and leadership traits were knocked out of them when teacher after teacher expected the students to be quiet and do what was told. You can't develop free thinking or creative thinking if you're going to expect students to answer, to obey without thinking everything you want them to do. This attitude was really prevalent in the Chinatown schools since all the Chinatown schools had a large number of teachers who had taught mainly Chinese students for many years. There were too many teachers making kids obey, treating kids as though they had no ability to think. That was the problem in Chinatown and the teachers got away with it since the Chinese students would never defy their elders nor their teachers.

*—Sandra Gin*

At my years in a Chinatown school, I think that the children were not being capitalized upon and developed to their fullest potential. They were thought of as being "Chinese" and not Americans. There should have been a stress on fostering competitive spirit, high expectancy in level of attainment, leadership development, etc. The academics were pursued and the children were kept happy, busy and quiet by many fine teachers. The system doesn't encourage the development of Chinese as individuals who can stand on their feet and speak out on issues of vital concern.

— *Patricia Lum*

## Discrimination by Race

A little over half of those interviewed said they experienced racial discrimination. The school district and teacher training institutions were faulted equally. The interviews tell the whole story:

I graduated from State College in 1942–43 and couldn't get a job as a teacher. There were no jobs. I was going to pay five dollars to the Teacher Placement Bureau but they said to me offhandedly, "There's no job for a Chinese in California. Why don't you go to Hawaii?" I said, "Hell, why should I give you $5.00 for something like that. I'll save my five bucks." That was during the wartime. . . . How else can I feel? How else would anybody feel? You go through five years of school to learn a profession. See, in my time, the idea is there's nothing you can do about it. They tell you that—you just take it and that's it. You don't say, "I'm going to defend my Constitutional rights." There's no rights for you to demand. Well, the next best thing was that, during wartime anyway, if you don't get into some kind of wartime activity, you'll be drafted. So I applied and got a job as an electrician's helper. . . . I didn't expect that [discrimination]. I thought, at this day and age, it's 1940 you know. You never look and say is it going to be discriminatory. Naturally I've known people that graduated in earlier times and they came out as engineers and they ended up as waiters and laundry workers. In a way you're sort of conditioned to that, and yet you hope the thing could change. Things didn't change until after World War II. Later on when in the '50s and '60s you had the Civil Rights and all this jazz-ma-tazz. Before that a lot of you guys used to say, "Oh Mr. Kim, boy, you sure had it easy then." What the hell, I had to fight my way to get into the damn thing. . . . After I worked over at the Naval Supply Depot for a year, I said to myself, "I'm not getting anywhere, I'm just a helper here. I'm doing the work of the other guy. What the hell, I might as well get out and see." Then I applied in San Francisco [to teach]. I never went outside [of San Francisco] to apply because I knew very well that all the jobs were frozen during that time. There was no hiring. In fact when I got on I was hired to replace somebody who had to go into the military service. The first thing I went down to Civic Auditorium [old site of the administrative office] and applied to see if there was any teaching job. I went to see the superintendent in charge of personnel. He sent me out to Denman. I had an interview with the principal there. Dierke was vice principal there. Dierke said, "I don't care what you are. I want a P.E. [physical education] teacher." But then the principal talked to me and right away I knew he wasn't interested. You say how do you know? You don't have to know. You know by the way they talk to you—you understand what I mean? I'm not bringing out stories. I'm telling you these are true facts. So the guy says, "You go back and see the superintendent of personnel." Right then and there I know he's writing me off. I'm a P.E. man, but I'm a P.E. man with a yellow face. I don't care about that. They don't want me, there's nothing you can do. So I went back to the superintendent of personnel and he sent me over to Francisco and that's where I started—November 8, 1943. I started as a long-term sub until August 1946 when I got appointed.  —*Tommy Kim*

During my senior year, I went to apply in the Teacher Placement Office and they said, "Now Miss Chan, you realize you are not going to have much of a chance getting a job teaching in the San Francisco schools." I said, "Gee, how come you're telling me now! That should have been brought to my attention in my junior year. At least I could have made a switch in my major." Then they said, "Well, you always have the opportunity of going back to teach your own people—you know, back in China." Well, that was in 1942. We were already in a war; China has been fighting ever since 1937. This was *crazy*. I was really pretty burned up. I said to myself, "Since I'm already a senior I might as well finish up and take my chances." The funny thing was that my mother was working in the shipyard at that time. She didn't speak much English but she was bringing money home. It was almost at the end of August when I was notified by the school board to report to Washington Irving School as a long-term substitute teacher. I remembered my first check was $90 and my mother was bringing home twice that much if not three times that much from the shipyard. She used to laugh at me and said, "You went through college all these years and you're bringing home $90?" I was almost tempted to quit teaching and go to work in the shipyard. I remained in teaching because I enjoyed teaching and working with the children; also, the principal was very nice and helpful.
  —*Rosemary Chan*

I was put in student teaching in Berkeley under this professor of education at UC. He was a very competent teacher at Oakland Tech as well as a part-time professor at Berkeley. For some reason, he chose to be my master teacher. I was to teach geometry under him. I did the best I could. Once in a while, because he was watching me like a hawk, I would hesitate or possibly grope for an idea. He'd jump up and correct me right in front of all those kids on some technicality in geometry. He did this a couple of times so you know how that must have gone across with the kids. By the end of the semester, I realized I'm going to have to get out from under his supervision if I'm going to survive this. So I requested a junior high school placement. I got placed in Berkeley under this very nice supportive teacher from whom I received a high rating. However the professor gave me a low rating which meant I could not apply to teach in Berkeley. When I was assured that I would receive my California teaching credential, I went and told the professor how I felt. I said to him, "I've done my student teaching under you. I have compared my notes with every other student in the department and my notebooks have been more extensive and more complete. You have embarrassed me in front of the class by correcting me and I do not consider that a good teaching method. Furthermore, you rated me low and I feel that I have done as well or better than any other person in student teaching this semester. I cannot now apply in Berkeley and I feel that this is based on prejudice." He just looked at me and didn't say a thing—just kind of surprised. Then the following semester I took another course from him because he was the only one who taught it. He gave me an A.

—Jannie Wu

In those days, people were afraid of the exams. So some people didn't even bother; they just went outside of the school district. But I could tell you before I got the city job, I had applied all over—Marin, San Jose, San Mateo—I never heard from some of those districts. And I'm sure I know why—with the last name of Wong.

—Helen Wong Lum

After you passed a certain score on the National Teachers Exam you were admitted to a committee interview. I felt very good in that interview because of a remark made by one of the panel members— a Miss Bell from Polytechnic High School. She said, "If you were available right now Mr. Lum, I would have you out at my school." I recalled going home and telling my wife about that; and my wife, who had graduated from Poly, said, "That was Edith Bell that you're talking about. She's the head of the English Department and one of the power-houses in the city. I believe she's related to the National Geographic Bell family as well too." I said, "If she took me at Poly tomorrow I think I would go over despite any reputation Poly may have. You stay with somebody who wants you." Interestingly enough, when the list was posted, I was number three on the English list. I felt really good about that because I knew practically everybody else on a list of about 57 to 60 names of people I have gone to school with and knew from different places. I called downtown to find out where would I be placed now that I was number three. And rather interestingly a few days after that, I had gotten a form letter— it was a mimeographed letter—from the district's Personnel Depart-

ment stating very simply that because a previous English and Social Studies list—they combined the two or they mentioned the two—had not been exhausted, I should not place any great hopes in getting a position that particular fall. I said all right—the hell with you. I am not going to bother with San Francisco. I had an offer from a Southern California district which was very, very tempting.... I decided to take that position and I informed the school district that I would be requesting a year's leave of absence for contract purposes. At that time the district automatically granted you such a leave of absence. When I was down in Southern California I got a special delivery letter one day that stated that I had been appointed by board action to Continuation High School. So I wrote back to the Personnel Director and said that I didn't feel that I was particularly suited to teach in a Continuation High School. I thought that placing high on a list like that would get me a school other than Continuation. I got a good exchange of letters going with him. In fact the first letter that came back from Ward Nichols (Personnel Director) was an offer for a position at Galileo High School. I kind of smiled to myself because I thought I was being stereotyped almost immediately—that I would be sent to a school with a predominantly Chinese population. So I wrote back that I had some hesitation about going to Galileo. I said as a matter of fact there are a number of people there—number of students there—whom I knew on a first name basis. The gap between my age then 25 years ago and the kids who were still in school wasn't that great. And I said for many reasons I just didn't think Galileo was suited to me. Then I got a strange letter back from Nichols saying he was perplexed as to my way of looking at it. He said why don't I list for him three schools that I would like to teach in and he would see what he could do about it. Well the three schools I had listed included number one, Polytechnic because of Edith Bell—my old stay-with-a-winner theory; number two, I put in Lowell because that's where I had done my student teaching experience; and the third one I was stumped. I was stumped because I didn't know all of the schools in San Francisco. I didn't realize that Balboa was this kind of a school and so forth. So I decided to jot down the name of Abraham Lincoln High School. To be frank with you, at that time I did not know where Abraham Lincoln was located. Ward Nichols wrote back again and said fine—the next time you're in the city, drop by and we'll have a talk and we'll see what we can do. I believe it was at Christmas time when we came up for a visit and I did drop by to see him. I was appointed to Abraham Lincoln.
— *Philip Albert Lum*

On one of my teaching assignments I was under an administrator who demonstrated discrimination against minorities and non-Catholics. I was never spoken to but always reprimanded to the point of tears. I was caused deep anxieties and a loss of personal worth as a human being. At the close of the school year I went down to Personnel and asked to be reassigned. The administrator gave me a satisfactory evaluation report in all areas for both semesters. This led me to conclude that I was being harassed to ask for a transfer. If I was unsatisfactory as a teacher, then it should have been documented in writing.

—*Patricia Lum*

The above interviews coupled with the information in the tables on Chinatown schools lead to the conclusion that Chinese American teachers had to cope with the discrimination of at least two bureaucracies—the teacher training institutions and the school district.

Chinese American teachers thought to have accents were judged unqualified to teach English-speaking children. Many were accepted into the school district only because of the growing numbers of Chinese-speaking children in the Chinatown schools. In the late 1950s, Chinese American teachers had to prove they were tough teachers before they would be "rewarded" with a Chinatown school assignment, provided that the quota at these schools hadn't been reached. Moreover, it meant that the few Chinese American teachers already in the Chinatown schools had to conform to the established rule of the day. Creative ideas in the classroom could mean a poor evaluation report, a transfer of assignment, or dismissal.

The majority of the teaching staff in the Chinatown schools was white. Chinese American students during this period were taught by old-timers set in their culturally biased ways and by ineffective teachers shunted to their assignment of last resort. The white teaching staff in the Chinatown schools failed to improve significantly the English-speaking ability of many of these Chinese American students. The practice of stressing reading and writing skills rather than verbal skills plagued those students who later sought to become teachers. It can never be determined how many prospective Chinese American teachers had their ambitions stifled by public schooling in the Chinatown schools. The number of Chinese American teachers up to 1959 in the San Francisco system would have been fewer if it had not been for Chinese American job seekers outside San Francisco. Available statistics indicate that 45 percent of all Chinese American teachers in San Francisco during this period came from out of town. Most pointedly, because San Francisco Chinese American teachers' aspirations were directed toward "getting into the system," they were blinded to the fact that the educational system represented only one small segment of the larger society. Consequently, in the civil rights era of the 1960s and 1970s, when teaching professionals became involved in the struggle of minorities for linguistic and cultural identity, the casualties of the movement were the "successful" Chinese American teachers who had put so much of their energies into speaking "good English" and "being an American." They consciously or unconsciously denied or suppressed their cultural heritage. The climb back to ethnic affirmation for this group of teachers was extremely bewildering, since an education that used the children's home language and culture had never been part of their public school experiences.

The three-tiered educational bureaucracies were major hurdles for Chinese Americans to overcome to get into the teaching profession. As far as can be ascertained, of the total of seventy-one teachers hired between 1926 and 1959, forty, including eleven who retired, remained with the district, twenty-seven left the district, and four died.

SOME CHINESE AMERICAN TEACHERS interviewed expressed an interest in educational administration.[102] Of the thirty-one teachers interviewed, about one-fifth mentioned this area. Many of the same obstacles that made their entry into teaching so difficult restricted them even more from administration. Cited again were racial and linguistic discrimination, indicated in the 1978 interviews.

In our days there were some discrimination in getting in [to teaching]; and so to even make it as a classroom teacher was what you might call an achievement. We were never encouraged to go into administration—perish the thought of being an administrator.
— *Wilbur Woo*

When I went for my administrative interviews, they always asked you what you think of yourself and about your racial background. The wrong answer would be, in those days, "I'm Chinese and I'm proud of it and all that." In those days, the right answer, which I always mouthed because I figured that was the right answer was, "You must think of yourself as part of the mainstream. You must never think of yourself as Chinese except when you look in the mirror and comb your hair. I'm a good American." That was the answer in those days and that was the climate in those days. In fact, they tell you that if you think of yourself as a minority, you'll never get ahead. In fact, you couldn't even get in. You've got to have a white mentality because you're a part of the system. That was my own thinking I have to admit. But let's face it, you can never be part of the white establishment.

—*Wellington Chew*

I went for a number of administrative interviews. Always came away feeling that I was just wasting my time with it. At one point, Alta Harris even told me I had a slight accent—big deal. They gave me a lot of baloney about getting the opinions of my peers. The school district has never, ever, for any administrator, found out from his peers what they felt about him. So if they don't want to give you a position, they'll just give you one kind of excuse after another.

—*Larry Lew*

Discrimination against administrative applicants continued on even into the 1960s:

To be very candid, in the late 1960s, when I was starting on my master's degree, I had a principal at a Chinatown school who felt probably that Orientals shouldn't be in administration. . . . That person so much as said that she didn't think the Orientals should be in it.

—*Rosemary Fong*

The issue of ethnicity in relationship to school administrative appointments was driven home to Chinese Americans in 1949 when two administrative appointments by Superintendent Herbert C. Clish to the Chinatown schools were held up by board members. Commissioner George W. Johns held up Rose Lagomarsino's appointment to Commodore Stockton because "several residents of Chinatown had asked him to consider the appointment of a qualified Chinese American to the vice principalship at this school."[103] And in the matter of a second appointment, Commissioner Joseph Alioto held up Victor Rossi's appointment as principal of Jean Parker–Washington Irving School. Alioto wanted to study Rossi's record and was particularly anxious to avoid appearing to push solely for the appointment of a fellow Italian.[104]

The commissioners' action angered the superintendent, who threatened to quit if politics rather than merit was the basis for appointments.[105] Two weeks later, Rossi's and Lagomarsino's appointments were approved by the board. Alioto and Johns found them to be "quite competent."[106] Johns defended his right as a board member to investigate appointments of the superintendent.[107]

Of the 71 Chinese American teachers employed in San Francisco between 1926 and 1959, only Elizabeth Hall became principal during this period. Personnel records and interviews with this pioneering school principal on October 28, 1977, and January 20, 1978, showed that her experiences were similar in substance to those faced by Chinese American teachers raised in San Francisco. There was, however, one major difference—she attended public schools outside of Chinatown. Thus, she did not share the "Chinatown accent" of Chinese American teachers who grew up there. Her personnel records showed no comments or remarks regarding her accent. On the other hand her ethnicity was noted: "The applicant is a cultured Chinese gentle woman," said a director of student teaching in 1940. One former employer mistook her ethnicity when he commented in the same year that:

Miss Hall combines the finest of both Japanese ancestral traits with learned American ones to make her the charming, gentle person she is....I hope her racial background will not hinder her progress for she is capable and deserving.

"I consider that Miss Hall, of Chinese ancestry, would be an asset to any school," said a principal in 1943.

Hall came from a traditional Chinese cultural background and her memories of those early school years in San Mateo were negative—she feared school, cried, and had nightmares about her new environment. By the time she returned to San Francisco in 1919 as a fourth grader, she had mastered English. Her parents wanted her to attend Pacific Heights School, because it was the school nearest their home. The principal refused, saying that Hall must attend the Oriental School in Chinatown. Hall's brother appealed to Superintendent Roncovieri, who granted Hall permission to attend her neighborhood school.

Hall's high school years were spent at Polytechnic High School, where she received a scholarship to enter the University of California. After two years at Cal, she transferred to San Francisco State College to obtain her A.B. degree and a teaching credential in 1931. While at San Francisco State she student taught at Jean Parker School under Rose Lagomarsino.

According to Hall, San Francisco had a moratorium on the hiring of teachers at the time of her graduation. Since she couldn't get a job with the school district, she tutored English in Chinatown, taught at a private school called Midtown Nursery, and was the head teacher at the Frederick Burk Nursery School—a student teacher training school for San Francisco State College.

She took her first teacher examination with San Francisco in

1934 or 1935, but was not notified of her standing. Although the authorities weren't usually questioned in those days, she did ask to see her test results. What she saw convinced her that she hadn't been fairly treated. In addition, she was told by the superintendent that there wasn't a need for any more Chinese teachers. She was told she would be called if the district needed another Chinese teacher at Commodore Stockton School. The feeling in those days, according to Hall, was that white teachers were essential in "Americanizing" the Chinese children.[108]

By 1940, she had again taken and passed the teacher examination. Sue Convery, then principal at Commodore Stockton School, asked Hall to join her staff in 1941, so that finally, after a wait of ten years, Hall gained entry into the San Francisco school system.

Hall taught at Commodore Stockton School for the next twelve years, with a slight break to do psychometric testing with the Bureau of Research in various city schools. Her appointment to Commodore was unique in two ways. Since her predecessors had worked part-time in the area of parent-community involvement, she was the first Chinese American teaching full-time in the classroom. Second, she was the first Chinese American teacher allowed to instruct English-speaking Chinese children, which was a first step toward the recognition that Chinese American teachers could "Americanize" Chinese American students as well as could white teachers.

Rose Lagomarsino encouraged Hall to go into administration and she returned to San Francisco State where she received her M.A. and administrative credential in 1953. In July of that year she was appointed vice principal of the Hancock–Sarah B. Cooper schools. Four years later she became principal in those two schools—the first Chinese American administrator in the San Francisco school system. (The first Chinese American male administrator was Wellington Chew, who was appointed as Chinese Bilingual Supervisor in 1967, ten years after he received his administrative credential.)

In one of the more ironic twists, Hall transferred to Spring Valley School in 1964, where she remained until her retirement in 1974. It was this very school that eighty years before had barred Chinese children.

# Completion of Commodore Stockton School

As THE YEARS WENT BY, the main building and annex of Commodore Stockton School couldn't house all the Chinese children. In 1928, the board added two rooms on top of the main building,[109] but this proved inadequate. It was at this time that the Chinese-American Citizens Alliance requested the school board to add another building to Commodore.[110] This request was postponed when the older male students of Commodore were allowed to go to nearby Washington Grammar School.[111]

By 1940, the overcrowded conditions at Commodore became unbearable, because the majority of Chinese children in San Francisco were still attending this school. The school board's response was to add bungalows to the side of the annex.[112]

The lack of space for housing the students plus the substandard condition of Commodore Stockton made it a prime target for rehabilitation when the citizens of San Francisco approved a new school bond in 1948. The Department of City Planning came out with a report on the Commodore Stockton service area.

According to the report, the present site was among the most deficient in the city in terms of total space. Prevailing standards for elementary schools provided for a minimum of 30 square feet of classroom space and from 50 to 100 square feet of playground space per pupil. Commodore's classroom space was 27 square feet per pupil. Playground space was 40 square feet per pupil.[113] The school plan originally provided for 24 classrooms, but inadequate office, storage, restroom, library, child care, and adult education facilities necessitated conversion of several classrooms to serve these needs.[114] Moreover, the annex building was poorly related to the main building and to the playgrounds, being separated from them by Washington Street, which, although it carried only neighborhood traffic, constituted a hazard to the schoolchildren and an obstacle to the efficiency of school activities.[115]

The report projected that the new school addition would be in conjunction with a new Chinatown that would be less congested and less densely populated, because the Chinese were beginning to move outside of the core area of Chinatown and their children were attending the Chinatown schools. With this in mind the city planners recommended that the main building be removed by 1965 and the space be utilized as a playground area. They also recommended that the annex building be removed by 1975 and the site be used for additional play space if needed, or otherwise be disposed of by the school district.[116]

By the time the board was ready to request the director of public works to call for bids on Commodore's new addition,[117] School Superintendent Herbert C. Clish was near retirement. He was to be replaced by Dr. Harold Spears. The soon-to-be superintendent emphasized the need to house students not only at Commodore but in the other Chinatown schools. The outstanding classroom problem in the city, he said, was the area of Chinatown. This area needed 15 to 20 new classrooms immediately. He left no doubt that this would be one of his first priorities upon taking office on July 1, 1955.[118]

Indeed, Spears had already alerted Clish two months earlier regarding the heavy increase in school enrollment not only at Commodore Stockton but the other Chinatown schools, particularly in the first three grades. In his memo, he said that as 200 to 250 sixth graders went on to junior high schools, they were being replaced by an entering kindergarten class of approximately 800 children. If this trend continued, he foresaw an increase of five to six hundred children each year. Commodore Stockton in 1955 was short four rooms, because there was a doubling of classes and teachers to handle the overload. Moreover, there were only ten classrooms available in the area, including three being used for adult classes.[119]

To handle the problem, Spears made the following suggestions:

1. Use the 10 available rooms in the neighborhood by redistricting some children and by transferring the 3 adult classes.
2. Use the auditoriums at Washington Irving, Cooper, Garfield, and Hancock Schools for classroom purposes. Those at Commodore Stockton and Jean Parker are already used to house children.
3. Transport older children by bus to out-of-neighborhood schools where space is available.[120]

In addition, he suggested that the building department take the following steps:

1. Determine if there are any auxiliary building facilities in that neighborhood that the School Department might use temporarily for classroom purposes.
2. Determine if any of the school yards could take bungalows.
3. Study the possibility of further building in the neighborhood.[121]

By the mid-1950s, the crowded conditions at the Chinatown schools extended to Francisco Junior High and Galileo High— secondary schools with large Chinese student populations. Superintendent Spears said in 1956 that Galileo High School might take over the ninth grade from Francisco Junior High by 1959 or 1960 to ease an anticipated housing problem at the lower school.[122]

As construction of the new addition to Commodore got under way, Superintendent Spears reported on the shameful condition of dozens of San Francisco school buildings. His comments of concern to this study are as follows:

1) Commodore Stockton School
   A. There are four classes in two kindergarten rooms.
   B. The auditorium has been given over to a child care center for pre-school children of working mothers. The overload has spilled over into an annex at the nearby Y.W.C.A.
   C. Each morning the third through the sixth grade students (300 students) are loaded on buses to be taken over to the less-crowded Sherman School at Union and Franklin Streets.
   D. Children spend their recess and noon periods in a roped-off alley.[123]
2) Jean Parker School
   A. Two or more classes held in one classroom.
   B. Classes are held regularly in the teachers' lounge and library.[124]

In 1957, the $790,000 Commodore Stockton addition was barely completed in time for the new semester. It had space for 200 children, a 250-capacity auditorium, and a gymnasium. Still, 120 students continued at Sherman School for six months until four more rooms were added to the new building.[125]

The additional rooms required more than six months to construct, and the project was granted an extension period of 116 days.[126] A year later, in 1957, at a cost of $108,000 the four new classrooms were opened to accommodate the 120 students who formerly had to ride buses to Sherman School. Commodore's enrollment was 1200, making it the city's largest elementary school.[127]

Another extension period of 42 calendar days was granted to the project[128] before the addition to Commodore Stockton was finally dedicated on May 22, 1958.[129] The newsworthy item for the press was the school's "charming, well-behaved children, wearing gay Oriental clothes, and singing songs with accents that were strictly San Francisco."[130]

One person who summed up the Chinese response to the Commodore Stockton addition was Doris Low Schultze, Commodore Stockton's PTA president in the late 1950s. She shared her experience with this researcher:

The school! How we got that school! The new addition—the new Commodore—I tell you—that was one big project. We used to have a thousand members in our PTA, and gee, about three to four hundred active members because we all spoke English and most of us were college graduates or had been to college. Coming back to the subject, Dr. Clish was the superintendent at the time. He said you [the parents] need a new school. His term was real short because he got a lot of threatening notes from somebody—I don't know who— we never did find out. Well, anyway, he started the ball rolling with the architect at City Hall. Oh, and then Dr. Spears too—they got us all together at a meeting. They knew we all needed the school. They took a survey that eventually we will have a lot of students. The Annex and the regular school is not enough. And they could very easily acquire all that land on Clay Street—the church and the apartments.... Then after that, they drew up plans for us and gave us the know-how on who to get to. Well, a nucleus of us haunted the district office. We tried to cut the red tape by going in there that we wanted the school. We said to them, "Get it [the school]! If not we're just going to camp here." We all practically did—the architect's office, the city planner for the school, you just name it—well, we put it on pretty thick. After all, we were born here. Why shouldn't we have the same privileges? What does race got to do with it? We just needed a school. You said we needed a school; well, go get it.— You see, the school board wanted that school site already. They couldn't do much because they couldn't speak Chinese. So they had us as the PTA do the footwork. We asked CACA and Chinese Six Companies what they thought of having another school. Alice Fong and Henry Tom were very helpful in talking to the Chinese community. Our [spoken] Chinese wasn't that good. You see, the Board might have bought the lot but they'll build the school on their own time. We wanted it right now! And Bret Harte School before had the same problem. But the Board figured that we need it more than Bret Harte. I guess we got a little more priority because we were just pretty persistent. I tell you—we wine and dine them out of our PTA funds [laughter]—we had to!...Boy, in less than a year, the school building was up. That's cutting it pretty thin! But we did get it though. In the meantime we were all bushed by then. Oh, then we got the Recreational Center too. So don't think that we haven't done anything. Our PTA was a showplace for a couple of years. People came over from Europe to come see how a group of mothers—Chinese especially—can get something like that, you know.[131]

In summary, the initial construction of Commodore Stockton School (Oriental Public School) in 1915 was the result of San Francisco's discriminatory school policy that barred the Chinese children from access to the city's public schools.[132] This separate all-Chinese school couldn't provide the necessary classroom space to house the city's Chinese children, so the much-needed annex was constructed in 1924. In the more enlightened eras of the 1940s and 1950s, there were more new arrivals from China and more Chinese American children born and raised in San Francisco Chinatown, so that by 1957 a third building became necessary. This three-stage construction in the San Francisco public school system stands as a permanent reminder of the city's response to state school law and has left the school with the dubious reputation of being a segregated, rather than a neighborhood, school. Lest it be forgotten, Commodore Stockton School's distinctiveness is that is was built amidst public protest against having a permanent Chinese school erected in a white neighborhood.

# Chapter 8
# Conclusion

THIS BOOK DOCUMENTS a century-long struggle against discrimination by the San Francisco Chinese community to gain a footing in the city's educational system. The Chinese had to confront racism from within the school system as well as the prejudices of society at large. The combined prejudice relegated them to a life of alienation from the city's mainstream.

San Francisco Superintendent of Schools George Tait's labeling in 1864 of the Chinese race as "unimpressible" helped perpetuate a false image of the Chinese people. This stereotype, also shared by other governmental units in the city, allowed free license for all levels of white society to harass or ignore the Chinese. This view of the Chinese became ingrained in the school bureaucracy and blighted the lives of many young Chinese Americans—a loss to the Chinese community as well as to the city of San Francisco. To a large extent this negative perception still lingers today.[1]

The Chinese fought discrimination not passively, but with positive action. They used the legal and political framework available to them in this country to demand their right to public schooling. The countless appeals and testimony of the Chinese before local, state, and federal officials for improved educational opportunities underscore their refusal to accept the discriminatory status quo. The most dramatic examples of this determination were the pivotal lawsuits of *Tape v. Hurley* (1885) and *Wong Him v. Callahan* (1902). The former gave American-born Chinese the right to public education, albeit segregated schooling. The latter was an unsuccessful attempt to allow Chinese parents to send their children to the schools nearest their place of residence or work.

The drive for educational rights became the focal point around which the Chinese community coalesced. The isolation of the

Chinese in American society was lessened as community groups worked together within the American system for a common goal. Although progress was slow to rectify educational malpractice, their limited success provided the foundation for later breakthroughs.

Also documented in this study are the instances of the more enlightened San Francisco superintendents, like John Pelton, and those school board members, administrators, and community leaders who pushed against the prejudicial tide of public opinion. Given the pervasive climate of discrimination that endured for over one hundred years until after World War II, the courage of these individuals is laudable. Particularly noteworthy are the actions of the missionaries, such as the Reverend Otis Gibson, Donaldina Cameron, and Claudia White, who were outspoken advocates for the rights of the Chinese. The full story of the religious community's contribution to the historical development of San Francisco's Chinatown has yet to be told.

Although the school laws of California and San Francisco discriminated against all non-white minority Americans, no evidence was found to document any effort by minority groups to pool their resources to combat these unfair laws. The differences among the races and the harsh social and economic pressures forestalled any collective action.

Obtaining a teacher credential was an arduous process for any student, but it was made even more difficult for the Chinese, because racial, linguistic, and cultural discrimination extended to the teacher preparation program itself. In the San Francisco school district, when Chinese American teachers were hired, it was in proportion to the numbers of overseas students and not because of the growing numbers of American-born, and particularly Chinatown-born, Chinese. In the district there was an unofficial quota of Chinese American teachers in Chinatown schools, and, with a few exceptions that prove the rule, Chinese American teachers were assigned the teaching of neither English-speaking Chinese nor non-Chinese students in San Francisco until the late 1950s. Their refusal to succumb to the racist training, hiring, and placement practices of the educational bureaucracy is a testament to their determination to enter the teaching profession.

Many San Francisco-born and/or -raised Chinese American college students who entered the teaching profession were given inadequate English language instruction. If—and the interviews for this study do so indicate—those educated at the Chinatown schools and particularly at Commodore Stockton, after twelve years of public schooling, still had problems with English, then the problems encountered by immigrant Chinese students must have been even greater.

At the present time and in the light of the *Lau* decision of 1974, the American educational structure is beginning to recognize and affirm cultural plurality. School districts have been required by this court decision to set up alternatives to traditional English-only instruction for children who have limited or no English ability.

Throughout the United States, the Chinese and other minority Americans have taken up the banner of bilingual education as a major legacy of the civil-rights activism of the 1960s. Leaders in the ethnic communities seek to replace the "melting pot" thinking that has dominated educational attitudes in the past.

Bilingual education as it is now conceived and funded is a compensatory model. That is, children who come to school with a language other than English need special remedial help to ease their way into the mainstream. The instructional program offered them is intensive English as a second language instruction (ESL), while they learn the subject matter from a bilingual staff. This transitional model is mandated by law. However, as soon as students demonstrate mastery in English, they are reassigned to their regular classes.

This writer would like to see bilingual education function as a maintenance model for immigrant students to maintain their own language and as an enrichment model for Chinese American students who have lost their language and want to reacquire it. From my perspective, the transitional bilingual approach hasn't shorn off the melting-pot philosophy. The role of public education still seems bound to the "melt the ethnics" thinking. Maintenance and enrichment bilingual instructional approaches would affirm, not dilute, the minority heritages in the United States. It is conceivable that these two models are attainable *without added cost* to school districts that have large language-minority enrollments. The bilingual-bicultural graduates from these programs would enrich themselves, their communities, and the United States.

The writing of this book has stimulated other concerns that, if

researched, might bring its contents into better focus. Such questions as the following need to be pursued:
• Were schools exclusively for Chinese established in other counties of California, and did the public support the establishment of these schools?
• Prior to 1906, many Chinese students attended private schools, particularly schools sponsored by the Protestant missions. Since some of the Chinatown churches have celebrated or will be celebrating their centennials, research into their archives would supplement this study.
• Many Chinese families moved over to Oakland and Berkeley after the 1906 earthquake. A study of the education of the Chinese in those nearby communities would shed light on this subject.
• Why were Chinese language schools established in Chinatown? Was it to perpetuate Chinese language and culture in America or to prepare young Chinese for service in China?
• Since Chinese American children were attending public schools in the North Beach district prior to the termination of *de jure* segregation, an examination of the PTA minutes of these schools might provide additional information on the reception of Chinese in these schools. Furthermore, research into the Italian press of the North Beach area could provide data on the encroachment of Chinese into their district, particularly when Chinese students entered Francisco Junior High School.
• From 1850 to 1920, Chinese was the dominant language spoken in the Chinese quarter of San Francisco. From 1920 to 1960, Chinese who lived in the Chinatown core area were apt to be bilingual and those outside Chinatown encountered an English-speaking society. From 1960 to the present, due to the abolition of inequitable immigration and residential laws, the Chinese-speaking population is no longer restricted to Chinatown. How can schooling meet the needs of this new student population?

# Challenge for the 1980s:
# Striving for Equal Educational Treatment

IT IS NOW 1982. In light of the current acceptance of Chinese today, it is hard to imagine that a century ago, American immigration and education laws barred them from entry and made life miserable for those already here. The slow educational headway made by the Chinese in San Francisco, chronicled in this book, was one form of response to elevate their status in an unfavorable social climate. Indeed, it was nothing short of remarkable that they made any advances given these circumstances. Each step gained chipped away at the tenaciously held stereotyping of the Chinese as unassimilable, passive, inscrutable, and "unimpressible." Nevertheless, the institutional practices of the old order and the distorted perceptions of Chinese remained impregnable during their long struggles.

Around the mid-1960s, the new order gradually replaced the old order with an emerging concept that defines an American not by race, color, or religion, but by dedication to the principles of equality and justice. Minority Americans benefited from this more inclusive definition and began entering the institutional life of mainstream America in greater numbers.

The challenge that lies ahead for ethnolinguistic communities is in the educational arena—for it is here that the old order is deeply rooted and it is here that language minorities are stripped of their language and cultural traditions.[2] As *reacting* was the appropriate response under the old order, so *seizing the initiative* is the appropriate response under the new. This means, among other things, demystifying the "good old days" of schooling, defining and embracing those values and customs that affirm one's identity, maintaining vigilance over school texts that perpetuate stereotypes or have serious omissions of minority Americans, and participating in the politics of education to ensure the systematic transmission of minority heritages as well as to humanize American public education.

The incentive for this response lies in the civil-rights movement of the 1960s, in general, and the *Lau v. Nichols* Supreme Court decision of 1974, in particular. The former reminded the general public of the need for fair play for all Americans. The latter is an educational extension of that principle. The unrest and agitation that led to these two events reminded our leaders of the serious cleavage between our nation's practices and its founding principles.

The humanization of America's institutions has begun, but the journey will be a long one. The most fundamental obstacle is the educational bureaucracy. The *Lau* ruling, won by Chinese Americans, released a torrent of long-fomenting energy. Minority

Americans have long wanted linguistic and cultural affirmation, and what had previously been pushed into an unnatural state as a melting pot has now become a boiling cauldron. Our nation's pedagogical leaders have cause to ponder, for there is pressure to cease educational policies and practices that are inconsistent with our country's democratic traditions. This achievement by the Chinese in San Francisco is both "impressible" and very American.

# Appendix A
## State School Superintendent
## Andrew Moulder's Annual Report of 1858

I regret to announce that the odious tastes of the Negrophilist school of mock philanthropists, have found their way, to some extent, into California. In several of the Counties, attempts have been made to introduce the children of Negroes into our Public Schools on an equality with the Whites.

Whenever consulted on the point, the State Superintendent has resolutely resisted such attempts, and employed all the power conferred upon him by law, to defeat them.

In his communications of the subject, he has instructed School officers that our Public Schools were clearly intended for white children alone. The Law provides that in the month of October, the School Marshals shall take the census of the white children between the ages of four and eighteen years.

Upon this census, the apportionment of the State and County School Funds is based. It matters not how many Negro children there may be in a School-District, it receives no funds for their education.

Had it been intended by the framers of the law that the children of the inferior races should be educated side by side with the whites, it is manifest the census would have included children of all colors.

If this attempt to force Africans, Chinese, and Diggers into our white Schools is persisted in, it must result in the ruin of our Schools.

The great mass of our citizens will not associate on terms of equality with these inferior races, nor will they consent that their children should do so. Grant, for the purpose of the argument, and only for that purpose, that this antipathy is unreasonable—that it is but a prejudice—the fact is patent that it is deeply rooted, and widespread. Until our people are prepared for practical amalgamation, which will probably not be before the millenium, they will rather forego the benefits of our Schools than permit their daughters—fifteen, sixteen, and seventeen years of age—to affiliate with the sons of Negroes. It is practically reduced to this, then, that our Schools must be maintained exclusively for whites, or they will soon become tenanted by blacks alone.

This intermingling of Negroes with Caucasians is, moreover, a positive cruelty to the former. They are, by the association when children, brought up in the belief that the intimacy can continue in after years. It can only bring mortification and chagrin—and that, the more their sensibilities are cultivated—when time disabuses them of this idea. For these reasons, the State Superintendent has emphatically prohibited their admission into our white Schools. At the same time, it is not desirable, neither does our School Law render it necessary, that they should be brought up in ignorance and heathenism. Any District may establish a separate School for the benefit of the inferior races, and apply a certain portion of the public funds to its support, provided the citizens do not object, which it is presumed they will not do, unless for cogent reasons.

The question involved in these remarks is not a mere abstraction. It is practical—now pressing upon us for solution. The purpose of this introduction, is to ask further legislation on the subject. Under the existing law, the State Superintendent could do nothing more than employ the influence of his official position to discourage the attempt referred to. He has no authority to punish for disobedience of his instructions. It is recommended, therefore, that power be conferred upon him to withhold the public moneys from any District that permits the admission of the children of inferior races—African, Mongolian, or Indian—into the Common Schools.

The State Superintendent disclaims any prejudice against a respectable Negro—in his place; but that place is not, in his opinion, an association, on terms of equality, with the white race.

Source: California State Superintendent of Public Instruction, *8th Annual Report*, 1858, pp. 14–15.

# Appendix B

## City School Superintendent James Denman's Annual Report of 1860

This school was first organized as a day school in September 1859 under the instruction of Mr. B. Lanctot and was, I believe, the first institution established in any Christian country, for the instruction of this large class of pagan worshippers. I regret that I am not able to present a more satisfactory report of the success of this experiment.

On the first of June last, the board suspended the school for want of scholars, and a lack of interest and appreciation of the benefits and blessing thus generously offered to them.

The teacher has been faithful and energetic in the discharge of his difficult duty; but the prejudices of caste and religious idolatry are so indelibly stamped upon their character and existence that his task of education seems almost hopeless. According to our laws, the Mongolian race can never be elevated to an equality with the Anglo-Saxon, and receive the title and immunities of American citizens. They therefore take but little interest in adopting our habits, or learning our language and institutions. The school, during the first term, until it was closed in June, numbered 77 scholars—8 girls and 69 males—while the average attendance, during the same time was only 12.

A few of the scholars were under the age of 18 years; but most of the regular attendants of the school ranged from 20 to 30 years of age.

It has since been reopened as an Evening School, with an increased number in attendance. Greater interest has been manifested by a few of the more intelligent Chinamen to sustain the school; but its final success is a doubtful experiment, which should receive the careful consideration of this Board, before appropriating the public funds for its support.

SOURCE: San Francisco Superintendent's *Annual Report*, 1860, pp. 30–31.

# Appendix C

## Chronology of Superintendents of Public Schools in San Francisco 1851–1887

| Name | Years in Service |
|---|---|
| *(Appointed by the Board of Education)* | |
| Thomas J. Nevins | 1851–1853 |
| William H. O'Grady | 1854–1855 |
| E. A. Theller | –1856 |

### County Superintendent
*(Elected by the people)*

| Name | Years in Service |
|---|---|
| John C. Pelton | –1856 |

### City and County Superintendents
*(Elected by the people)*

| Name | Years in Service |
|---|---|
| John C. Pelton | –1857 |
| Henry B. Janes | 1857–1859 |
| James Denman | 1859–1860 |
| George Tait | 1861–1864 |
| John C. Pelton | 1865–1867 |
| James Denman | 1868–1870 |
| J. H. Widber | 1871–1873 |
| James Denman | 1874–1875 |
| H. N. Bolander | 1876–1877 |
| Azro L. Mann | 1877–1880 |

### Under New Constitution
*(Elected by the people)*

| Name | Years in Service |
|---|---|
| John W. Taylor | 1880–1883 |
| Andrew Moulder | 1883–1887 |

SOURCE: Francis Yung Chang, "A Study of the Movement to Segregate Chinese Pupils in the San Francisco Public Schools up to 1885," doctoral dissertation, Stanford University, 1936, p. 400.

# Appendix D

# Mrs. Tape's Letter

1769 Green Street
San Francisco, April 8, 1885

To the Board of Education—Dear Sirs: I see that you are going to make all sorts of excuses to keep my child out off the Public Schools. Dear sirs, Will you please tell me! Is it a disgrace to be born a Chinese? Didn't God make us all!!! What right! have you to bar my children out of the school because she is a chinese Descend. They is no other worldly reason that you could keep her out, except that I suppose, you all goes to churches on Sundays! Do you call that a Christian act to compel my little children to go so far to a school that is made in purpose for them. My children don't dress like the other Chinese. They look just as phunny amongst them as the Chinese dress in Chinese look amongst you Caucasians. Besides, if I had any wish to send them to a chinese school I could have sent them two years ago without going to all this trouble. You have expended a lot of the Public money foolishly, all because of a one poor little Child. Her playmates is all Caucasians ever since she could toddle around. If she is good enough to play with them! Then is she not good enough to be in the same room and studie with them? You had better come and see for yourselves. See if the Tape's is not same as other Caucasians, except in features. It seems no matter how a Chinese may live and dress so long as you know they Chinese. Then they are hated as one. There is not any right or justice for them.

You have seen my husband and child. You told him it wasn't Mamie Tape you object to. If it were not Mamie Tape you object to, then why didn't you let her attend the school nearest her home! Instead of first making one pretense Then another pretense of some kind to keep her out? It seems to me Mr. Moulder has a grudge against this Eight-year-old Mamie Tape. I know they is no other child I mean Chinese child! care to go to your public Chinese school. May you Mr. Moulder, never be persecuted like the way you have persecuted little Mamie Tape. Mamie Tape will never attend any of the Chinese schools of your making! Never!!! I will let the world see sir What justice there is When it is govern by the Race prejudice men! Just because she is of the Chinese descend, not because she don't dress like you because she does. Just because she is decended of Chinese parents I guess she is more of a American then a good many of you that is going to prewent her being Educated.

Mrs. M. Tape

SOURCE: *Alta*, April 16, p. 1, col. 3.

# Appendix E

## Researcher's Letter to
## Chinese American Teachers

Dear ———:

My name is Victor Low. I have been teaching in the San Francisco Unified School District for the past 18 years. Currently I am on sabbatical leave and am attending the University of San Francisco as a doctoral student in the Multicultural Program. My dissertation topic is an historical study of the Chinese in the San Francisco Public Schools from 1859–1959. I hope to document the Chinese struggle to overcome the many educational obstacles in order to obtain a fair and equitable treatment in the public schools. Therefore my theme throughout deals with exclusion to inclusion.

One of my chapters is on the exclusion/inclusion of Chinese Americans as public school teachers. I have a graph showing the number of Chinese American teachers appointed in San Francisco from 1926 to 1959 which might be of interest to you. I not only want to show this graph to you, but would also want to interview you about your personal experiences as a student and as a teacher in order to provide the human dimension to my study. Information from you that is helpful to my topic will be incorporated into the dissertation with the understanding that no names will ever be mentioned unless permission has been granted by you.

I hope you will share this concern with me as well as allow me to interview you at your convenience. From my perspective, your experience is the heart of my study. I will telephone you within the week to request an appointment.

Sincerely,

(signed)
Victor Low

# Appendix F

# Questions Used in Interview with Chinese American Teachers

1. Why did you become a teacher?

2. Describe some unforgettable experiences when you were a child attending the San Francisco Public Schools that would be relevant to my dissertation topic.
   A. elementary school
   B. junior high school
   C. high school

3. Describe some unforgettable experiences during your teaching career that would be relevant to my dissertation topic.
   A. teacher preparation
   B. student teaching
   C. teacher examination
   D. probationary teacher
   E. tenured teacher

4. Were some of your friends discouraged from going into the field of teaching? What were the reasons?

5. What do you feel is the primary role of the public schools in educating Chinese American students?

# Bibliography

## Documents

California. *Amendments to Codes of California* (Annotated Ed.), 1873–1874.
———. *Assembly Journals*, 1874, 1875.
———. *California Constitution, 1879.*
———. *California Legislature: Chinese Immigration—The Social, Moral and Political Effect of Chinese Immigration. Testimony Taken Before a Committee of the Senate of the State of California, Appointed April 3, 1876*, Sacramento: State Superintendent of Public Printing, 1876.
———. *First Biennial Report, 1864–1865.*
———. *School Code of the State of California, 1929.*
———. *Second Biennial Report, 1866–1867.*
———. *Senate Journals, 1852, 1855, 1874, 1880, 1885.*
———. *State Superintendent of Public Instruction, 1863–1873.*
———. *Statutes, 1856–1874.*
———. *Statutes and Amendments to the Codes, 1885, 26th Session; 1909, 38th Session; 1921, 44th Session; 1947.*
———. *The Law Establishing and Regulating Common Schools in the State of California*, Sacramento: B. B. Redding, State Printer, 1855.
Chinese Consolidated Benevolent Association, *Memorial of the Six Chinese Companies: An Address to the Senate and House of Representatives of the United States.* Testimony of California's Leading Citizens Before the Joint Special Congressional Committee. San Francisco: Alta Print, 1877.
Department of the Interior, Bureau of Education, *The Public School System of San Francisco, California, Bulletin, 1917, No. 46*, Washington Government Printing Office, 1917.
*Lau v. Nichols*, 414 U. S. Reports 563, 1974.
*Minutes of Chinese-American Citizens Alliance, 1923–1928* (同源會記錄).
*People v. Hall*, 4 California Report 399.
*Plessy v. Ferguson*, 163 U. S. 537, at 550–551 (1896).
San Francisco. *By-Laws of the Board of Education of City and County of San Francisco*, San Francisco: C. A. Calhoun, Printers, 1856.
———. *Certificated Payroll Records of the San Francisco School District, 1939–1959.*
———. *Circulars and Memoes of the School Superintendents*, July 6, 1875 to January 7, 1929.
———. Department of City Planning, *Report on a Population and Site Analysis of the Commodore Stockton School Service Area*, San Francisco: August 1950.

————. Moulder, Andrew Jackson, *Appendix to the Commentaries on the School Law*, San Francisco: Department of Instruction, 1860.

————. *School Superintendents' Annual Reports, 1858–1933.*

————. *School Board Minutes, 1906–1959.*

*Tape v. Hurley*, 66 California Reports 473–474 (1884–1885).

*Treaties and Conventions Since June 4, 1776*, Vol. 2, 1870–1871.

*U. S. Congress Joint Special Committee to Investigate Chinese Immigration.* Report on the Joint Special Committee to Investigate Chinese Immigration. Feb. 27, 1887, Washington: Government Printing Office, 1877.

*Ward v. Flood*, 48 California 36–43 (1874).

*Westminster School District v. Mendez*, 161 Fed. (ed.) 774 (1947).

*Wong Him v. Callahan*, 119 Fed. 381–382 (1903).

## Books

Baccari, Alessandro, Project Coordinator, *San Francisco Chinese Community Citizen's Survey and Fact Finding Committee Report*. Abridged Edition, Co-Chairmen Lim P. Lee, Albert Lim and H. K. Wong, August 1969. Bank of Canton sponsored, condensed version printing, November 1969.

Chinn, Thomas W., *A History of the Chinese in California*. San Francisco: Chinese Historical Society of America, 1969.

Cloud, Roy W., *Education in California*, Stanford: Stanford University Press, 1952.

Coolidge, Mary R., *Chinese Immigration*, New York: Henry Holt and Company, 1909.

Cowan, Robert Ernest, and Dunlap, Boutwell, *Bibliography of the Chinese Question in the United States*, San Francisco: A. M. Robertson, 1909.

Davis, Winfield, Jr., *History of Political Conventions in California, 1849–1892*, Sacramento, California State Library, 1893.

Dobie, Charles Caldwell, *San Francisco Chinatown*, New York: Appleton Century, 1936.

Dohrmann, Frederick Jr., *Three Years on a Board*, San Francisco: written and published for private circulation, December 1924.

Eaves, Lucile, *A History of California Labor Legislation With an Introductory Sketch of the San Francisco Labor Movement*, Berkeley: The University Press, 1910.

Farwell, William B., *The Chinese at Home and Abroad Together With the Report of the Special Committee of the Board of Supervisors of San Francisco, on the Condition of the Chinese Quarter of that City*, San Francisco: A. L. Bancroft and Company, 1885.

Ferrier, William Warren, *Ninety Years of Education in California, 1846–1936*, Berkeley: Sather Gate Book Shop, 1937.

Fishman, Joshua A., *Language in Sociocultural Change*, Stanford, California: Stanford University Press, 1972.

Gibson, Rev. Otis, *Chinese in America*, Cincinnati: Hitchcock and Walden, 1877.

Glazer, Nathan, and Moynihan, Daniel P., *Beyond the Melting Pot*, Cambridge, Massachusetts: M.I.T. Press, 1963.

Hansen, Gladys C., *The Chinese in California, a Brief Bibliographic History*, Portland, Oregon: Richard Abel and Company Inc., 1970.

Healy, Patrick, and Ng Poon Chew, *A Statement for Non-Exclusion*, San Francisco, 1905.

Hendrick, Irving G., *Final Report, Public Policy Toward the Education of Non-White Minority Group Children in California, 1849–1970*, National Institute of Education, Project No. NE-G-003-0082, School of Education, University of California, Riverside, March 1975. Revised to *The Education of Non-Whites in California, 1849–1970*, San Francisco: R & E Research Associates, Inc., 1977.

Hittell, Theodore H., *History of California*, San Francisco: N. J. Stone and Company, 1897.

Hoy, William, *The Chinese Six Companies*, San Francisco: Lawton R. Kennedy, 1942.

Huang, Joe, and Wong, Sharon Q., *Chinese Americans: Realities and Myths Anthology*, San Francisco: The Association of Chinese Teachers, 1977.

Jacobs, Paul, and Landau, Saul, *To Serve the Devil: Volume 2: Colonials and Sojourners*, New York: Vintage Books, 1971.

Lai, Him Mark, and Choy, Philip P., *Outlines: History of the Chinese in America*, San Francisco: Fong Brothers Printing, 1971.

Lanctot, Benoni, *Chinese and English Phrase Book, with the Chinese Pronunciation Indicated in English, Specially Adapted for the Use of Merchants, Travelers and Families* (華英通語), San Francisco: A. Roman and Company, 1867.

Lee, Rose Hum, *The Chinese in the United States of America*, Hong Kong: Hong Kong and Oxford University Press, 1960.

Liu, Pei Chi, *A History of the Chinese in the United States of America*, Taiwan, 1976. Chinese reference is 劉伯驥，美國華僑史，(台灣，黎明文化事業公司印行)，一九七六年

McGloin, John Bernard, *Eloquent Indian: The Life of James Bouehard, California Jesuit*, Stanford, California: Stanford University Press, 1949.

Melendy, H. Brett, and Gilbert, Benjamin F., *The Governors of California: Peter H. Burnett to Edmund G. Brown*, Georgetown, California: Talisman Press, 1965.

Millard, Bailey, *History of the San Francisco Bay Region*, Volume I, San Francisco: The American Historical Society Inc., 1924.

Miller, Stuart Creighton, *The Unwelcome Immigrant*, Berkeley: University of California Press, 1969.

Nee, Victor G. and Brett De Bary, *Longtime Californ'*, New York: Pantheon Books, 1972.

Sandmeyer, Elmer Clarence, *The Anti-Chinese Movement in California*, Urbana, Illinois: University of California Press, 1939.

Saxton, Alexander, *The Indispensable Enemy*, Berkeley, California: University of California Press, 1971.

Shuck, Oscar T., *Historical Abstract of San Francisco*, San Francisco, 1897.

Soule, Frank; Gihon, John H.; and Nisbet, James, *The Annals of San Francisco Together With the Continuation Through 1855*, Palo Alto: Lewis Osborne, 1966.

Stone, Irving, *Men to Match My Mountains*, New York: Doubleday and Co., Inc., 1956.

Sung, Betty L., *Mountain of Gold*, New York: The Macmillan Company, 1967.

Townsend, Luther Tracy, *The Chinese Problem*. Boston: Lee and Shepard, 1876.

## Articles

Andrews, Sidney, "Wo Lee and His Kinsfolk," *Atlantic Monthly*, Vol. XXV, February 1870.

Baldwin, Rev. S. L., "The Education of the Mongolian, or Chinese," *The Journal of Proceedings and Addresses of the National Educational Association*, 1886 session at Topeka, Kansas, Salem: Observer Book and Job Print, 1887.

Chang, Francis Y., "An Accommodation Program for Second-Generation Chinese, *Sociology and Social Research*, Vol. XVIII, No. 6, pp. 541–553, July–August, 1934.

Chin, Lonnie, "Chinese and Public School Teaching," *Chinese Americans: School and Community Problems*, Integrated Education Associates, Chicago, Illinois, 1972, pp. 58–59.

Chinn, Thomas W., "New Chapters in Chinese American History," *California History*, Volume LVII, No. 1. San Francisco: California Historical Society, Spring 1978.

Chow, Christopher, and Leong, Russell, "A Pioneer Chinatown Teacher: An Interview with Alice Fong Yu," *Amerasia Journal*, Volume 5, Number 1, Asian American Studies Center, University of California at Los Angeles, 1978.

Cowdery, J. F., "The Word 'White' in the California School Laws," *Pacific Appeal*, February 14, 1874, pp. 1–2.

Dyer, Francis John, "A Chinese Public School," *World Today*, Volume 8, Chicago: The World Today Company, 1905.

Inglis, William, "The Width of a School Bench: Reasons for California's Defiant Decree Against the Japanese in Her Public Schools," *Harper's Weekly*, Volume 51, January 19, 1907.

Joe, Kenneth, "The Oriental School" (遠東學校), *East/West, Chinese American Weekly*, January 1, 1970.

Lai, Him Mark, "The Chinese and Public Education in San Francisco," Parts 1–3, *East/West, Chinese American Weekly*, August 18, September 1 and 8, 1971.

Laughlin, Rev. John Hood, "Chinese Children in American Schools," *Overland Monthly*, May 1911.

Lee, Chingwah, "Remember When?" *Chinese Digest*, March 6, 1936.

Lee, Lim P., "The Political Rights of the American Citizens of Chinese Ancestry," *Chinese Digest*, October 23, 1936.

Lee, Samuel D., "A Chinese Community Center," *Chinese Digest*, December 6, 1935.

Newhall, Cecilia, "The Chinese Public School of San Francisco," *Dragon Student*, published by the Chinese Students' Alliance of America,( 中西日報承印), 1905.

Polos, Nicholas C., "Segregation and John Swett," *Southern California Quarterly*, Vol. 46, 1964.

Wang, L. Ling Chi, "Lau v. Nichols: History of a Struggle for Equal and Quality Education," *Counterpoint: Perspectives on Asian America*, Asian American Studies Center, University of California at Los Angeles," 1976.

———. "The Chinese American Student in San Francisco," *Chinese Americans: School and Community Problems*, Integrated Education Associates, Chicago, Illinois, 1972, pp. 53–57.

### Pamphlets

Jue, George K., *Chinatown, Its History, Its People, Its Importance*, San Francisco: San Francisco Chamber of Commerce, May 1951.

Kerr, J. G., *The Chinese Question Analyzed. A Lecture Delivered in the Hall of the Young Men's Christian Association, Nov. 13th, 1877*, San Francisco: printed for the author, 1877.

Lee, Samuel D., *San Francisco's Chinatown—History, Function and Importance of Social Organization*, San Francisco for the Central District Coordinating Council, 1940.

Pro-Chinese Minority of California. *To the American President and Congress*, San Francisco, 1882.

Swett Papers, "Have Negroes Been Taught in Classes on Terms of Equality in a Public School Under the Charge of Mr. John Swett?" Bancroft Library, University of California, 1862.

Williams, S. Well, "Chinese Immigration," a paper read before the Social Science Association at Saratoga, September 10, 1879, New York: Scribner, 1879.

## Unpublished Dissertations

Butzbach, Arthur Graham, "The Segregation of Orientals in the San Francisco Schools," master's thesis, Stanford University, 1928.

Chang, Francis Yung, "A Study of the Movement to Segregate Chinese Pupils in the San Francisco Public Schools Up to 1885," doctoral dissertation, Stanford University, 1936.

Dolson, Lee Stephen, Jr., "The Administration of the San Francisco Public Schools 1847–1947," doctoral dissertation, University of California at Berkeley, 1964.

Fernandes, Norman Almeida, "The San Francisco Board of Education and the Chinese Community: Segregation-Desegregation, 1850–1975," doctoral dissertation, University of Denver, 1976.

Lee, Mary Bo-Tze, "Problems of the Segregated School for Asiatics in San Francisco," master's thesis, University of California at Berkeley, 1920.

Lum, Philip Albert, "The Chinese Freedom Schools of San Francisco: A Case Study of the Social Limits of Political System Support," doctoral dissertation, University of California at Berkeley, 1975.

Myers, James Edwards, "The Educational Work of Andrew Jackson Moulder in the Development of Public Education in California, 1850–1895," doctoral dissertation, University of California at Berkeley, 1961.

Shih, Hsien-Ju, "The Social and Vocational Adjustment of the Second Generation High School Students in San Francisco," doctoral dissertation, University of California at Berkeley, 1937.

## Published Dissertations

Cather, Helen V. "The History of San Francisco's Chinatown," master's thesis, University of California, 1932. Reprinted in 1974 by R & E Research Associates, San Francisco, California.

Courtney, William J., "San Francisco Anti-Chinese Ordinances 1850–1900," master's thesis, University of San Francisco, 1956. Reprinted in 1974 by R & E Research Associates, San Francisco, California.

Ng, Pearl, "Writings on the Chinese in California," master's thesis, University of California, 1939. Reprinted in 1972 by R & E Research Associates, San Francisco, California.

Wollenberg, Charles, *All Deliberate Speed*, Berkeley, California: University of California Press, 1976.

## English Newspapers

*San Francisco Daily Alta California*
*San Francisco Evening Bulletin*
*Daily Morning Call*
*San Francisco Chronicle*
*San Francisco Examiner*
*San Francisco News*
*San Francisco Call Bulletin*
*San Francisco Call*
*San Francisco Bulletin*
*San Francisco Call/Post*
*San Francisco Post*
*San Francisco California Journal*
*San Francisco Journal of Commerce*
*San Francisco California Hayes Valley Advertiser*
*Sacramento Union*

## Chinese Newspapers

*Golden Hill News*
*The Oriental or Tung Ngai San Luk,* 東涯新錄
*San Francisco China News,* 舊金山唐人新聞紙
*Chinese Record,* 華人記錄
*Chinese World,* 世界日報
*Chung Sai Yat Po,* 中西日報
*Chinese Digest,*
*Chinese Press,* 華美週報
*Chinese News*
*East-West,* 東西報

## Formal Interviews

Chan, Agnes. May 31, 1978; San Francisco residence.
Chan, Mee Chee. May 16, 1978; San Francisco residence.
Chan, Rosemary. May 15, 1978; San Francisco residence.
Chang, Susan. June 15, 1978; San Rafael residence.
Chew, Wellington. May 19, 1978; First Chinese Baptist Church.
Chin, Rose. May 17, 1978; San Francisco residence.
Chinn, Mayme. June 21, 1978; Area Office.
Fong, Rosemary. June 13, 1978. Yerba Buena School.
Gin, Sandra. June 16, 1978; San Francisco Board of Education.
Hall, Elizabeth. October 28, 1977;
Hom, Mildred. June 16, 1978; First Chinese Baptist Church.
Kim, Tommy. May 17, 1978; First Chinese Baptist Church.
Lai, Roberta. June 20, 1978; San Francisco residence.
Lau, Dorothy. May 20, 1978; First Chinese Baptist Church.
Lew, Larry. May 26, 1978; First Chinese Baptist Church.

Lim, Nora. May 31, 1978; San Francisco residence.
Look, Louise. June 7, 1978; Corbett School.
Low, Lily. June 20, 1978; San Francisco residence.
Lum, Helen. June 15, 1978; Daly City residence.
Lum, Patricia. June 21, 1978; San Francisco residence.
Lum, Phil. June 12, 1978; Roosevelt Middle School.
Wing, Anita. June 14, 1978; Chinese Education Center.
Wing, Peggy. June 14, 1978; First Chinese Baptist Church.
Wong, Anna. June 23, 1978; San Francisco residence.
Wong, Darlene. June 12, 1978; Visitacion Valley School.
Wong, Doris. June 23, 1978; San Francisco residence.
Wong, Elsie. May 20, 1978; San Francisco residence.
Wong, Jim. June 5, 1978; Everett Middle School.
Woo, Wilbur. June 7, 1978; San Francisco residence.
Wu, Jannie. June 2, 1978; Counseling Office.
Yu, Alice Fong. October 10, 1977; Piedmont residence.

## Informal Interviews

### *Commodore Stockton's PTA Presidents*

Lee, Flora. June 28, 1979; San Francisco Board of Education.
Loo, Florence. April 28, 1978; San Francisco residence.
Schultze, Doris Low. April 17, 1978; San Francisco residence.
Tom, June. March 10, 1978; San Francisco residence.

### *Community Representatives*

Chinn, Thomas, publisher and editor of *Chinese Digest*. January 14, 1979; San Francisco residence.
Lai, Him Mark, Chinese American history lecturer and researcher; president of Chinese Historical Society of America. January 21, 1979; San Francisco residence.
Lai, S. K., editor of *Chinese Times*. May 20, 1978; *Chinese Times* office.
Lee, Ching Wah, Chinatown and Chinese culture lecturer; graduate of the Oriental School. January 19, 1979; Kong Chow Temple.
Ng, Jerry, son of Suey Ng, pioneering Chinese American teacher. May 24, 1978; Woodland Hills residence.
Tom, Henry, executive secretary of Chinese YMCA. September 13, 1978; Chinese American Citizens Alliance office.
Whang, Paul, recreation director of Chinatown. September 20, 1978; San Francisco residence.

# Notes

## INTRODUCTION

1 San Francisco School Superintendent's *Annual Report*, 1864, pp. 31-32.

2 *Lau v. Nichols*, 414 U.S. Reports 563, 1974.

3 For a history of this lawsuit, see Ling-chi Wang's article, *Lau v. Nichols:* History of a Struggle for Equal and Quality Education," *Counterpoint: Perspectives on Asian America*, Asian American Studies Center, University of California at Los Angeles, 1976, pp. 240-263.

4 The Chinese have traditionally called San Francisco's Chinatown "the big city" (dai fow 大埠)

5 Charles Wollenberg, *All Deliberate Speed*, (Berkeley, California: University of California Press, 1976), p. 4.

6 Lee Stephen Dolson, Jr., "The Administration of the San Francisco Public Schools, 1847-1947," Doctoral Dissertation, University of California, Berkeley, 1964.

7 Norman Almeida Fernandes, "The San Francisco Board of Education and the Chinese Community: Segregation-Desegregation, 1850-1975," Doctoral Dissertation, University of Denver, 1976.

8 Irving G. Hendrick, *The Education of Non-Whites in California, 1849-1970*, San Francisco: R & E Research Associates, Inc., 1977.

9 Charles Wollenberg, ibid.

10 Philip Albert Lum, "The Chinese Freedom Schools of San Francisco: a Case Study of the Social Limits of Political System Support," Doctoral Dissertation, University of California, Berkeley, 1975.

11 Walter R. Borg and Meredith Damien Gall, *Educational Research, An Introduction*, Third Edition, (New York: Longman Inc., 1979), pp. 372-403.

12 The primary source for research was the school district's archives. Superintendents' *Annual Reports*, circulars, memorabilia, press clippings on education and dissertations were available in the Teachers' Professional Library. Board minutes were in a special room on the second floor. The San Francisco School District personnel office had information on Chinese American teachers and their research office had attendance data on the schools surrounding Chinatown.

School Superintendents' *Annual Reports* missing from the school district's archives were found in the History Room of the city's main library. Reports of early school board meetings were available through microfilm of the early newspapers of the city. These early press reports supplemented meager information from school years prior to 1906, since board minutes were destroyed by the great earthquake and fire.

Another major source was the state library in Sacramento, the only library that indexes the topic by referring to page and column number in the newspapers. The Bancroft Library at the University of California provided verification of school laws and microfilm of early San Francisco newspapers. The Law Library at City Hall in San Francisco provided information on Chinese seeking legal redress. Particularly relevant to this study were the details of *Tape v. Hurley* and *Wong Him v. Callahan*.

The minutes of the Chinese American Citizens Alliance are located at the headquarters of that organization in San Francisco. Chinese American English language sources include the *Chinese Digest* and *East/West Journal*, a weekly newspaper published in San Francisco.

This study was limited by the fact that school minutes up to 1905 were destroyed by the fire of 1906. Also, the minutes of the Chinese Consolidated Benevolent Association (commonly called Chinese Six Companies) were not kept systematically. Since they did not show any information on the Chinese community's early role regarding the city school board, Chinese responses to school district discrimination prior to 1900 were obtained mainly from English sources.

13 Named after Donaldina Cameron, a Presbyterian missionary, who originally established this mission to shelter Chinese girls who were brought over to America for illegal purposes. Cameron House later became a religious/social center for the youths of Chinatown.

## CHAPTER ONE

1 The first known Chinese to set foot in the United States were three seamen, named Ashing, Achun and Accun, who were on board the Pallus when it docked in Baltimore in 1785. They were stranded with other crew members when the ship's captain decided to quit the sea and settle down. A Philadelphia merchant petitioned the Continental Congress to assist the seamen. Their presence in the United States is documented by the petition, which is now in the National Archives.
2 State of California, *Senate Journal*, 1852, p. 15.
3 *San Francisco Daily Alta California*, May 12, 1851, p. 2, col. 3. (hereafter cited as *Alta*).
4 Frank Soule, John H. Gihon, and James Nisbet, *The Annals of San Francisco Together With the Continuation Through 1855*, (Palo Alto: Lewis Osborne, 1966), p. 381.
5 Mary Roberts Coolidge, *Chinese Immigration*, (New York: Henry Holt, 1909), p. 56.
6 State of California, *Senate Journal*, 1852, pp. 376, 378.
7 Frank Soule, ibid., p. 381.
8 Theodore H. Hittell, *History of California*, (San Francisco: N.J. Stone and Co., 1897), p. 108.
9 Francis Yung Chang, "A Study of the Movement to Segregate Chinese Pupils in the San Francisco Public Schools Up to 1885," Doctoral Dissertation, Stanford University, 1936, p. 63.
10 Frank Soule, ibid., p. 381. Soule made no mention of the contents of the letter.
11 Mary Roberts Coolidge, ibid., p. 55.
12 Ibid., pp. 57-58.
13 *Alta*, May 21, 1853, p. 2, col. 1.
14 Ibid., June 23, 1853, p. 2, cols. 2-3.
15 By printing Lo Chum Qui's letter, the term "fan qui"番鬼made its appearance in an American newspaper. What the editor might not have known was the "fan qui" means foreign devils or barbarians in Chinese (Cantonese). This term is still used in Chinatowns today when one refers to white Americans. The usage, however, no longer carries the bitterness intended by Nineteenth Century Chinese.
16 Ibid.
17 Frank Soule, ibid., p. 381.
18 *Alta*, November 21, 1853, p. 2, col. 3.
19 Robert Ernest Cowan and Boutweel Dunlap, *Bibliography of the Chinese Question in the United States*, (San Francisco: A.M. Robertson, 1909), p. 23.
20 *Golden Hill News*, June 10, 1854.
21 Ibid., July 29, 1854.
22 *People v. Hall*, 4 *California Report* 399.
23 Mary Roberts Coolidge, ibid., p. 409.
24 State of California, *Senate Journal*, 1855, p. 54.
25 *The Oriental: or Tung-Ngai San Luk*, February 1, 1855.
26 *The Chinese Digest*, Jan. 1940, p. 19, col. 2. An editorial tracing the history of Chinese in San Francisco.
27 Francis Yung Chang, ibid., p. 104
28 For a history of the city's "colored school," see Lee Stephen Dolson Jr.'s, "The

Administration of the San Francisco Public Schools, 1847-1947," Doctoral Dissertation, University of California, Berkeley, 1964, pp. 116-120.

29 *The Law Establishing and Regulating Common Schools in the State of California,* (Sacramento: B.B. Redding, State Printer, 1855), p. 31.

30 *California Statutes,* 1856, p. 155. Also *By-Laws of the Board of Education of City and County of San Francisco,* (San Francisco: C.A. Calhoun, printers, 1856), p. 13.

31 Readers interested in the history of education of non-whites in California are referred to Irving G. Hendrick's *The Education of Non-Whites in California, 1849-1970,* (San Francisco: R & E Research Associates, Inc., 1977). Also see Charles Wollenberg, *All Deliberate Speed,* (Berkeley: University of California Press, 1976).

32 *San Francisco Evening Bulletin,* January 14, 1857, p. 2, col. 1. The evening school was established to assist working adults and older children who could not attend the day schools.

33 Ibid., January 15, 1857, p. 3, col. 5.

34 Ibid., January 14, 1857, p. 2, col. 1.

35 Ibid., January 20, 1857, p. 1, col. 1.

36 Ibid.

37 Ibid., February 18, 1858, p. 3, col. 2.

38 Ibid., February 24, 1858, p. 2, col. 1.

39 Ibid.

40 James Edward Myers, "The Educational Work of Andrew Jackson Moulder in the Development of Public Education in California, 1850-1895," Doctoral Dissertation, University of California at Berkeley, 1961, p. 50.

41 For the full report of State Superintendent Andrew Moulder see Appendix A.

42 Francis Yung Chang, ibid., p. 150.

43 *Evening Bulletin,* February 18, 1858, p. 3, col. 2.

44 San Francisco School Superintendent's *Annual Report,* 1858, p. 16.

45 Letter dated July 29, 1862. Found in handbill, "Have Negroes been taught in Classes on Terms of Equality in a Public School Under the Charge of Mr. John Swett?" Located in *Swett Papers,* Bancroft Library, University of California, Berkeley, California.

46 Letter dated August 11, 1862, ibid.

47 Ibid.

## CHAPTER TWO

1 *Evening Bulletin, January 19, 1859.* Cited in Francis Yung Chang, ibid., p. 259.

2 Ibid., March 3, 1859, p. 2, col. 1.

3 Ibid., August 24, 1859, p. 3, col. 6.

4 Ibid., August 31, 1859, p. 3, col. 3.

5 *Alta,* September 13, 1859, p. 2, col. 2.

6 San Francisco School Superintendent's *Annual Report,* 1859, p. 64. Hereafter cited as *Annual Report.*

7 Ibid., p. 12.

8 *Evening Bulletin,* December 31, 1859, p. 3, col. 3-4.

9 Ibid.

10 *Alta,* January 1, 1860, p. 2, col. 1.

11 *Evening Bulletin,* January 4, 1860, p. 3, col. 4.

12 Ibid. Two separate articles were published this day.

13 Ibid., April 18, 1860, p. 3, col. 3.

14 Ibid., April 25, 1860, p. 3, col. 2.

15 Ibid., July 25, 1860, p. 3, col. 4.

16 Ibid., October 26, 1860, p. 3, col. 3.

17 Ibid.

18 Ibid., October 31, 1860, p. 3, col. 3.

19 *Annual Report,* 1860, pp. 30-31. See Appendix B, for full report.

20  *California Statutes,* 1860, p. 325.
21  Andrew Jackson Moulder, *Superintendent of Public Instruction, Appendix to the Commentaries on the School Law,* (San Francisco: Department of Instruction, 1860), p. 11.
22  *Alta,* May 23, 1861, p. 1, col. 1.
23  *Evening Bulletin,* May 25, 1861, p. 3, col. 3.
24  Ibid., September 4, 1861, p. 3, col. 3.
25  Ibid., September 18, 1861, p. 3, col. 3.
26  Ibid., November 27, 1861, p. 3, col. 2.
27  H. Brett Melendy and Benjamin F. Gilbert, *The Governors of California,* (Georgetown, California: Talisman Press, 1965), p. 118.
28  Lucille Eaves, *History of California Labor Legislation,* (Berkeley: The University Press, 1910), pp. 14-15.
29  Victor and Brett de Bary Nee, *Longtime Californ',* (New York: Pantheon Books, 1972), p. 44.
30  *Evening Bulletin,* September 27, 1861, p. 3, col. 3.
31  Nicholas C. Polos, "Segregation and John Swett," *Southern California Quarterly,* Vol. 46, 1964, p. 70.
32  Ibid., p. 79.
33  Irving G. Hendrick, *The Education of Non-Whites in California, 1849-1970,* (San Francisco: R & E Research Associates, 1977), p. 14.
34  *First Biennial Report,* 1864-1865, p. 57.
35  Francis Yung Chang, "A Study of the Movement to Segregate Chinese Pupils in San Francisco Public Schools, Up to 1885," Doctoral Dissertation, Stanford University, 1936, pp. 175-176.
36  *California Statutes,* 1863, pp. 202-203.
37  State Superintendent of Public Instruction, *13th Annual Report,* 1863, p. 67.
38  Ibid., 1864, p. 213.
39  *California Statutes,* 1865-1866, pp. 395-398.
40  *Second Biennial Report,* State Superintendent of Public Instruction, California, 1866-1867, p. 22. Separate schools were permitted under Section 57 rather than Section 58.
41  Ibid.
42  *Annual Report,* 1864, p. 45.
43  Ibid., pp. 31-32.
44  *Daily Morning Call,* January 11, 1865, p. 2, col. 2.
45  *Evening Bulletin,* January 25, 1865, p. 3, col. 3.
46  Ibid., February 8, 1865, p. 3, col. 3.
47  Ibid., November 14, 1866, p. 5, col. 4.
48  Ibid., December 12, 1866, p. 5, col. 4.
49  Ibid., January 4, 1867, p. 5, col. 4.
50  Ibid., February 27, 1867, p. 5, col. 4.
51  *Alta,* August 21, 1867, p. 1, col. 2.
52  *Evening Bulletin,* January 10, 1865, p. 3, col. 3.
53  Ibid., October 26, 1860, p. 3, col. 3.
54  *Alta,* February 13, 1867, p. 1, col. 2.
55  *Evening Bulletin,* February 13, 1867, p. 3, col. 5.
56  Annual Report, 1867, p. 55.
57  Ibid., p. 31.
58  Ibid., p. 78.
59  See Appendix C for a chronology of San Francisco city school superintendents.
60  *Evening Bulletin,* February 26, 1868, p. 3, col. 3.
61  Ibid., April 15, 1868, p. 3, col. 4.
62  Ibid., March 10, 1869, p. 3, col. 4.
63  *Annual Report,* 1869, p. 356.
64  *Call,* March 11, 1894, p. 7, col. 1.
65  *Evening Bulletin,* February 15, 1871, p. 1, col. 2.
66  Irving Hendrick, ibid., p. 17.
67  *California Statutes,* 1869-1870, p. 839.

68 Nicholas Polos, ibid., p. 75.
69 *Annual Report, 1870, p. 54.*
70 *Evening Bulletin,* March 1, 1871, p. 1, col. 1.
71 Samuel D. Lee, "A Chinese Community Center," *Chinese Digest,* December 6, 1935, p. 10, cols. 1-2. To this day, America is still called "Gum Shan." (金山) *The Chinese Times,* one of San Francisco Chinatown's daily papers, is called "Gum Shan Sze Bo," 金山時報.
72 Ibid.
73 Mary Roberts Coolidge, ibid., p. 269.
74 Lucile Eaves, ibid., p. 125.
75 Helen Virginia Cather, *The History of San Francisco's Chinatown,* (San Francisco: Reprinted by R. and E. Research Associates, 1974), p. 15.
76 Pearl Ng, *Writings on the Chinese in California,* (San Francisco: Reprinted by R. and E. Research Associates, 1972), p. 16.
77 Winfield Davis, Jr., *History of Political Conventions in California, 1849-1892,* (Sacramento: 1893), p. 265.
78 H. Brett Melendy and Benjamin F. Gilbert, ibid., p. 149.
79 Pearl Ng, ibid., pp. 16-17.
80 Winfield Davis, Jr., ibid., p. 290.
81 Pearl Ng, ibid., p. 16.
82 Victor and Brett De Bary Nee, ibid., p. 43.
83 *Treaties and Conventions Concluded Between the United States of America and Other Powers Since July 4, 1776, Vol. 2,* (Washington: Government Printing Office, 1889), p. 181.
84 Irving G. Hendrick, ibid., p. 25. See also Lucile Eaves, ibid., p. 135. Further substantiation was found in Patrick J. Healy and Ng Poon Chew, *A Statement for Non-Exclusion,* (San Francisco: November 1905), p. 24.
85 Mary Roberts Coolidge, ibid., p. 351.
86 Victor G. and Brett De Bary Nee, ibid., p. 44.
87 Patrick J. Healy and Ng Poon Chew, *A Statement for Non-Exclusion,* (San Francisco: 1905), pp. 25, 28.
88 *Alta,* July 16, 1870, p. 1, col. 1.
89 Lucile Eaves, ibid., p. 137.
90 Pearl Ng, ibid., p. 25.
91 *Sixteen United States Statutes at Large,* (Washington: Government Printing Office, 1872), p. 144.
92 Victor and Brett De Bary Nee, ibid., p. 45.
93 Sidney Andrews, "Wo Lee and His Kinsfolk," *Atlantic Monthly* Vol. XXV, (Bostch, Fields, Osgood and Co., February 1870), p. 229.
94 *Evening Bulletin,* April 18, 1860, p. 3, col. 3; ibid., July 25, 1860, p. 3, col. 4. Also *Annual Reports,* 1860, p. 31; 1869, p. 301; 1870, pp. 53-54.
95 *Annual Report,* 1859, p. 64.
96 *Evening Bulletin,* December 31, 1859, p. 3, cols. 3-4; also *Alta,* January 1, 1860, p. 2, col. 1.
97 *Alta,* August 21, 1867, p. 1, col. 2.
98 *Annual Reports,* 1860, p. 31; 1870, pp. 53-54. Also *Evening Bulletin,* April 18, 1860, p. 3, col. 3.
99 *Annual Reports,* 1869, p. 301; 1870, pp. 53-54.
100 *Daily Morning Call,* January 11, 1865, p. 2, col. 2.
101 *Evening Bulletin,* December 31, 1859, p. 3, cols. 3-4.
102 Ibid., August 31, 1859, p. 3, col. 3.
103 *Alta,* August 27, 1864, p. 1, col. 1.
104 *Evening Bulletin,* January 10, 1865, p. 3, col. 3.
105 Ibid.
106 *Alta,* August 21, 1867, p. 1, col. 2.
107 *Evening Bulletin,* August 31, 1859, p. 3, col. 3.
108 *Annual Report,* 1860, p. 31.
109 *Evening Bulletin,* May 8, 1861, p. 3, col. 3.
110 Ibid., January 10, 1865, p. 3, col. 3.

111 *Annual Report*, 1871, no page number. Cited in back of report.
112 *Evening Bulletin*, April 18, 1860, p. 3, col. 3.
113 *Annual Report*, 1860, p. 31.
114 *Evening Bulletin*, January 10, 1865, p. 3, col. 3.
115 *Annual Report*, 1861, p. 48.
116 *Alta*, February 13, 1867, p. 1, col. 2.
117 *Evening Bulletin*, February 13, 1867, p. 3, col. 5.
118 *Annual Report*, 1861, p. 47.
119 Ibid., p. 48.
120 *Evening Bulletin*, December 31, 1859, p. 3, cols. 3-4.
121 *Annual Report*, 1864, p. 32.
122 *Evening Bulletin*, January 10, 1865, p. 3, col. 3.
123 *Alta*, May 23, 1861, p. 1, col. 1.
124 Ibid., August 27, 1864, p. 1, col. 1.
125 Ibid., August 21, 1867, p. 1, col. 2.
126 *Evening Bulletin*, January 10, 1865, p. 3, col. 3.
127 *Annual Report*, 1861, p. 47. 'John' was a commonly used term referring to the Chinese.
128 *Alta*, August 27, 1864, p. 1, col. 1.
129 *Evening Bulletin*, January 10, 1865, p. 3, col. 3.
130 *Alta*, August 27, 1864, p. 1, col. 1.
131 *Evening Bulletin*, January 10, 1865, p. 3, col. 3.

## CHAPTER THREE

1 Mary Roberts Coolidge, *Chinese Immigration*, (New York: Henry Holt and Company, 1909), p. 351.
2 Victor and Brett De Bary Nee, *Longtime Californ'*, (New York: Pantheon Books, 1972), pp. 45-46.
3 *California Statutes*, 1871-72, p. 970.
4 Ibid., 1873-74, p. 979.
5 Lucile Eaves, *A History of California Labor Legislation*, (Berkeley: The University Press, 1910), p. 147.
6 *Chinese Record*, May 21, 1877, p. 4, cols. 2 and 3.
7 Ibid.
8 Ibid.
9 John Bernard McGloin, *Eloquent Indian: The Life of James Bouchard, California Jesuit*, (Stanford: Stanford University, 1949), pp. 184-185.
10 Oscar T. Shuck, *Historical Abstract of San Francisco*, (San Francisco: 1897), p. 45.
11 For a study of Chinese Six Companies' history and organization, see William Hoy, *The Chinese Six Companies*, (San Francisco: Lawton R. Kennedy,), 1942. For a study of its waning influence in Chinatown, see *Longtime Californ'*, Chapter IX.
12 Ibid.
13 *Alta*, June 25, 1873, p. 4, col. 1.
14 Ibid.
15 Mary Roberts Coolidge, ibid., pp. 66-67.
16 Victor and Brett De Bary Nee, ibid., p. 46.
17 Mary Roberts Coolidge, ibid., p. 131.
18 Helen V. Cather, *The History of San Francisco's Chinatown*, (San Francisco: R & E Research Associates, Reprinted in 1974), p. 23.
19 Mary Roberts Coolidge, ibid., p. 396.
20 *Alta*, April 3, 1876, p. 1, col. 1.
21 Mary Roberts Coolidge, ibid., p. 110.
22 Victor and Brett De Bary Nee, ibid., p. 46.
23 Mary Roberts Coolidge, ibid., p. 46.
24 *Alta*, April 6, 1876, p. 1, col. 3.

25 Victor and Brett De Bary Nee, ibid., p. 46.
26 *Chronicle*, April 6, 1876, p. 3, col. 3.
27 *Evening Bulletin*, May 11, 1876, p. 1, col. 4.
28 Victor and Brett De Bary Nee, ibid., p. 49.
29 Mary Roberts Coolidge, ibid., p. 114.
30 Ibid., p. 47.
31 Ibid.
32 Mary Roberts Coolidge, ibid., p. 114.
33 Ibid.
34 *Chinese Record*, June 30, 1877, p. 1, col. 4.
35 Mary Roberts Coolidge, ibid., p. 115.
36 *Chronicle*, July 24, 1877, p. 3, col. 5.
37 Pearl Ng, ibid., p. 22.
38 Victor and Brett De Bary Nee, ibid., p. 47.
39 Lim P. Lee, "San Francisco Chinatown's Labor Problems," *Chinese Digest*, July, 1938, p. 6, col. 3.
40 Mary Roberts Coolidge, ibid., p. 115.
41 Elmer Clarence Sandmeyer, *The Anti-Chinese Movement in California*, (Urbana: University of Illinois Press, 1939), p. 65.
42 Victor and Brett De Bary Nee, ibid., p. 48.
43 *Evening Bulletin*, September 25, 1877, p. 2, col. 4.
44 Victor and Brett De Bary Nee, ibid., p. 48.
45 Betty Lee Sung, *Mountain of Gold*, (New York: The Macmillan Company, 1967), p. 43.
46 *Alta*, November 4, 1877, p. 1, col. 1. Also in Winfield Davis, ibid., pp. 371-372.
47 Elmer Clarence Sandmeyer, ibid., p. 66.
48 Ibid., p. 110.
49 California *Constitution*, 1879, Article XIX.
50 Six Chinese Companies, *Memorial— An Address to the Senate and House of Representativies of the United States*, (San Francisco: December 8, 1877), pp. 1, 53.
51 *The Chinese Record*, March 26, 1878, p. 1, cols. 1-3.
52 Lucile Eaves, *A History of California labor Legislation*, (Berkeley: The University Press, 1910), p. 172.
53 Betty Lee Sung, ibid., pp. 49-50.
54 Ibid.
55 H. Brett Melendy and Benjamin F. Gilbert, *The Governors of California*, (Georgetown, California: Talisman Press, 1965), p. 118.
56 Him Mark Lai and Philip P. Choy, *Outlines, History of the Chinese in America*, (San Francisco, California: Fong Bros. Printing, 1971), p. 88.
57 Victor and Brett De Bary Nee, ibid., pp. 53-54.
58 Ibid.
59 Lim P. Lee, ibid., p. 7, col. 1.
60 Victor and Brett De Bary Nee, ibid., pp. 54-55.
61 *Senate Journal*, (20th Session), 1874, p. 604.
62 Ibid., p. 683.
63 *Assembly Journal*, (20th Session), 1874, pp. 1085-1086.
64 *Ward v. Flood*, 48 California 36-43.
65 *Amendments to Codes of California*, (Annotated Ed.) 1873074, p. 211.
66 Superintendent of Public Instruction, *6th Biennial Report*, 1874 and 1875, p. 144.
67 Charles Wollenberg, ibid., p. 24.
68 Arthur G. Butzbach, "The Segregation of Orientals in the San Francisco Schools," Master's Thesis, Stanford University, 1928, p. 10.
69 *Senate Journal* (23rd Session), 1880, pp. 381-4, 389, 405-7, and 451-4.
70 *Annual Report*, 1873, pp. 93-94. See also pp. 62, 75, 82 and 89 for other anti-Chinese compositions.
71 Ibid., p. 79.
72 *San Francisco China News*, April 3, 1875, p. 3, col. 5.

73 *Annual Report*, 1874, p. 37.
74 Ibid., 1875, pp. 54-55.
75 Ibid., 1878, pp. 116-117.
76 Ibid., 1875, pp. 132-133.
77 Ibid., 1860, pp. 30-31.
78 Ibid., 1870, p. 73.
79 Ibid., 1879, p. 333; 1880, p. 51; 1882, p. 30.
80 Ibid., 1869, p. 301.
81 Ibid., 1878, p. 106.
82 State Superintendent of Public Instruction, *5th Biennial Report*, 1872 and 1873, p. 126.
83 *California Statues*, 1865-1866, pp. 395-396.
84 S. Well Williams, "Chinese Immigration;" a paper read before the Social Science Association's Annual Convention at Saratoga, September 10, 1879, (New York: Scribner, 1879), p. 43.
85 *Evening Bulletin*, October 23, 1872, p. 1, col. 3.
86 Ibid., November 9, 1876, p. 3, col. 3.
87 *Report of the Joint Special Committee to Investigate Chinese Immigration*, (Washington: Government Printing Office, 1877), pp. 400-401
88 Ibid., pp. 432-433.
89 Rev. Otis Gibson, *Chinese in America* (Cincinnati: Hitchcock and Walden, 1877), pp. 381-383.
90 *Chronicle*, July 24, 1877, p. 3, col. 7.
91 Luther Tracy Townsend, *The Chinese Problem*, (Boston: Lee and Shepard, 1876), pp. 40-41.
92 J.G. Kerr, "The Chinese Question Analyzed," a Lecture Delivered in the Hall of the Young Men's Christian Association, November 13, 1877, San Francisco, p. 16.
93 Six Chinese Companies, *Memorial—An Address to the Senate and House of Representatives of the United States*, (San Francisco: 1877), p. 11.
94 *Chinese Record*, February 5, 1877, p. 1, par. 2.
95 Ibid., May 21, 1877, p. 1, col. 1.
96 *Evening Bulletin*, August 22, 1877, p. 1, col. 1.
97 *Sacramento Union*, August 22, 1877, p. 3, col. 4.
98 *Alta*, August 22, 1877, p. 1, col. 5.
99 *Evening Bulletin*, October 3, 1877, p. 2, col. 2.
100 *Daily Morning Call*, March 7, 1878, p. 2, col. 3.
101 Ibid.
102 *Evening Bulletin*, July 8, 1882, p. 3, col. 7.
103 Ibid., p. 2, col. 1.
104 Ibid., p. 3, col. 7.

## CHAPTER FOUR

1 Willard B. Farwell, *The Chinese at Home and Abroad* together with "The Report of the Board of Supervisors of San Francisco on the Condition of the Chinese Quarter of that City," (San Francisco: A.L. Bancroft & Co., 1885), pp. 58-62.
2 Francis Yung Chang, "A Study of the Movement to Segregate Chinese Pupils in the San Francisco Public Schools Up to 1885," Doctoral Dissertation, Stanford University, 1936, p. 306.
3 *Evening Bulletin*, September 29, 1884, p. 1, col. 6.
4 Ibid.
5 Ibid., October 22, 1884, p. 1, col. 5.
6 Ibid., October 11, 1884, p. 4, col. 3.
7 Ibid.
8 Ibid., October 22, 1884, p. 1, col. 5.

9 Ibid.
10 Ibid.
11 Ibid., November 13, 1884, p. 1, col. 7.
12 Ibid.
13 Ibid., January 10, 1885, p. 2, col. 3.
14 Ibid.
15 Ibid.
16 Ibid., January 15, 1885, p. 1, col. 5.
17 Ibid.
18 Ibid.
19 Ibid.
20 Ibid.
21 66 *California* 473-474.
22 Ibid.
23 *Evening Bulletin*, January 10, 1885, p. 2, col. 3
24 Charles Wollenberg, *All Deliberate Speed*, (Berkeley: University of California Press, 1976), pp. 41-42.
25 *Evening Bulletin*, March 4, 1885, p. 2, col. 5.
26 *Journal of the Assembly*, California, 26th Session, 1885, p. 92.
27 *Evening Bulletin*, March 4, 1885, p. 2, col. 5. For background on the omission of Chinese children from apportionment, see Norman Almeida Fernandes; "The San Francisco Board of Education and the Chinese Community: Segregation-Desegregation, 1870-1975," Doctoral Dissertation, University of Denver, 1976, pp. 67-69.
28 Ibid., March 5, 1885, p. 1, col. 7. For details on how the new legislation was passed through the Assembly, see *Journal of the Assembly*, California, 26th Session, 1885, pp. 229, 544.
29 Ibid.
30 Ibid., March 7, 1885, p. 4, col. 3.
31 Ibid. For details on how the bill moved through the Senate, see *Senate Journal*, California, 26th Session, 1885, pp. 523-524, and 535.
32 *Statutes and Amendments to the Codes*, California, 1885, 26th Session, pp. 99-100.
33 Francis Yung Chang, ibid., p. 323.
34 *Evening Bulletin*, March 19, 1885, p. 1, col. 5.
35 Ibid., April 2, 1885, p. 1, col. 5.
36 Ibid.
37 Ibid.
38 Ibid.
39 Ibid., April 7, 1885, p. 2, col. 4.
40 Ibid.
41 Ibid., April 8, 1885, p. 1, col. 7.
42 Ibid.
43 Ibid.
44 *Alta*, April 16, 1885, p. 1, col. 3. See Appendix D for full text.
45 *Evening Bulletin*, April 14, 1885, p. 3, col. 4. School for Chinese children was used interchangeably by the city press as "Chinese Public School," "Chinese Primary School" and "Chinese School."
46 Ibid., April 16, 1885, p. 3, col. 8
47 *Annual Report*, 1885, pp. 106-107.
48 Him Mark Lai, "The Chinese and Public Education in San Francisco," Part 2, *East-West*, September 1, 1971, p. 5, col. 4.
49 *Evening Bulletin*, April 16, 1885, p. 3, col. 8.
50 *Annual Report*, 1885, p. 107.
51 *Evening Bulletin*, April 16, 1885, p. 3, col. 8.
52 *Alta*, April 17, 1885, p. 4, col. 1.
53 *Daily Morning Call*, March 21, 1886, p. 5, col. 1.
54 *Evening Bulletin*, March 25, 1886, p. 1, col. 4
55 Circular No. 56, April 1, 1886.

56 Betty Lee Sung, *Mountain of Gold*, (New York: The Macmillan Company, 1967), p. 55.
57 *Daily Morning Call*, October 2, 1888, p. 2, col. 3.
58 Mary Roberts Coolidge, *Chinese Immigration*, (New York: Henry Holt and Company, 1909), p. 203.
59 Betty Lee Sung, ibid., pp. 55-56.
60 Samuel D. Lee, "A Chinese Community Center," *Chinese Digest*, December 6, 1935, p. 10, col. 3.
61 Norman Almeida Fernandes, ibid., p. 42. Cited California *Statutes and Amendments to the Codes*, 1891, pp. 185-191.
62 Victor and Brett De Bary Nee, ibid., p.55.
63 Lim P. Lee, "The Political Rights of the American Citizens of Chinese Ancestry," *Chinese Digest*, October 23, 1936, p. 11, col. 1.
64 Interview with S.K. Lai, past editor of *Chinese Times*, May 20, 1978.
65 Rose Hum Lee, *The Chinese in the United States of America*, (Hong Kong University Press, 1960), p. 180.
66 Betty Lee Sung, ibid., p. 139.
67 Thomas W. Chinn, *A History of the Chinese in California*, (San Francisco: Chinese Historical Society of America, 1969), p. 79.
68 *Evening Bulletin*, November 23, 1901, p. 4, col. 2.
69 Ibid., November 18, 1901, p. 6, col. 2.
70 Elmer Clarence Sandmeyer, *The Anti-Chinese Movement in California*, (Urbana: University of Illinois Press, 1973), p. 107. Published originally in 1939. Cited House Doc. No. 1, 57th Congress, 1st Session, p. XVIII.
71 Him Mark Lai and Philip P. Choy, *Outlines: History of the Chinese in America*, (San Francisco: Fong Bros. Printing, 1971), p. 92.
72 Lim P. Lee, ibid., p. 11, cols. 1-3.
73 *Examiner*, February 23, 1909, p. 3, col. 2.
74 H. Brett Melendy and Benjamin F. Gilbert, *The Governors of California*, (Georgetown, California: Talisman Press, 1965), pp. 266-267.
75 *Annual Report*, 1886, pp. 60-61.
76 Ibid., p. 90.
77 *Evening Bulletin*, June 17, 1886, p. 1, col. 7 and July 1, 1886, p. 4, col. 1.
78 *Daily Morning Call*, November 30, 1886, p. 2, col. 1.
79 Rev. S.L. Baldwin, "The Education of the Mongolian, or Chinese," *The Journal of Proceedings and Addresses of the Educational Association*, 1886 Session at Topeka, Kansas, (Salem: Observer Book and Job Print, 1887), pp. 211-221.
80 *Annual Reports*, 1887, p. 19; 1888. p. 80; 1889, p. 6.
81 Ibid., 1893, p. 25; 1894, p. 59; 1895, p. 122; 1897, p. 44.
82 Ibid., 1898, p. 67.
83 *Daily Morning Call*, January 23, 1898, p. 26, col. 1.
84 Ibid., August 4, 1897, p. 5, col. 1.
85 *Annual Report*, 1891, p. 16.
86 Ibid., 1892, pp. 97-98; 1893, p. 7; 1894, pp. 36-37,, 54.
87 Ibid., 1897, p. 44.
88 *Daily Morning Call*, March 13, 1894, p. 3, col. 7.
89 *Evening Bulletin*, March 1, 1894, p. 6, col. 4.
90 *Daily Morning Call*, March 13, 1894, p. 3, col. 7.
91 Ibid., March 1, 1894, p. 10, col. 5.
92 *Examiner*, March 1, 1894, p. 10, col. 2.
93 *Daily Morning Call*, March 1, 1894, p. 10, col. 5.
94 *Chronicle*, March 1, 1894, p. 4, col. 6.
95 *Examiner*, March 1, 1894, p. 10, col. 2.
96 *Call*, March 1, 1894, p. 10, col. 5.
97 Ibid., March 11, 1894, p. 7, col. 1
98 Ibid.
99 Ibid., p. 7, cols. 1-2.
100 Ibid., March 12, 1894, p. 6, col. 2.
101 Ibid., March 13, 1894, p. 3, col. 7.

102 Ibid.
103 Ibid., March 15, 1894, p. 3, col. 3.
104 Ibid.
105 *Chronicle*, March 15, 1894, p. 3, col. 3
106 Ibid.
107 *Daily Morning Call*, January 23, 1898, p. 26, col. 1.
108 Ibid., April 4, 1897, p. 27, col. 1.
109 Ibid., January 23, 1898, p. 26, col. 1.
110 Ibid., April 4, 1897, p. 27, col. 1. The term "Fon Gwai" (番鬼) was used twice by the reporter in this article. This derisive term, coined by the Chinese toward white Americans who mistreated them, evidently was a common enough phrase for the reporter to understand that it referred to white Americans. Whether the reporter knew this term carried negative connotations could not be ascertained. That it was first noted in the early 1850s, became part of the idiom and is still a contemporary term demonstrate the depth of the bitterness long after the events occurred.
111 Mary Roberts Coolidge, ibid., p. 436. The date of this incident was confusing as Coolidge used 1905 in another section of her book. Other substantiating evidence to support this incident could not be found.
112 Mary Roberts Coolidge, ibid., p. 438.
113 See *Wong Him v. Callahan*, et. al., 119 Federal Reporter 381-383 (1903). The litigation stated that Dr. Wong Him's child's name was Henry. Newspapers covering this case at times used "Katie" and at times used "Henry." See newspaper footnotes in this section for reference.
114 *San Francisco Call*, August 20, 1902, p. 6, col. 6.
115 Philip Albert Lum, "The Chinese Freedom Schools of San Francisco: A Case Study of the Social Limits of Political System Support," Doctoral Dissertation, University of California, Berkeley, 1975, p. 81.
116 *San Francisco Call*, June 19, 1902, p. 10, col. 1.
117 Ibid., August 20, 1902, p. 6, col. 6.
118 *Statutes and Amendments to the Codes*, California 1885, 26th Session, pp. 99-100.
119 *San Francisco Bulletin*, June 19, 1902, p. 10, col. 1.
120 Ibid., August 20, 1902, p. 6, col. 6.
121 Ibid. By the time the lawsuit got under way, the principalship at Clement School was changed from McFarland to Callahan. The legal challenge followed accordingly; hence it was *Wong Him v. Callahan* and not *Wong Him v. McFarland*.
122 *Chronicle*, November 30, 1902, p. 12, col. 1.
123 Ibid.
124 *Wong Him v. Callahan*, 119 F. 382 (1903).
125 *Plessy v. Ferguson*, 163 U.S. 537, at 550-551 (1896).
126 *Examiner*, February 20, 1903, p. 4, col. 1.
127 Ibid.
128 Ibid.
129 Ibid., February 19, 1903, p. 8, col. 2.
130 Ibid., February 20, 1903, p. 4, col. 1. No record was found describing the consequences of her trip.
131 Ibid.
132 *Annual Reports*, 1891, p. 36; 1892, p. 161; 1893, p. 28.
133 *Chronicle*, June 15, 1893, p. 5, col. 5.
134 Superintendents *Letters to Principals*, April 28, 1896; September 18, 1897; May 24, 1899.
135 Ibid., Circular No. 12, February 28, 1902; Circular No. 13, April 16, 1903; Circular No. 3, September 13, 1904; Circular No. 1, August 10, 1905.
136 *Chronicle*, May 7, 1905, p. 25, cols. 6-7.
137 Lee Stephen Dolson, Jr., ibid., p. 349. Cited Walton Bean, *Boss Ruef's San Francisco*, (Berkeley: University of California Press, 1952), p. 22.
138 Irving G. Hendrick, ibid., p. 39.

139 *Examiner*, May 15, 1905, p. 4, col. 3.
140 *Chronicle*, December 19, 1906, p. 1, col. 5.
141 Superintendent's *Letter to Principals*, Circular No. 8, January 12, 1906.
142 *Daily Morning Call*, January 13, 1904, p. 11, col. 1.
143 Ibid., January 14, 1904, p. 9, col. 4.
144 Cecilia Newhall, "The Chinese Public School of San Francisco," *Dragon Student* (published by the Chinese Students' Alliance of America, 1905), p. 20. Since Newhall, the Chinese Primary School has been called Chinese Public School.
145 Ibid.
146 *Daily Morning Call*, November 28, 1908, p. 2, cols. 3-7.
147 Cecilia Newhall, ibid., p. 21.
148 Francis John Dyer, "A Chinese Public School," *World Today*, Volume 8, (Chicago: The World Today Company, 1905), pp. 333-334.

## CHAPTER FIVE

1 *Chinese Digest*, June 26, 1936, p. 1, col. 1.
2 Helen V. Cather, *The History of San Francisco's Chinatown*, (San Francisco: R & E Research Associates, Reprinted in 1974), p. 44.
3 Lee Stephen Dolson, Jr., "The Administration of the San Francisco Public Schools, 1847-1947," Doctoral Dissertation, University of California, Berkeley, 1964, p. 345. Cited Hubert D. Russell, *Complete Story of the San Francisco Horror*, (San Francisco: The Author, 1906), p. 256.
4 Ibid.
5 *Chronicle*, December 7, 1902, p. 6, col. 4; December 14, 1902, p. 6, col. 2.
6 Thomas W. Chinn, "New Chapters in Chinese American History," *California History*, Volume LVII, No. 1, (San Francisco: California Historical Society, Spring 1978), p. 7.
7 Norman Almeida Fernandes, "The San Francisco Board of Education and the Chinese Community: Segregation-Desegregation, 1850-1975," Doctoral Dissertation, University of Denver, 1976, p. 94.
8 *Daily Morning Call*, May 27, 1906, p. 31, col. 1.
9 Rev. John Hood Laughlin, "Chinese Children in American Schools," *Overland Monthly*, May 1911, p. 503.
10 Philip Albert Lum, "The Chinese Freedom Schools of San Francsico: A Case Study of the Social Limits of Political System Support," Doctoral Dissertation, University of California at Berkeley, 1975, p. 80.
11 Charles Wollenberg, *All Deliberate Speed*, (Berkeley, California, University of California Press, 1976), p. 54.
12 *Minutes of San Francisco Board of Education*, September 27, 1906. Hereafter written "Board Minutes." The writer is of the opinion that Mason Street was a typographical error. The correct location should be between Powell and Stockton Streets. The struggle of relocating the Chinese Public School in 1894 and the later incident of a permanent structure for the Oriental School in 1915, showed that Powell Street was already "Caucasian territory." Since Mason Street is a block above Powell, it is highly unlikely that this location was the intent of the school authorities.
13 For an elaboration of this distinction, see Robert Kwan's article "Asian vs. Oriental: A Distinction Worth Making," *East/West*, June 4, 1980.
14 *Board Minutes*, October 11, 1906.
15 *Chronicle*, November 11, 1906, p. 66, col. 3.
16 Ibid., March 14, 1907, p. 4, col. 1.
17 *Board Minutes*, March 13, 1907.
18 Irving G. Hendrick, *The Education of Non-Whites in California, 1849-1970*, (San Francisco: R & E Research Associates, 1977), p. 40. Cited *Board Minutes*, June 6, 1907. The names of the five other schools were not indicated.
19 Philip Albert Lum, ibid., p. 82.

20 Bailey Millard, *History of the San Francisco Bay Region*, Volume I (San Francisco: The American Historical Society Inc., 1924), p. 357.
21 William Inglis, "The Width of a School Bench: Reasons for California's Defiant Decree Against the Japanese in Her Public Schools," *Harper's Weekly*, Volume 51, January 19, 1907, pp. 83-84.
22 *Chronicle*, October 12, 1906, p. 10, col. 4.
23 Ibid.
24 *Daily Morning Call*, October 12, 1906, p. 11, col. 7.
25 William Inglis, ibid., p. 83.
26 Superintendent's *Letter to Principals*, April 25, 1905.
27 Arthur Graham Butzbach, "The Segregation of Orientals in the San Francisco Schools," Master's Thesis, Stanford University, 1928, p. 81, citing *Christian Advocate* (San Francisco), November 29, 1906.
28 Lee Stephen Dolson, Jr., ibid., pp. 725.
29 *Board Minutes*, September 23, 1908.
30 *Chronicle*, August 29, 1908. p. 16, col. 4.
31 *Daily Morning Call*, August 23, 1908, p. 48, col. 1.
32 *Chronicle*, August 30, 1908, p. 28, col. 4.
33 Ibid.
34 *Daily Morning Call*, August 23, 1908. p. 48, col. 1.
35 *San Francisco News*, October 17, 1908, p. 1, cols. 1-2.
36 *Chronicle*, October 18, 1908, p. 52, col. 5.
37 Ibid. The class was established at the Presbyterian Mission across the street from the Oriental School.
38 *San Francisco News*, October 17, 1908, p. 1, cols. 1-2.
39 *Daily Morning Call*, November 28, 1908, p. 2, cols 3-7.
40 *San Francisco News*, October 17, 1908, p. 1, col. 2.
41 *Chronicle*, October 18, 1908, p. 52, col. 5.
42 Ibid., August 25, 1908, p. 5, col. 6.
43 *Examiner*, August 26, 1908, p. 3, col. 6.
44 *Examiner*, February 10, 1909, p. 1, cols. 5-6.
45 Ibid., p. 2, col. 7.
46 California *Statutes and Amendments to the Codes*, 1909, 38th Session, pp. 903-904.
47 *Examiner*, October 14, 1908, p. 5, col. 4.
48 *Chronicle*, October 14, 1908, p. 16, col. 4.
49 *Daily Morning Call*, March 21, 1910, p. 14, col. 3.
50 *Chronicle*, June 2, 1910, p. 4, col. 1.
51 *Daily Morning Call*, September 1, 1910, p. 7, col. 2.
52 Ibid.
53 Newspaper Files, Teachers' Professional Library, San Francisco Unified School District, 1910-1911, Volume 12, p. 160. Cited *San Francisco Post*, February 15, 1911.
54 *Chronicle*, February 16, 1911, p. 10, col. 3.
55 Ibid., February 21, 1911, p. 4, col. 1.
56 Ibid.
57 *Daily Morning Call*, February 23, 1911, p. 6, col. 2.
58 Ibid., April 8, 1911, p. 15, col. 5.
59 *Chinese World*, September 2, 1910, p. 4, col. 3; April 10, 1911, p. 4, col. 1. Its Chinese title is 世界日報
60 *Chronicle*, April 27, 1911, p. 10, col. 2.
61 *Examiner*, May 28, 1911, p. 80, cols. 5-6.
62 Victor and Brett De Bary Nee, ibid., p. 72. Dr. Sun Yat-Sen's party overthrew the Manchu government and established the Republic of China.
63 Thomas W. Chinn, *A History of the Chinese in California*, (San Francisco: Chinese Historical Society of America, 1969), p. 79. See also Paul Jacobs and Saul Landau, *To Serve the Devil*, Vol.2: Colonials and Sojourners, (New York: Vintage Books, 1971), pp. 114-115.

64 Pei Chi Liu, *A History of the Chinese in the United States of America,* (Taiwan: Li-Ming Cultural Enterprise Publisher, 1976), p. 372.
65 Ibid.
66 *Chronicle,* January 16, 1909, p. 20, col. 1
67 Him Mark Lai, "The Chinese and Public Education in San Francisco," Part 3, *East-West,* Chinese-American Weekly, September 8, 1971, p. 5, col. 1.
68 See Mary Bo-Tze Lee, "Problems of the Segregated School for Asiatics in San Francisco," Masters Thesis, University of California at Berkeley, 1920, p. 3. See also Samuel Lee, *San Francisco's Chinatown — History, Functions and Social Importance of Social Organizations,* (San Francisco Chamber of Commerce, 1936), p. 10.
69 Rev. John Hood Laughlin, "Chinese Children in American Schools," *Overland Monthly,* May 1911, p. 507.
70 *Chronicle,* March 19, 1908, p. 13, col. 3.
71 *Board Minutes,* September 1, 1909.
72 *Daily Morning Call,* March 29, 1908, p. 39, col. 1.
73 *Board Minutes,* February 3, 1909.
74 Ibid., April 21, 1909; April 17, 1912; May 22, 1912.
75 Ibid., October 6, 1909.
76 Ibid., September 21, 1910.
77 Ibid., April 3, 1912.
78 *Examiner,* April 9, 1912, p. 12, col. 3.
79 *Board Minutes,* April 24, 1912.
80 Ibid., June 13, 1912.
81 *Examiner,* September 22, 1912, p. 88, col. 4.
82 *Chronicle,* September 25, 1912, p. 18, col. 6.
83 Ibid.
84 Ibid., October 3, 1912, p. 8, col. 1.
85 Ibid. For race war see *Examiner,* October 3, 1912, p. 8 col. 1. For fatality see *Chronicle,* February 2, 1912, p. 2, col. 4; August 3, 1912, p. 4, col. 4.
86 *Chronicle,* October 3, 1912, p. 9, col. 1.
87 Ibid.
88 *Daily Morning Call,* October 8, 1912, p. 7, col. 1.
89 *Examiner,* October 8, 1912, p. 12, cols. 2-3.
90 *Board Minutes,* October 16, 1912.
91 Ibid., October 24, 1912.
92 *Daily Morning Call,* November 5, 1912, p. 18, col. 2.
93 *Board Minutes,* November 13, 1912. This is the official version. The *Call* reported that the recommended site by the delegation was the lot on Stockton Street near Sacramento. See *Daily Morning Call,* November 14, 1912, p. 17, col. 7.
94 *Chronicle,* January 31, 1913, p. 10, col. 1.
95 *Board Minutes,* February 13, 1913.
96 Ibid., February 26, 1913.
97 Newspaper Files, Teachers' Professional Library, San Francisco Unified School District, 1913, Volume 24, p. 58. From *Call,* April 24, 1913.
98 *Board Minutes,* April 26, 1913.
99 Newspaper Files, Teachers' Professional Library, San Francisco Unified School District, 1913, Volume 24, p. 85. From *Post,* May 6, 1913.
100 Ibid. Both the *Evening Bulletin,* May 6, 1913, p. 2, col. 1, and *San Francisco Daily News,* May 6, 1913, p. 2, cols. 2-3, singled out the Oriental School as the notable reason why Le Conte would not be built.
101 *Board Minutes,* May 9, 1913.
102 *San Francisco Daily News,* May 13, 1913, p. 6, col. 3.
103 Ibid.
104 Ibid.
105 *Board Minutes,* October 28, 1913.
106 *San Francisco Daily News,* October 30, 1913, p. 1, col. 4.
107 Ibid.

108  Ibid.
109  Ibid.
110  *Board Minutes*, November 4, 1913.
111  *Chronicle*, December 20, 1913, p. 11, col. 7.
112  *San Francisco Daily News*, January 6, 1914, p. 2, col. 6.
113  *Chronicle*, January 8, 1914, p. 8, col. 3.
114  Ibid.
115  Ibid.
116  Ibid.
117  *Examiner*, January 18, 1914, p. 32, col. 6.
118  *San Francisco Daily News*, January 20, 1914, p. 6, col. 3.
119  Ibid.
120  Ibid.
121  *Examiner*, January 20, 1914, p. 3, col. 2.
122  *Chronicle*, January 20, 1914, p. 3, col. 2.
123  *San Francisco Journal of Commerce*, January 20, 1914 p. 2, col. 2.
124  *Board Minutes*, March 10, 1914.
125  *Examiner*, April 9, 1914, p. 9, col. 1.
126  *Board Minutes*, July 23, 1914.
127  *San Francisco Call and Post*, January 21, 1915, p. 10, col. 7.
128  *Board Minutes*, October 19, 1915.
129  *Chronicle*, October 21, 1915, p. 4, col. 4.
130  Ibid., October 20, 1915, p. 10, col. 4.
131  Chung Sai Yat Po, October 21, 1915, p. 3. Its Chinese title is 中西日報
132  Chingwah Lee, "Remember When?" *Chinese Digest*, March 6, 1936, p. 9, col. 3.
     See also *Chinese World*, December 17, 1910, p. 3, col. 3.
133  Sources were San Francisco newspapers from June 1907, to June 1915.
134  Department of the Interior, Bureau of Education, *The Public School System of
     San Francisco, California*, Bulletin, 1917, No. 46, (Washington: Government
     Printing Office, 1917), pp. 546-547.
135  Mary Bo-Tze Lee, ibid., pp. 9, 16, 30, 31.
136  Ibid., pp. 9, 12.
137  Ibid., pp. 29-32.
138  Interview with Him Mark Lai, president of Chinese Historical Society of
     America, January 21, 1979.
139  May Bo-Tze Lee, ibid., p. 5.
140  Francis John Dyer, "A Chinese Public School," *World Today*, Volume 8, (The
     World Today Company, Chicago, 1905), p. 334.
141  Ibid.
142  Kenneth Joe, "The Oriental School," *East-West*, January 1, 1970, p. 19, Chinese
     Language Section.
143  Mary Bo-Tze Lee, ibid., pp. 6-7.
144  Ibid., p. 7.
145  Ibid.
146  Him Mark Lai, "The Chinese in Public School," ibid.
147  *Statutes and Amendments to the Codes*, California, 1921, 44th Session, p.
     1161.

## CHAPTER SIX

1  *Chronicle*, January 18, 1922, p. 8, cols. 1-4. Dr. Ng's Chinese name is 伍盤照
   博士
2  Ibid. Part of the assimilation process was to have names like other American
   children and to do away with the phonetic transcription of the Chinese names
   into English—thus Low Teen Chee becomes Victor Low. A look at the city's
   newspapers would show that by 1922, "American" names began outnumber-
   ing the phonetic transcription of the Chinese names among the Oriental

School graduates. See *San Francisco California Journal*, June 17, 1922. Cited from Newspaper Files of San Francisco Unified School District, Volume 35, Part II, 1922, p. 131. Compare this with *Chronicle*, June 4, 1915, p. 10, col. 8.

3  *Minutes of Native Sons of the Golden State*, December 6, 1921.
4  *Board Minutes*, January 17, 1922; February 7, 1922.
5  Ibid., March 7, 1922.
6  Ibid., August 15, 1922.
7  *Examiner*, August 24, 1922, p. 15, col. 8.
8  *San Francisco Journal*, November 3, 1922. In Newspaper Files of San Francisco Unified School District, Volume 35, Part I, April-December 1922, p. 90.
9  *Examiner*, April 18, 1922, p. 15, col. 5.
10  *Board Minutes*, September 5, 1922.
11  Ibid., October 3, 1922.
12  *San Francisco Daily News*, November 13, 1922, p. 9, col. 5. See also *Call/Post*, November 14, 1922, p. 17, col. 8.
13  *Chronicle*, November 25, 1922, p. 3, col. 1.
14  Ibid., January 31, 1923, p. 8, col. 8. Francisco Primary School would later be part of the narrative when it was redesignated as a junior high school.
15  *Examiner*, April 14, 1923, p. 7, col. 3.
16  *Board Minutes*, May 1, 1923.
17  Ibid., October 2, 1923.
18  *San Francisco California Journal*, March 17, 1923. Cited in Newspaper Files of the San Francisco Unified School District, Teachers' Professional Library, Vol. 36, 1922-23, p. 95.
19  *Chung Sai Yat Po*, March 19, 1924, pp. 2-3.
20  *Board Minutes*, April 22, 1924.
21  *Minutes of Native Sons*, September 13, 1923.
22  *Chung Sai Yat Po*, January 5, 1924, p. 3.
23  *Board Minutes*, February 19, 1924.
24  Ibid., February 26, 1924.
25  Ibid.
26  Ibid., April 1, 1924.
27  Ibid., March 11, 1925.
28  Ibid., March 24, 1925.
29  Ibid., June 16, 1925. This was also the time that Jean Parker Girls School and Washington Grammar Boys School became co-educational. These schools were located on the fringes of Chinatown.
30  Ibid., April 8, 1925.
31  Ibid., May 12, 1925.
32  *Minutes of Native Sons*, June 3, 1925.
33  *Board Minutes*, June 16, 1925.
34  Ibid.,
35  Ibid., June 23, 1925.
36  Ibid., August 25, 1925.
37  *San Francisco Bulletin*, September 3, 1925, p. 6, col. 1. See also *Chung Sai Yat Po*, September 3, 1925, p. 3. The reporter reverted back to the old name of Commodore Stockton School.
38  *Chung Sai Yat Po*, February 4, 1926, p. 2.
39  *Chronicle*, February 6, 1926, p. 15, col. 4.
40  *Chung Sai Yat Po*, February 6, 1926, p. 3.
41  *San Francisco Daily News*, February 6, 1926, p. 3, col. 6.
42  *Chronicle*, February 6, 1926, p. 15, col. 4. Washington Grammar School was located on Washington and Mason Streets—one and a half blocks away from Commodore Stockton School.
43  *Chung Sai Yat Po*, February 19, 1926, p. 2. The Chinese Consul-General's name is 葉可探領事
44  *Chung Sai Yat Po*, February 20, 1926, p. 2. Mr. Fung's Chinese name is 馮汝達
45  Ibid.
46  Ibid.

47 Ibid.
48 *San Francisco Daily News*, March 5, 1926, p. 11, col. 5.
49 *Chung Sai Yat Po*, March 6, 1926, p. 3.
50 Ibid.
51 Ibid.
52 *Chronicle*, March 20, 1926, p. 3, col. 1.
53 Ibid.
54 Ibid.
55 Ibid.
56 Ibid.
57 *Chung Sai Yat Po*, March 20, 1926, pp. 2-3.
58 *Board Minutes*, March 23, 1926.
59 Ibid., March 30, 1926.
60 Ibid., April 6, 1926.
61 Ibid., May 11, 1926.
62 Ibid.
63 Ibid., May 18, 1926.
64 Ibid., June 29, 1926.
65 *Examiner*, June 30, 1926, p. 6, cols. 6-8.
66 *Chonicle*, June 30, 1926, p. 17, col. 8.
67 Ibid.
68 *Board Minutes*, June 29, 1926.
69 *Examiner*, June 30, 1926, p. 6, col. 8.
70 *Minutes of Native Sons*, July 7, 1926.
71 *San Francisco Bulletin*, May 31, 1929, p. 4, col. 3.
72 Wellington Chew, the first Chinese supervisor in Bilingual Education, attended Jean Parker School in 1930. Jim Wong, a teacher at Everett, attended Washington Irving School in 1935. Chinese living outside of Chinatown had to apply for special permission to attend their neighborhood schools as in the case of Elizabeth Hall, the first Chinese principal in San Francisco.
73 *School Code of the State of California*, 1929, p. v. Cited in Francis Yung Chang, "A Study of the Movement to Segregate Chinese Pupils in the San Francisco Public Schools up to 1885," Doctoral Dissertation, Stanford Univ., 1936, p. 222.
74 Interview with Alice Fong Yu, October 10, 1977.
75 *Board Minutes*, October 6, 1925.
76 Interview with S.K. Lai, past editor of *Chinese Times*, May 20, 1978.
77 Christopher Chow and Russell Leong, "A Pioneer Chinatown Teacher: An Interview with Alcie Fong Yu," *Amerasia Journal*, Volume 5, Number 1, Asian American Studies Center, University of California at Los Angeles, 1978, p. 81.
78 Ibid., p. 79.
79 Interview with Alice Fong Yu.
80 Ibid.
81 Teacher Efficiency Report, May 10, 1928.
82 Personnel File, June 6, 1927.
83 Ibid., June 10, 1927.
84 Ibid., June 6, 1927.
85 *Call Bulletin*, June 19, 1952, p. 7F, cols. 1-2.
86 Letter to placement office secretary, November 29, 1929.
87 Ibid.
88 Letter to placement office secretary, November, 1929.
89 Memo to personnel committee from assistant director of personnel, April 18, 1932.
90 *Amerasia Journal*, ibid., p. 81.
91 Teacher efficiency report, August 10, 1931.
92 Letter from deputy superintendent in charge of personnel to Francisco's principal, March 11, 1931.
93 Letter from deputy superintendent to Suey Ng, March 12, 1931.
94 Letter from Francisco's principal to assistant director in charge of personnel, March 20, 1931.

95  Ibid.
96  Letter from Suey Ng to assistant director of personnel, March 20, 1931.
97  Letter from assistant director in charge of personnel to principal of Francisco, March 24, 1931.
98  Letter from deputy superintendent in charge of personnel to state board of education, February 10, 1932.
99  Teacher's efficiency report, March 30, 1933.
100  Teacher transfer request, June 21, 1939.
101  Teacher efficiency report, January 5, 1940.
102  Ibid., May 1941.
103  Interview with Jerry Ng, May 24, 1978.
104  This situation obviously had an impact on Chinese students and their perceptions of their future careers in America. For an in-depth treatment on this subject, see Hsien-Ju Shih's "The Social and Vocational Adjustment of the Second Generation Chinese High School Students in San Francisco," Doctoral Dissertation, University of California at Berkeley, 1937.
105  Interview with Paul Whang, May 8, 1979.
106  *Chinese Digest*, May 15, 1936, pp. 3, 13; May 22, 1936, pp. 3, 14; May 29, 1936, pp. 11, 15; June 5, 1936, p. 5; June 12, 1936, pp. 5, 14; July 3, 1936, pp. 5, 14; July 17, 1936, p. 14.
107  *San Francisco News*, August 10, 1933, p. 11, col. 3.
108  Ibid., December 27, 1933, p. 4, col. 5.
109  Ibid.
110  *Board Minutes*, January 9, 1934 and January 30, 1934.
111  *San Francisco News*, August 10, 1933, p. 11, col. 3.
112  *Call Bulletin*, November 21, 1934, p. 3, col. 1.
113  *San Francisco News*, November 21, 1934, p. 5, cols. 2-3. The original name of this organization was called Native Sons of the Golden State. It was changed to Chinese American Citizens Alliance on December 14, 1928.
114  Ibid.
115  *Chinese Digest*, October 30, 1936, p. 11, col. 2.
116  Ibid., *San Francisco News*, November 21, 1934. Washington Grammar School eventually became the Chinese Recreation Center to address the growing recreational needs of Chinatown. Heretofore the only play facility offered to the young was the Chinese Playground on Sacramento Street which was built in 1925. See *Chinese Digest*, October 30, 1936, p. 15, col. 1.
117  *San Francisco California Hayes Valley Advertiser*, November 27, 1934. Cited in Newspaper File of San Francisco Unified School District, Teachers' Professional Library, Vol. 9, July-December 1934.
118  *Chinese Digest*, October 30, 1936, p. 11, cols. 2-3.

## CHAPTER SEVEN

1  Rose Hum Lee, *The Chinese in the United States of America*, (Hong Kong: Hong Kong University Press, 1960), p. 117.
2  Paul Jacobs and Saul Landau, *To Serve the Devil*, 3 Volumes, Volume II, "Colonials and Sojourners," (New York: Vintage Books, 1971), p. 117.
3  *Board Minutes*, Febraury 23, 1943.
4  *San Francisco News*, March 17, 1943. Cited in Newspaper Files, San Francisco United School District, Teachers' Professional Library, Volume 30 January-June 1943.
5  Interview with Elizabeth Hall, October 10, 1977.
6  *Chinese Press*, October 29, 1943, p. 4, col. 1.
7  Betty Lee Sung, *Mountain of Gold*, (New York: The Macmillan Company, 1967), pp. 78-80.
8  Him Mark Lai & Philip P. Choy, *Outlines: History of the Chinese in America*, (San Francisco, California: Fong Bros. Printing, 1971), p. 145. See advertisement to repeal Chinese Exclusion Act in *Chinese Press*, September 10, 1943, p. 8 and

in Joe Huang and Sharon Quan Wong, *Chinese Americans: Realitites and Myths, Anthology*, (San Francisco: The Association of Chinese Teachers, 1977), pp. 44-45.

9 Rose Hum Lee, ibid.

10 Paul Jacobs and Saul Landau, ibid.

11 Victor G. & Brett De Bary Nee, *Longtime Californ'*, (New York: Pantheon Books, 1972), p. 155.

12 Rose Hum Lee, ibid., p. 314.

13 Ibid.

14 *Chronicle*, March 3, 1941, p. 24, cols. 1-2. See Thomas W. Chinn, *A History of the Chinese in California: A Syllabus*, Chinese Historical Society of America, San Francisco, California, 1969, pp. 78-79 for a list of Chinatown organizations.

15 *San Francisco News*, October 9, 1942, p. 2, cols. 1-4.

16 *Chronicle*, February 6, 1943, p. 20, cols. 4-5.

17 *San Francisco. News*, March 3, 1943. Cited in Newspaper Files, San Francisco Unified School District, Teachers' Professional Library, Volume 30, January-June 1943. This was the first time Chinese students were considered as Americans by a city paper.

18 Ibid., April 26, 1943.

19 *Examiner*, June 25, 1944, Smart Set Section, p. 3, col. 1.

20 *San Francisco News*, October 26, 1944, p. 10, cols. 3-6. Even overseas Chinese were called young Americans or Chinese-Americans.

21 Ibid., June 15, 1946, p. 10.

22 *Examiner*, July 25, 1954, Smart Set Section, p. 7, cols. 6-8.

23 *Westminister School District v. Mendez*, 161 F. (ed.) 774 (1947).

24 California *Statutes and Amendments to the Codes*, 1947, Sections 8003 and 8004, p. 1792.

25 Charles M. Wollenberg, *All Deliberate Speed* (Berkeley: University of California Press, 1976), pp. 108, 132.

26 Philip Albert Lum, "The Chinese Freedom Schools of San Francisco: a Case Study of the Social Limits of Political System Support," Doctoral Dissertation, University of California at Berkeley, 1975, pp. 90-91. Also Norman Almeida Fernandes, "The San Francisco Board of Education and the Chinese Community: Segregation-Desegregation, 1850-1975," Doctoral Dissertation, University of Denver, 1976, p. 122. It is beyond the scope of this study to describe the conflict between the Chinese community and the school board over "desegregation" in the late 1960s and early 1970s. The reader is referred to Lum's and Fernandes' dissertations for a study of this issue.

27 *Board Minutes*, April 15, 1924.

28 Ibid., March 3, 1925. See page 48 of the *Board Minutes* for the exact dimensions of the additional area.

29 Ibid., June 9, 1926.

30 Ibid., September 6, 1927.

31 Ibid., July 29, 1930. It could not be found that the Board acted on this resolution. *Boards Minutes* showed that Superintendent Gwinn and his deputy would investigate and report back.

32 *Board Minutes*, March 18, 1941.

33 *Call Bulletin*, March 27, 1941, Editorial Page, col. 1.

34 Ibid. Chinatown's petition for addiitonal playground space went hand-in-hand with the attempt to acquire low-cost housing. See also *San Francisco News*, April 8, 1941, p. 4, col. 3.

35 *Chronicle*, April 9, 1941, p. 9, cols. 7-8.

36 *Board Minutes*, April 8, 1941.

37 *Call Bulletin*, April 9, 1941, p. 7, cols. 6-8. Thanks to the effort of Susie J. Convery, principal of Commodore Stockton School and one of the members of the Chinatown Improvement Association, Chinatown's problems of congestion, traffic hazard, and lack of play space attracted the attention of the Junior Safety League of California. This organization started a drive to transform Portsmouth Square into a playground for Chinese children. Portsmouth Square

is located two blocks east of Commodore Stockton School. See *Examiner*, October 5, 1941, p. 5, col. 4 and *Chronicle*, November 17, 1941, p. 13, cols. 1-2.

38 *Board Minutes*, April 29, 1941.
39 Ibid., August 12, 1941.
40 Ibid., August 19, 1941.
41 Ibid., August 26, 1941.
42 Ibid., December 2, 1941.
43 Ibid., January 13, 1942.
44 Ibid., February 10, 1942. The actual measurement of the play space is recorded here as well as on December 2, 1941.
45 Ibid., June 30, 1942.
46 Ibid.
47 Ibid.
48 Ibid., April 9, 1946.
49 Ibid., May 7, 1946.
50 Ibid., February 25, 1947.
51 Ibid., August 19, 1947.
52 Ibid.
53 Ibid., August 26, 1941.
54 *Call Bulletin*, April 9, 1941, p. 7, col. 6.
55 The drive by the Chinese Community for recreational facilities resulted in a new Chinese Recreation Center in 1951 on Washington and Mason Streets—the site of the old Washington Grammar School. See *Examiner*, August 15, 1955, p. 6, col. 3.
56 Interview with Florence Loo, April 28, 1978, P.T.A. President, 1945.
57 *Examiner*, January 4, 1945, p. 18, col. 1.
58 Ibid., March 13, 1945. Cited in Newspaper Files, San Francisco Unified School District, Teachers' Professional Library, Vol. 32, July 1944-June 1945.
59 Interview with June Tom, March 10, 1978, P.T.A. President, 1949.
60 Ibid.
61 Ibid.
62 Ibid.
63 Ibid.
64 *Examiner*, May 21, 1948, p. 26, cols. 3-4.
65 *Call Bulletin*, May 20, 1948. Cited in Newspaper Files San Francisco Unified School District, Teachers' Professional Library, Vol. 35, July 1947-June 1948.
66 *Examiner*, May 26, 1948, p. 22, cols. 3-4.
67 *Chronicle*, May 26, 1948, p. 10, col. 4.
68 Interview with Flora Lee, June 28, 1979, former P.T.A. President (date of office uncertain).
69 Rose Hum Lee, *The Chinese in the U.S.A.* (Hong Kong: Hong Kong University Press, 1960), p. 81.
70 Betty Lee Sung, *Mountain of Gold*, (New York: The Macmillan Company, 1967), p. 118.
71 Ibid., pp. 82, 156. Chinese American Citizens Alliance played an important role in bringing this Act into being. See *Chinese Press*, July 1, 1949.
72 Department of City Planning, *Commodore Stockton School Service Area*, August, 1950, p. 3.
73 *San Francisco News*, December 30, 1952, p. 9, col. 3.
74 Lee, ibid., pp. 115-116.
75 Paul Jacobs and Saul Landau, *To Serve the Devil*, Volume II, (New York: Vintage Books, 1971), p. 117. The same thought was expressed in the *San Francisco News*, February 14, 1951. Cited in Newspaper Files, San Francisco Unified School District, Teachers' Professional Library, Vol. 38, July 1950-June 1951.
76 *San Francisco News*, May 27, 1948, p. 17, col. 3; February 20, 1951, p. 22, col. 2; December 30, 1952, p. 9, col. 3. Also *Call Bulletin*, March 31, 1949, p. 15, cols. 1-2.
77 *San Francisco News*, December 30, 1952, p. 9, col. 4.
78 *Call Bulletin*, September 1, 1953, p. 1, col. 1, Tong, (堂), freely translated

means lodge or fraternal organization. The reader is referred to the Chinese Historical Society of America's syllabus, *A History of the Chinese in California*, pp. 67-68, for further treatment on this subject.
79 *Examiner*, March 29, 1954, p. 1, col. 1; also p. 28, col. 3.
80 Ibid.
81 Ibid.
82 Ibid. The name of the Chinatown leader was not mentioned in the article.
83 Ibid.
84 *San Francisco News*, March 17, 1954, p. 9, col. 4.
85 *Examiner*, March 29, 1954, p. 28, col. 3.
86 Ibid., August 15, 1955, p. 6, cols. 2-5.
87 Schools with large concentrations of Chinese students.
88 *San Francisco News*, March 17, 1954, p. 9, cols. 2-3.
89 *Call Bulletin*, March 31, 1949, p. 15, cols. 1-2.
90 *San Francisco News*, February 20, 1951, p. 22, col. 2.
91 *Chronicle*, April 3, 1952, p. 9, col. 7.
92 *San Francisco News*, December 30, 1952, p. 9, col. 5.
93 *Examiner*, March 29, 1954, p. 28, col. 3.
94 Ibid.
95 *San Francisco News*, December 30, 1952, p. 9, col. 4. The staff at Francisco found 44 boys living alone.
96 Ibid., March 17, 1954, p. 9, cols. 2-5.
97 *Examiner*, August 15, 1955, p. 6, cols. 2-5.
98 *San Francisco News*, December 30, 1952, p. 9, col. 4.
99 See Appendices E and F for initial contact and questionnaire used in interviews.
100 Letter from Wellington Chew to researcher. May 21, 1978.
101 All teachers are eligible for a sabbatical leave for study or travel after seven consecutive years of teaching.
102 For more current information of Chinese Americans in administration, see Philip Albert Lum's study, ibid., pp. 127-130.
103 *Chronicle*, February 17, 1949, p. 1, cols. 3-5.
104 *Examiner*, February 17, 1949, p. 5, cols. 1-2.
105 *Call Bulletin*, February 17, 1949, p. B, col. 7.
106 *Chronicle*, March 2, 1949, p. 1, cols. 2-3.
107 Ibid.
108 Interview with Elizabeth Hall, October 28, 1977.
109 *Board Minutes*, January 3, 1928.
110 *Minutes of Chinese-American Citizens Alliance*, September 5, 1928, and October 3, 1928.
111 Ibid., October 3, 1928.
112 *Board Minutes*, May 13, 1941.
113 Department of City Planning, ibid., p. 5.
114 Ibid., p.6
115 Ibid.
116 Ibid., p. iii.
117 *Board Minutes*, April 12, 1955.
118 *Call Bulletin*, April 20, 1955, p. 14, col. 3.
119 *Board Minutes*, February 10, 1955.
120 Ibid.
121 Ibid.
122 *Examiner*, May 2, 1956, p. 12, col. 1.
123 *Chronicle*, October 22, 1956, p. 38., cols. 4-5.
124 *Examiner*, October 22, 1956, Section II, p. 20, col. 1. See also *San Francisco News*, October 24, 1956, p. 25, cols. 4, 9.
125 *San Francisco News*, February 4, 1957, p. 11, col. 2.
126 *Board Minutes*, March 12, 1957.
127 *Examiner*, February 3, 1958, p. 23, col. 4.
128 *Board Minutes*, February 18, 1958.

129  *San Francisco News,* May 23, 1958, p. 5, cols. 1-3.
130  Ibid.
131  Interview with Doris Lowe Schultze, April 17, 1978.
132  In 1971, Commodore Stockton School, along with other schools in San Francisco, was desegregated. See dissertations of Fernandes and Lum for coverage of this issue.


## CHAPTER EIGHT

1  See Philip Albert Lum, ibid., p. iv. See also *East/West,* April 29, 1981, p. 16, cols. 2-3. *Asian Week,* Vol. 2, No. 37, May 14, 1981, p. 1, col. 1.
2  For an elaboration of this concept, read the author's "Education as De-ethnization" in the forthcoming *Proceedings of the 1980 National Conference on Chinese American Studies* published jointly by the Chinese Historical Society of America and the Chinese Culture Foundation of San Francisco with the collaboration and support of the Asian American Studies Center of the University of California, Berkeley.

# Name Index

# Subject Index